The Ports of the British Isles

LIVERPOOL AND THE MERSEY

PORTS AND HARBOURS OF THE BRITISH ISLES

Series Editor: *Dr Gordon Jackson, Lecturer in Economic History, University of Strathclyde*

LIVERPOOL AND THE
MERSEY

*Professor F. E. Hyde
Chaddock Professor of Economic
History, University of Liverpool*

in preparation

PORTS OF THE BRITISH
ISLES: AN HISTORICAL
SURVEY

*Dr Gordon Jackson, Lecturer in
Economic History,
University of Strathclyde*

EAST ANGLIA

Dr Wilfred J. Wren

EASTERN SCOTLAND

*Bruce Lenman, Lecturer in
Modern History, University
of Dundee*

Liverpool and the Mersey

AN ECONOMIC HISTORY OF A PORT 1700–1970

FRANCIS E. HYDE

*Chaddock Professor of Economic History
in the University of Liverpool*

DAVID & CHARLES: *Newton Abbot*

ISBN 0 7153 5241 5

Set in 11/12pt Granjon and printed in Great Britain by Western Printing Services Limited Bristol for David & Charles (Publishers) Limited South Devon House   Newton Abbot   Devon

Contents

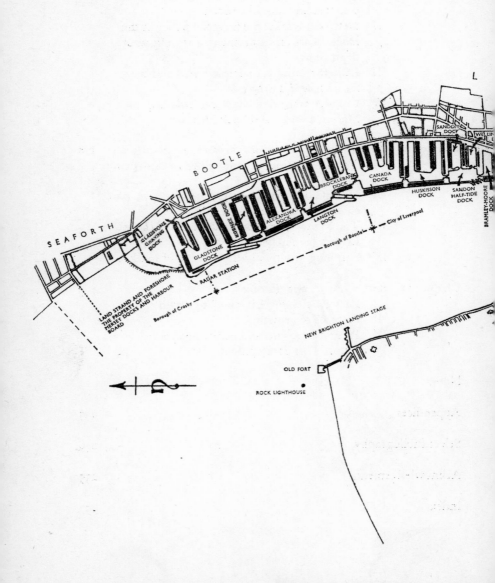

SEAFORTH

BOOTLE

L

GLADSTONE GRAVING DOCK

GLADSTONE DOCK

ALEXANDRA DOCK

LANGTON DOCK

BROCKLEBANK DOCK

CANADA DOCK

HUSKISSON DOCK

SANDON HALF-TIDE DOCK

SANDON DOCK

WELLINGTON DOCK

BRAMLEY-MOORE DOCK

LAND STRAND AND FORESHORE THE PROPERTY OF THE MERSEY DOCKS AND HARBOUR BOARD

RADAR STATION

Borough of Bootle

Borough of Crosby

City of Liverpool

NEW BRIGHTON LANDING STAGE

OLD FORT

ROCK LIGHTHOUSE

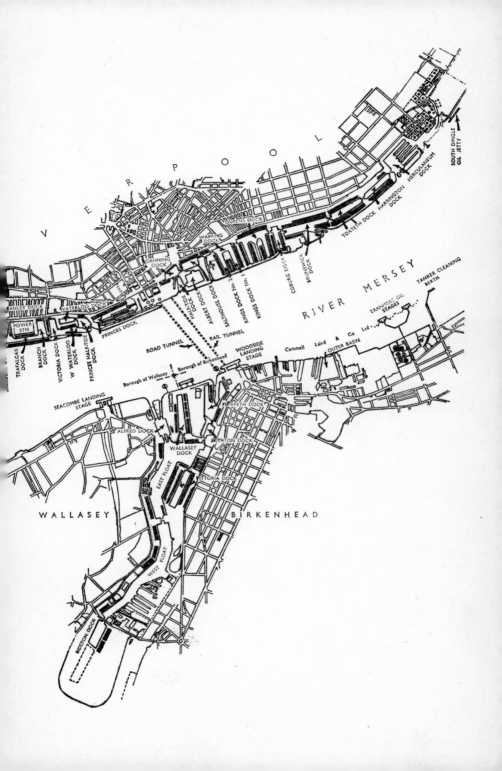

List of Illustrations

The said port of Leverpool extends from Red Stones on the Point of the Point of Worrall southerly, to the foot of Ribble Water in a direct line northerly, and so upon the South Side of the said River to Hesketh Bank easterly.[1]

[1] Commissions Returned into the Court of Exchequer, Michaelmas Term, 32 Car. II (1680); see R. C. Jarvis, 'The Head Port of Chester; and Liverpool, its Creek and Member', *Transactions of the Historic Society of Lancashire and Cheshire*, vol. 102, 1950, p. 83.

Introduction

A large number of scholarly histories of Liverpool have been written. Most of these have been based on the Municipal Records and are concerned with topography, the administration of corporate sanctions, political and social events, and specific aspects of shipping development in the port. Of them all, Thomas Baines's *History of the Commerce and Town of Liverpool*, published in 1852, was primarily concerned with the impact of commercial wealth upon the growth of Liverpool itself and, in the process of such development, the extension of Liverpool's influence throughout the world. This present volume seeks to broaden the scope of enquiry and to link growth with the aims and aspirations of an acquisitive society.

For a period of 300 years, the river Mersey has been a highway of commercial expansion, from the traffic in local products at the beginning of the eighteenth century to the flooding imports from a colonial empire and, in the nineteenth century, to the trade of a manufacturing nation. Since 1914, however, the relative importance of Liverpool and its river has declined, owing to a complex pattern of causes. It is hoped that the multitudinous threads of the port's fluctuating progress will have been given adequate degrees of emphasis to make clear a history in economic terms.

In order to undertake such a task, the author has not only drawn on traditional sources of information, but has brought within analysis the archives of Liverpool-based shipping companies, the Registers of Merchant Ships, the files of the Mersey Docks and Harbour Board, and a wide variety of manuscript sources relevant to the narrative. In addition, the latest publications, involving original research, have been used. Simple forms of measurement have been adopted in order to obtain comparative statements of growth in such essential features as tonnage using the port, investment in dock schemes, imports and exports, population and relative shares of trades. Above all, the story has been set against the background of human endeavour and enterprise in which the ideas of Liverpool's own men and women helped not only in the fashioning of their environment, but also in providing facilities for industrial and commercial expansion which ultimately changed the face of Britain.

As a broad generalisation, it might well be true that, in order to understand the nature of the Industrial Revolution, the Atlantic economy and, later, the opening up of the world to British shipping, one should have a real appreciation of what was happening in Liverpool. The author is aware that many themes in this book have not been given sufficient emphasis and that the picture has been painted on a broad canvas. It is hoped, however, that this general approach will be accepted and that future economic historians will, through further research, add to detail and thus give greater depth to Liverpool's economic history than has been possible in this present study.

University of Liverpool   F.E.H.
May 1971

CHAPTER ONE

Liverpool before 1700

A turbulent river estuary with high tides, treacherous sandbanks and shifting channels, a flat windswept shore, a curving inlet from the river known as the Pool; these were the chief features of the future site of the port of Liverpool. Further eastwards, at a distance of some two miles from the shore, was an encircling high sandstone ridge pitted with bogs and mosses, making communication with the hinterland difficult and, during winter months, extremely hazardous. It was not a prepossessing place and, when settlement was made, it must have been with the agricultural rather than with the seafaring potentialities of livelihood in mind.

It is, perhaps, of some interest to enquire into the state, extent, and relative importance of Liverpool before it became a prosperous industrial and trading centre, that is to say roughly before 1680. It is a fact that King John visited Liverpool and that, under Letters Patent of 1207, he conferred borough status upon it. He also made arrangements 'while awaiting a wind to carry him to Ireland' to build a castle on the north side of the junction between the Pool and the river.[1] This Bastille-like structure dominated the landscape and the few houses around it for nearly four centuries, but, by the end of the seventeenth century, it had become ruinous and was an eyesore. For a period of three centuries, the records indicate that the two chief occupations of Liverpool's citizens were fishing and agriculture. What ships there were in the Pool or in the river (apart from small craft) more often than not belonged to the king or to his representative, Lord Molyneux, the Constable of the castle. The Stanleys of Knowsley, later Earls of Derby, had, since the fifteenth century, commanded the use of ships in connection with their over-lordship of the Isle of Man and in pursuit of the king's business in Ireland. Even by the sixteenth century, very few ships could be claimed as merchant ships and these were owned jointly by one or two of a small number of burgesses.[2]

Thus, up to Elizabeth's reign, agriculture was a main source of sustenance for a population which, according to various estimates, numbered about 500.[3] They tilled the fields and gathered the harvests in much the same way as many another manorial community. The Town Books confirm this.[4] The great townfields lay to the north and to the east and beyond them were pastures and wastes, almost to the edge of the sandstone ridge. To the south, across the Pool, lay the great heath, the commons and the moss lake where burgesses had grazing rights and customary privileges over the cutting of peat and turf.[5] Nearer to the town were the heys or enclosed lands, usually in the possession of burgesses or leased from the more wealthy landholders. By 1670, the Moore and Crosse families owned a large number of these enclosures, while the Derby and Molyneux families held scattered lots; the remainder of the burgage lands being in small tenements and owned by the Houghtons, Athertons, Shaws, Moorcrofts, Johnsons, Williamsons, Benns, and Seels. The tithebarn was near to present-day Byrom Street and the manorial mill but a short distance away. The latter, however, had ceased to function in the seventeenth century and Sir Edward Moore and Richard Crosse both owned mills, their families having purchased the milling rights from manorial jurisdiction. They ground the wheat into flour for the whole community and charged an appropriate fee in kind for the service. Though many a vestige of an ancient feudal autonomy persisted as late as the third quarter of the seventeenth century, it is reasonably safe to assume that, up to the middle years of the sixteenth century, Liverpool was primarily dependent on agriculture; the only visible sign that it was connected with the sea (apart from the fishery) was on those occasions when it became necessary for the king to mount an expedition to quell an insurrection in Ireland or in Wales.

By the beginning of the seventeenth century, however, it is clear that fundamental changes had taken place affecting the basis of Liverpool's whole economy. The town had become a focal point for the import and export of goods. There are records of Breton salt being imported as early as 1566.[6] This commodity was also re-exported, mainly for agricultural purposes, to the Isle of Man, Workington and other small ports on the Lancashire coast. The trade was undoubtedly lucrative (the shrewd business sense of the Norris family led them to engage in it) and there is evidence that, by 1570, Liverpool men were seeking to control the sources of supply by trading in Cheshire rather than in Breton salt.[7] Thomas

Sekertson, for example, had interests in a salt house at Nantwich.[8] Some years later, in 1611, an immigrant named Atkinson established a salt works in a building called Mardyke at the bottom of Chapel Street. Thus, by producing salt within the town, the costs of importing the commodity were removed and, as a result, exports of the locally produced salt (viz., from Cheshire and Liverpool) could enter trade with a distinct price advantage over cargoes imported from Brittany.[9] This was a vital turning-point in the growth of Liverpool's trade. Traffic in salt not only extended the line of Liverpool's communication into the hinterland to the salt fields of Cheshire via the river Weaver, it was also the basis of a coastal trade and a growing cross-channel trade with Ireland. During Elizabeth's reign, therefore, trading contacts were made with Dublin, Carrickfergus, Dundalk, and Drogheda. In return for salt, coal, iron, copper, hops, Yorkshire cloth, alum, soap and other luxuries brought from abroad, Liverpool ships began to bring back sheepskins, tallow, linen, flax, frieze and mantles, wool, salt herrings, and salt beef in increasing quantities.

Meanwhile, Liverpool ships had been voyaging further afield. A small trade for the importation of Spanish iron from Bilbao had been started by Christopher Crosse in the 1560s and this had been extended through the activities of Edward and Thomas Tarleton, both listed as shipowners in the 1590s.[10] The Williamson family, whose main occupation was that of tanners, leather workers, and shoemakers, also embarked their capital in overseas trade, bringing back hides and skins from Irish, French, and Spanish ports.[11] In general, the trade with Spanish markets brought back iron, copper, train oil, sherry, Castile soap, figs, dates, oranges, and spices.[12] French ports of call on the voyage to Spain, such as Bordeaux, provided wine, tar, and resin. Very occasionally, there were cargoes of grain from Denmark and Hamburg. It was about this time (ie 1590–1600) that Liverpool ships began to carry outward cargoes of Manchester cottons, not perhaps the true cotton piece-goods of a later century, but a mixed fabric of cotton and linen for which Manchester had been famous since the days of Henry VIII. Thus, by the beginning of the seventeenth century, there are signs of a growing consciousness of the value of trade. This consciousness was heightened by the undoubted privileges which Liverpool's freemen, as merchants, enjoyed in foreign ports; for freemen of Liverpool became equal in status either by individual grant or general ordinance with nations in such ports as Wexford, Bordeaux, and Bilbao. This was a circumstance which facilitated the free movement of goods and freedom from discriminatory duties. Liverpool was beginning to enjoy a new-found prosperity with new sources of capital flowing into the pockets of her principal burgesses. From their number were elected the mayor, bailiffs and aldermen, and, in this way, trade and wealth which it brought in its train became associated with the town's governors.

Unfortunately, this burst of activity, with the anticipation of future expansion, was not maintained. The cause of this was twofold. In the first place, the Civil War interrupted the more peaceful pursuits of private enterprise and diverted funds from the financing of trade to the fortification and defence of the town. Secondly, regulation by Parliament very largely inhibited the more lucrative forms of trade with the Irish market. It was, therefore, not until the 1670s, when sugar refining in the town stimulated existing contacts with the West Indies, that the 'sources for the employment of capital in trading ventures were again opened and a more vigorous and prosperous system of merchanting began to develop'.[13]

In saying this, one must not discount the many efforts which were made during the century to maintain Liverpool's trading contacts with the outside world, however tenuous those contacts may have been. The Norris family continued to trade with Bordeaux, Spain, and Turkey. Through London, they sent merchandise to India. The oft-quoted despatch of Sir William Norris as royal ambassador extraordinary to the court of the Mogul emperor, in 1699, had, however, very little bearing on Liverpool's trading ventures. As is well known, all trade to the East was contained within the monopoly of the East India Company whose ships sailed from London. Nevertheless, there were a few Liverpool men engaged in the Indian trade, witness one, Thomas Plumbe of Wavertree Hall, who established himself as a merchant in Madras. There were also one or two connections maintained with the Mediterranean, surviving from Elizabethan times. Apart from the activities of the Norrises, there are records of cargoes from southern France, Italy, and north Africa. The hazards and dangers of such trade were emphasised in Thomas Lurting's account of 1681, in which there is a first-hand description of his capture by Barbary pirates. Voyages to the West Indies, after 1640, were perhaps more frequent and more remunerative. One of the earliest records of this trade dates from 1641, when John Moore of Bank Hall went to law concerning the ship, *William and Thomas* 'late of Barbados and now of Liverpool', in which he had an interest.[14] This ship was engaged in trade with the Barbados. After the Civil War, Liverpool ships were used to carry political prisoners and refugees from religious persecution to the West Indian Islands. Thus there were undoubted contacts between Liverpool and other countries which might be regarded as previous to the development of the town, but such contacts were usually in the nature of individual ventures and were in no way regular or sustained.

Meanwhile, by 1670, the physical extent of the town had changed. Much of our knowledge about this changing environment is derived from Sir Edward Moore's Rental, a document listing and valuing his various properties within the borough with shrewd advice to his son as to future exploitation and development. Moore's keen observations not only on the state of his property, but upon the character, demeanour and behaviour of his tenants, provide us with a picture of Liverpool which, when supplemented from the municipal records, is clear in detail and precise in description.

What had been the effect of this broadening of economic and commercial interests on the physical environment of Liverpool itself? The extent and layout of the town had changed by 1670, though the built-up area had not greatly increased beyond the boundaries of Tudor Liverpool. The principal streets were Tithebarn Street (a straggling winding way), Dale Street (built up on the north side but with fields to the south), Chapel Street and Water Street with the cross streets of Juggler (running to the east side of the 'town house') and Castle Street (wide at the top and becoming narrow at the south end where it stopped at Castle moat). There were some new streets in the course of construction. Moore Street, a fine broad walk from Fenwick Street down to the river and Fenwick Street itself (so named after Sir Edward Moore's wife) were built in the 1670s. The line of present Old Hall Street was also being laid out. To the east of the Castle, Lord Molyneux, after bitter controversy with the Corporation over his rights as lord of the manor (to which we shall refer later) was beginning to develop his land running down to the Pool by building houses along the line of present Lord Street. The lesser by-ways, Dig Lane, running from Tithebarn Street into Dale Street, and Pool Lane skirting the east side of the castle and following the line of what was later South Castle

Street, completed the plan of Liverpool in 1670. In 1677—that is ten years after the date of Moore's Rental—a list of streets is given in the municipal records, the additional streets being Lord Street, Lancelot's Hey, Hackin's Hey, Castle Hill, Preeson's Row, Redcross Street, and James Street, making a total of 18 streets altogether. By 1697, a new survey gives Chapel Yard, Common Garden (sic), Moorfields, Back of the Castle, St John's Street, Castle Hey or Harrington Street, Cook Street, Atherton Street, Pool Lane and Waterside. This made a total of 28 streets in all and covered an area very largely identifiable with Liverpool's present-day downtown business quarter.

Despite Edward Moore's native pride, Defoe's eulogistic description and Blome's rather inaccurate account, the main architectural features of the town were not particularly edifying. The Derby Tower at the bottom of Water Street looked like (and at a later date was in fact) a common gaol. The old chapel of St Mary le Quay, part of which probably dated from Norman times, had been sequestered in 1553 and had successively become a warehouse, a free school,[15] and (post-1700) a tavern and two dwelling houses. The castle had become ruinous and unsafe; the Old Hall, the seat of the Moore family since the time of Henry III, was dank and gloomy and in a state of disrepair. It was now under lease as the Moores had removed to a new house at Bank Hall. Only the ancient dwelling of the Crosse family had the semblance of style, and this was badly sited between Pool end and Dale Street. The old mediaeval clusters of alleys and courts behind the principal streets housed the majority of the population in unhealthy and insanitary overcrowding. The whole town must have presented a curious and not very impressive aspect to the visitor, not comparing in wealth or style with other seaports of like size. Within a period of fifty years, when Defoe wrote his much-quoted description,[16] the town had become greatly enlarged and the flow of new wealth, accompanying the expansion of trade, had led to new building and much rebuilding of the older parts of the inhabited area skirting the shore.

What is known about the principal citizens of Liverpool at this time? According to Moore, whose views were coloured by the way his tenants voted at election time, they were in general 'mercenary fellows'. 'Such a nest of rogues', he wrote to his son, 'was never educated in one town of that bigness.' His estimation of Alderman Andow (or Anido), to whom he had leased Old Hall, was typical of his descriptive powers: 'one of the lurchingest knaves in all the town', he called him. Of Thomas Row, who lived in Castle Street, his advice was: 'pretty honest, but trust him not'. Richard Williamson also lived in Castle Street, his family, as we have seen, having been settled in Liverpool since Tudor times. 'A most notorious knave', wrote Moore: 'remember that you never trust any of that name in this town for there is a great faction of them and their relations.' His opinion of John Pemberton, apothecary, was that he was a 'base, ill-contrived fellow'. Baillie Johnson he described as 'one of the hardest men in town'. In the end, however, even Moore's vituperation was not inexhaustible and he had to admit to some well-disposed characteristics in his tenants and neighbours. Despite what has been said about the general appearance of Liverpool, there were, even in Moore's day, a few well-built houses belonging to burgesses or to wealthy merchants. The Tarleton family house, a half-timbered structure, adjacent to the old chapel and known as Church Stile House, was worthy of notice. In Tithebarne Street, there was the house of one John Hacking (sic), through whose hey or field Moore recommended the building of a street to join Tithebarne Street with Dale Street. Another of Moore's tenants, Roger James, had a fine house and croft on the site of the street which now bears his name. The Johnson family lived in Dale Street on the site of the present Municipal Buildings, with fields running down to the Pool. It was through this land that Sir Thomas Street was cut and named in honour of Baillie Johnson's son, Sir Thomas Johnson. William Clayton, the son of Robert Clayton of Fulwood, built a large house in Moore Street which he rented to William Bushell, rope maker. Clayton was subsequently mayor and represented the borough in six Parliaments.[17]

William Blundell had a stone house in Tithebarn Street and Thomas Blundell a fine brick house in Dale Street. The Houghton family house was in Chapel Street, not very far from that of the Tarletons. Apart from houses such as these, however, one suspects that the majority of the town's citizens lived in varying degrees of evil-smelling discomfort, their lives being made tolerable (and perhaps healthy) only by the keen air and the sea breezes sweeping across Liverpool Bay.

Apart from the enlivening of his narrative with personal epithets, however, there is much valuable information in Moore's Rental concerning Liverpool's prospective development as a port. Referring to one of his tenements near to the shore, Moore stated that the sea was washing away the land so rapidly that the annual value had fallen from £10 a year in his grandfather's time to less than five shillings in his. He urged his son to construct a sea wall 'and, if it be possible, to get warehouses and dwelling houses built along the wall and also to make a street to go up the middle of it'—a shrewd prognostication of events. Again, in describing Baillie Johnson's land he said: 'remember there belongs a great close to this house . . . which runs down to the Pool. If ever the Pool shall be cut so as shipping comes up to the back of the Town, this will be a most especial place to make a street.' In another reference to the same project he added: 'if ever the Pool be cut and become navigable . . . there being no other place in Liverpool the like for cellars and warehouses . . . the shipping must be all along these closes and the trade will be all in them for the whole town. You may have building here worth more than £20,000.'[18] From this it is obvious that improvements to the docking and berthing facilities of the port were under consideration some fifty years before the first dock was in use. In the intervening period, however, some improvements had been made to the navigation in the river itself. In particular, work had been put in hand in 1694 by Thomas Patten, to make the river accessible to ships between Runcorn and Warrington. Such improvements not only led to an increase in traffic (estimated by Patten at 2,000 tons a year), but opened up new routes inland to Manchester and parts of Cheshire. In short, Liverpool, in seeking its own salvation, was being materially assisted by a similar spirit of enterprise in the hinterland.

Finally, it is necessary to mention one other important fact which had great bearing upon the course of the town's future development. We have mentioned the controversy which took place between Lord Molyneux and the Corporation. In fact, this controversy marked a turning point in the history of Liverpool. Lord Molyneux had bought the Crown rights over the town in 1632. As a consequence, he considered that he, as lord of the manor, was entitled to rights over the town wastes and common lands. When Caryl Molyneux decided, in 1668, to build his street and bridge the Pool, his plans included the continuation of that street (along present Church Street) over the common. This the Corporation strenuously opposed on the grounds that they, and not Lord Molyneux, had seignorial rights over the common. After some years of litigation a compromise was reached in 1672. Lord Molyneux was allowed to proceed with his street and to build his bridge on the payment of a nominal rent. He on his part sold to the Corporation all his rights to the overlordship of Liverpool with all dues and customs on a lease for 1,000 years at an annual rent of £30, the burgage rents and ferries only being excepted. This arrangement was of considerable significance in economic terms. When the time came for an extension of the town across the Pool to take place, and streets were laid out on the great heath, the Corporation began to reap the benefit in the rents and fines which they received for their leasehold property. By the end of the nineteenth century these rents amounted to £75,000; while for the tolls and dues, which were leased in 1672 for £30 per annum, the sum received when sold under Parliamentary power in 1856 was £1,500,000.

There was a parallel and equally significant change in Liverpool's commercial development. Up to 1699, the town had been included, for customs' administration, within the authority of the port of Chester. After 1700, however, Liverpool had its own Customs House with the implied right of official administration. Thus, by the end of the seventeenth century, Liverpool had virtually complete administrative control over its own affairs. It had at last become free from the inhibiting restrictions of a manorial overlordship. There was, therefore, no check upon economic growth provided always that resources could be made available and men with enterprise and initiative could take advantage of new opportunities. How this happened and how Liverpool burst the bounds of local confinement to become one of the world's largest ports is the subject of this present study.

CHAPTER TWO

The Emergence of Liverpool as a Port, 1680-1780

I

What, in historical terms, are the attributes of a port? The first and most obvious is that, by virtue of its situation, it can provide a safe haven for ships; secondly, that it is easy of access; thirdly, that it provides a convenient centre for the collection and distribution of goods, supplying the needs of its immediate hinterland and having time and space advantage on a variety of sea routes. Above all, in the course of any port's historical development, it must have evolved a system of administration in the handling and berthing of ships, in the management of cargo and in the commercial services necessary for the functioning of such activity.

If the foregoing attributes are translated into economic terms, one presupposes a growing accumulation of resources. These take the form of capital works, such as the provision of docks, wharves and warehouses; of merchant bodies with capital for the conduct of business; of banks to ensure flows of cash, and of institutional factors such as the establishment of a merchants' Exchange, commodity markets and trade associations. Behind all this, and in support of it, there must be an industrial organisation for the building and equipment of ships, for repair, maintenance, and salvage. In addition, and perhaps of fundamental importance, there should be a constant flow of resources into the development of efficient systems of transport between the port and the hinterland. In other words, the growth of a port in historical terms must have coincidence in economic terms. Essentially, a port comes into being and ultimately survives for the provision of a multitude of services. This involves the daily exercise of a complex logistical operation in which industrial, commercial and management skills have interplay. The purpose of this present study is to discover how Liverpool and associated dock systems on

Merseyside assumed, by reason of compelling geographical, historical and economic circumstances, the specific and sometimes peculiar characteristics which have, over the past two hundred years, influenced her rise to a position of major international status.

II

A cursory view of Liverpool's history might lead to a superficial conclusion that conditions for growth were generally unfavourable and that it was a matter of accident that a port was created. The river Mersey is like a bottle with a narrow neck; on the north side of the neck stands Liverpool, on the south, Birkenhead, Wallasey, and New Brighton. The estuary is subject to strong tides and the pressure of water into, and out of, the great pool which forms the main container of the bottle, creates strong currents and a high rise and fall of water. It was precisely at this point in the neck of the estuary that the early sailing ships had to berth and load cargo. Further out to sea the channel of the Mersey was, until cut in 1890, obstructed by a sand bar. Until the Crosby and other channels were charted, the easier way into and out of Liverpool was by the old course, half-way along the flat top of Wirral peninsula and thence outwards across the currents and shifting sands of the Dee estuary to the North Wales coast. The Collins' chart of 1689[1] and the later cartographic representations of Liverpool Bay,[2] show the many sitings which sailing ships had to make in tacking to a safe refuge in Hoyle Lake at the mouth of the Dee. The more heavily laden ships, anchored in Hoyle Lake, would usually transfer part of their cargo to flat-bottomed barges. Thus lightened, they could then sail the narrow channel round Black Rock Point into Liverpool. It is, therefore, not surprising that in 1698 Celia Fiennes should have regarded the great press of masts, spars and sails in Hoyle Lake with some degree of astonishment;[3] nor that William III should have chosen Deeside rather than the Mersey as the chief point for the embarkation of his troops en route for Ireland. Thus, to seaward, the hazards of adverse winds and tides, the treacherous state of shoals and sandbanks, made Liverpool a haven difficult of access to sixteenth- and seventeenth-century seamen.

To the landward, Liverpool's means of access were for many centuries equally unpropitious. As we have seen, the great marshy pool acted as a confining moat to the south and east. It curved inwards along the line of present-day Paradise Street, Whitechapel and Old Haymarket to the point where one now enters the Mersey Tunnel; it also formed part of the defences for King John's four-towered castle on its site at the end of Old Castle Street, presently the site of Queen Victoria's monument. To the east and north lay the sandstone ridge of Everton Brow and Edgehill interspersed with pockets of peat moss, highly dangerous to the traveller in wet weather. Further east lay marshland and heathland and the all-embracing barrier of Chat Moss. Before 1700, only one major road penetrated outwards as far as Warrington, running along the line of present-day Dale Street; while to the north there were trackways through the open fields and brecklands to help the traveller on his way to Preston and Lancaster.

If Liverpool was to become a port with potentialities for future expansion, the most obvious attributes which had to be acquired were those of accessibility and facility for the anchoring and berthing of ships. As a powerful stimulus to improvement, the scope of Liverpool's trade during the reign of Queen Anne became diversified. The evidence for this is to be found in the Port Books.[4] In some products, her share in the export trade was already considerable; outstanding examples of these products were white salt, English linen, refined sugar, metal products (including nails), leather goods, glass, coal, hops, textiles, earthenware, and, most important of all, coarse salt for agricultural purposes. Apart from textiles, coal, hops, and earthenware, the majority of these cargoes were beginning to be supplied from Liverpool's own growing industrial capacity, a capacity which, as we shall see later, increased rapidly after 1715. In addition, however, the figures for many of the items in the cargo lists reflect a growing awareness of Liverpool's hinterland, of the links with the Cheshire salt fields, with the south-west Lancashire coalfield, with the infant glass industry in St Helens and with the emerging pottery industry in Staffordshire. In Liverpool's import trade there was still a predominant emphasis on the long-established trade with Ireland, together with the newly acquired market in the West Indies. The chief imports were Irish linen cloth, muscovado sugar, tobacco, tallow, and hides. There was also a small trade with Europe including iron from Sweden and Spain and wine and other Mediterranean products from Spain and Portugal. It is also of some interest to note that, although Liverpool had a lively trade with the West Indies, that with Africa (1700-1714) had not yet seriously begun. Nevertheless, there was an incipient interest in West Africa as evidenced in the petition from Liverpool's merchants against the monopoly of the West Africa Company. Trade with British possessions overseas was chiefly with Virginia, Maryland, and the West Indies to which general consignments of goods, chiefly household requirements, farm supplies and clothing, were sent in increasing quantities. We shall deal with the expansion of these trades in a subsequent chapter. It is necessary to mention them here only as an indication of growing pressure upon Liverpool's facilities as a port.

What, in fact, was done to give accessibility to this increasing volume of trade? There were two primary objectives. In the first place, it was essential that better communication be established between Liverpool and her adjacent markets in Lancashire and Cheshire. This was effected by the improvement of various river navigation systems such as those on the Mersey, Irwell, Weaver, and Douglas rivers, and by the opening up of roads. Chadwick's map of 1725 indicates something of the effort already expended in the linking of Liverpool by road with Lancaster, York, and Manchester.[5] We shall deal with further extensions of the lines of communication by road and canal in a later chapter. In the second place, it was imperative that better berthing facilities be provided along Liverpool's shore line and that the mouth of the estuary be given a safer system of navigation. In the development of navigational facilities, siting beacons were placed at strategic points at the mouth of the estuary, the more dangerous sandbanks were marked and channels were improved. Above all, however, Sir Edward Moore's aspiration to make the Pool navigable came to realisation.

Thomas Johnson and Richard Norris, the town's MPs, were the prime movers in the promotion of Liverpool's first dock. It was largely through John's influence that Thomas Steers was brought up from London to make a new survey. Initially, in March 1709, Johnson and Norris had persuaded George Sorrocold, a reputable engineer, to make a plan for a four-acre dock, open for three hours each tide and able to accommodate a hundred ships. The whole work was estimated at a cost of £6,000.[6] Sorrocold's plan met considerable opposition, in particular, from the London cheesemongers whose ships, loading Cheshire cheese in the Mersey, would henceforth have to pay dock dues.[7] Sorrocold's scheme, however, never came to fruition owing to his sudden death. A new plan, submitted by Thomas Steers and supported by Johnson and Norris, was thereupon put into execution. Steers had previous experience of dock construction through his connection with the Rotherhithe project in London. His survey for a dock at Liverpool was original in the sense that it proposed to create a dock, of three and a half acres, not by carving it out of the land, but by using the natural features of the Pool and enclosing the water area therein by means of a sea wall. This was the first commercial dock in Britain. The scheme was sanctioned by the Common Council of Liverpool and the Steers plan was ratified by an Act of Parliament in 1709. The works proceeded very slowly and it was not until 1715 that ships were beginning to find anchorage in the dock. Even so, because of shortage of funds, the dock walls were not finally completed until 1719. It should be emphasised that this promotion was very largely the result of private enterprise and that the dry dock and retaining wall, built subsequently by Richard Norris, did not become a public dock until taken over by the Dock Trustees in 1740.[8] A certain amount of land behind the new sea wall to the south of the dock was reclaimed from the river, thus pushing the river bank outwards from the old mediaeval Strand. The Customs House was removed from its first site at the bottom of Water Street and a new building was erected at the east end of this wet dock. This was the beginning of Liverpool's vast dock estate and the spur to future commercial and industrial expansion.

The cost of these works had amounted to upwards of £30,000, to which must be added some £20,000 for the building of warehouses, offices, commercial buildings and dock appurtenances.[9] The dock gave Liverpool a focal point for development, for where cargoes were loaded and discharged, there was pressure for the employment of resources. A whole new town of streets began to be built beyond the Pool, running in a half semicircle to Hanover Street and Ranelagh Street; in fact a small building boom took place in which private capital, variously estimated at between £100,000 and £120,000, was expended.[10] In this new town were to be found evidence, not only of a quickening conscience by the building of a new church, St Peter's (presently the site of Woolworth's store, Church Street) and a charity school, the Bluecoat Hospital, but also the beginnings of a diversified industrial economy. At the waterside, adjacent to the new dock, were situated a glass works, Blackburne's salt works, sugar refineries and later an iron foundry (in association with Coalbrookdale), a copper works (probably associated with the Roe interests)[11] and many metal working establishments. Here also were the shipbuilding yards of John Fisher, the Graysons and Fearons, the timber yard of the Rathbones, together with ship repair facilities and shipping equipment houses. In the area between Parker Street and Ranelagh Street, there were the rope walks belonging to Charles Goore and Thomas Staniforth. Thus, from the time of Queen Anne to the middle of the eighteenth century, the expansion of resources in shipping, docks, industrial establishments and houses had gone on continuously. From what scanty evidence exists, it is possible to make the following approximate estimate of employed resources between 1710 and 1750: in docks and warehouses £50,000,[12] in ships £347,000,[13] in industrial plant £55,000, in housing £120,000,[14] making a total of £572,000. This is probably a conservative estimate, but it is an indicator to Liverpool's rapidly expanding trade. Capital accumulation was in fairly rapid process and the essentials of commercial and industrial enterprise were providing a generating influence for future economic expansion.

III

Parallel to the acquisition of physical attributes in the port's development was the growth of commercial expertise. This was an essential element in the process of satisfying the demands from Liverpool's own growing population, as well as from those from an expanding hinterland. These efforts led, not only to a widening of overseas markets, but to an ordering of commercial practice through the development of institutions within the port itself. In short, Liverpool was becoming possessed of all the physical and economic potentialities necessary for acquisitive growth and the spontaneous generation of resources.

In the years from 1680 to 1715, the driving force of commercial enterprise sprang from the income of landholders. In the first place, there were the long-established promotional activities of the ancient landowning families such as the Derbys of Knowsley, the Molyneux of Croxteth (created Earls of Sefton, 1771) and the Blundells of Crosby Hall. The leasing and mortgaging of parcels of land led to developments in non-agricultural pursuits and the raising of resources on land frequently provided liquid assets for shipping and commercial enterprise. Secondly, there were men of ancient lineage, not owners of vast estates, but whose families had accumulated blocks of property in Liverpool and the neighbourhood. Such men were the Moores of Bank Hall, the Crosses of Crosse Hall, the Norrises of Speke, the Claytons of Fulwood and Parr and other burgesses such as the Williamsons, the Houghtons, and the Tarletons. These men derived substance from the rents they charged for the use of property and very often invested surplus income in commercial ventures. Thirdly, there were those who came to Liverpool from other parts of the country bringing with them the ready resources for the establishment of new industrial processes. For example, it is estimated by Moore that Danvers and Smith brought in £40,000 as initial capital for the sugar refining industry and that the return value of trade in that commodity amounted annually to the capital sum expended.[15] Similarly, the returns on Blackburne's salt works, the glass, copper, and iron works, together with those on the shipbuilding yards must have had a precise dynamic effect. Finally, there were the new men, seamen such as Richard Rathbone, small traders such as Ralph Earle and craftsmen such as John Shaw who, in course of time, built up flourishing businesses as manufacturers, merchants, shipbuilders, ships' chandlers and metal producers. By establishing contacts between Liverpool and the outside world they created powerful vested interests in both the government and economic prosperity of the port. These were professional business men whose job it was to make money and to promote trade. They came more prominently into Liverpool's mercantile development after 1730; they had a continual turnover of funds and ploughed back their profits with the speculative intention of increasing their wealth and power. In political terms, they gave a new and insistent voice to Liverpool's economic demands through their activity as members of the Corporation. In London, they represented the borough as Members of Parliament and promoted the interests of trade.

Who were some of these men and how did they use their resources? John Ashton, the father of Nicholas Ashton of Woolton Hall, was Bailiff in 1749. He was listed as a merchant and was one of the promotors of the Sankey Navigation. His investment in this enterprise is said to have laid the foundation of the family fortune. Be that as it may, his capital was well employed, in his capacity as merchant and as shipowner, some time before it had the opportunity of augmentation in canal enterprises. John Gregson, Receiver of the Land Tax, was a banker and merchant, as also were Arthur and Benjamin Heywood, Richard Caldwell, Jonas Bold, and Thomas Leyland. The latter's initial wealth was variously alleged to have been derived from a lottery or from the Canadian timber trade; he was certainly an active slave trader after 1775 and ultimately died leaving upwards of £100,000.[16] In later life he purchased Walton Hall, seat of the Atherton family. James Atherton and Thomas Seel were property developers on an extensive scale; the former laying out streets in Everton and founding the site of what is now New Brighton, the latter in building up the area from the bottom of Seel Street to Colquitt Street. Moses Benson, after having made a fortune in the West Indies, bought an estate at Luttwych, but settled in Liverpool where he carried on business as an African trader. His personal estate at death amounted to £90,000.[17] John Colquitt was a merchant with a warehouse and counting house adjacent to his family house. John Earle began as an ironmonger in Castle Street, but laid the foundations of his wealth by ventures in the African trade. His estate was reported to be worth £100,000 with considerable proprietorship in land, most of which had been acquired by purchasing part of the old Moore estate. The connection between Liverpool and iron-founding was given impetus through the marriage, in 1768, between Joseph Rathbone and Mary Darby, the daughter of Abraham Darby of Coalbrookdale. Charles Goore and Thomas Staniforth were both shipowners and owners of extensive ropewalks on the south side of Lime Street. In fact, Thomas Staniforth was a man of parts. Besides being a shipowner, a banker and a rope-maker, he was interested in property development. In 1797 he was involved in financial arrangements for the transfer of about four acres of land in the old townfield known as Higher Weaver, Lower Weaver, and Black Half Acre. This land passed from John Shaw to Peter Atherton and was eventually developed by Edward Jones, builder, in a series of streets (including Prince Edwin and Iliad Streets), mainly running between Scotland Road and Great Homer Street.[18]

In the immediate vicinity of Liverpool there was considerable employment of resources in the raising of coal and in the manufacture of glass and salt. The Dungeon works produced fine white salt for export; there was considerable industrial development in and around St Helens and, in Nicholas Blundell's diary for 1719, there is a most interesting account of a new phenomenon. Visiting Thomas Case of Red Hazels, Huyton, Blundell records the working of coal pits and the sight of a small glass-works. In order to improve the efficiency of these pits and work the pumps, Case had installed a Newcomen engine at a cost of £1,500. This was probably the first application of steam to industrial processes on Merseyside.[19]

According to Baines, there were about a hundred merchants in Liverpool engaged in the African trade in 1752;[20] some forty-five of the general merchant body were also listed as shipowners. The principal capital holders were William Gregson, John Parr, Ralph Earle, Charles Goore, William Fleetwood, William Trafford, George Drinkwater, William Williamson, John Ashton, John and William Crosbie, John Tarleton, James Gildart, and Scroop Colquitt. Of the ships they owned, 106 vessels traded with the West Indies and North America, 88 were engaged in the African trade, 28 in various European trades and 125 in the coasting and Irish trades, in all amounting to 17,323 tons. In addition, there were 80 sloops owned by manufacturers, coal-owners and merchants engaged in salt and river trades.[21] The latter kept up communication between Warrington and Manchester by the Mersey and Irwell river navigation, bringing salt from the Weaver and coal from Wigan via the river Douglas. In 1750, the capital assets involved in these various shipping activities amounted to £347,000.[22] An analysis of the Liverpool Registers of Merchant Ships for 1789 shows that the stock of ships owned by the port amounted to 76,251 tons (see R. Craig and Rupert Jarvis, *The Liverpool Registry of Merchant Ships* (1967), Table 3, p. 148). This represented a more than fourfold increase over a period of thirty-six years.

It is, perhaps, a fact that the growth of banking and insurance in the town was coincidental with the involvement of merchants in the West Indian and African trades. As we shall see later, merchants and shipowners very largely insured their own ventures themselves, but the need for discounting facilities arose after 1750 with the growing volume of bills drawn against West Indian merchants. Thus some of the more important Liverpool merchants began to exercise the functions of banking. Accordingly, Liverpool was well served by a growth of merchant capital. Among the fourteen banks of any importance listed, after 1750, ten were founded by merchants.

Heywoods and Caldwells were West Indian merchants; Moss of
Moss, Dale & Rogers, owned sugar plantations in Demerara;
Thomas Leyland, a partner in Clarke's bank before he joined with
his nephews, Christopher and Richard Bullin, in a more famous
banking venture, was an African trader. For the most part, the
distinctive role of these bankers was in the acceptance and discounting business, though on occasion they performed civic and
sometimes national services. They remitted customs and excise
duties, and very often gave security against excise.[23] Following the
crash of Caldwell's bank, in 1793, both Heywoods and Gregsons
undertook the acceptance of Liverpool's own note issue and in so
doing helped to assuage the effects of crisis conditions by restoring
confidence.[24] The one other bank with a distinctive mercantile backing was that of Staniforth, Ingram, Bold & Dealtra. According to
Presnell, all of these houses could command assets of between
£200,000 and £300,000.

IV

This short cross-section of some of Liverpool's more important
citizens in the years from 1700 to 1775 is sufficient to indicate the
strength of growing enterprise, particularly that in commercial
affairs. It does not, however, cover two of the more distinctive craft
industries which were established in Liverpool during the latter half
of the eighteenth century. The first of these was pottery and china
manufacture, the second was clock- and watch-making. Samuel
Shaw built his pottery on Shaw's Brow (now William Brown
Street) and its importance as a centre of employment can be judged
from the fact that, by 1790, when the trade was in decline, there
were 74 houses on the Brow occupied by 374 persons, all of whom
were engaged in the various processes of pot-making. The most dis-
tinguished among them had been Richard Chaffers who, having
served his apprenticeship with the Shaws, began business on his own
account at the bottom of Shaw's Brow sometime before 1750. In
1755, Chaffers and an associate, Philip Christian, induced Robert
Podmore to sign an agreement whereby a secret process used in the
Worcester factory was passed to them, Podmore having been previously employed there.[25] Thereupon, Chaffers began to manufacture porcelain characterised by a bluish milky glaze. In fact, he

produced a heat-resistant soapstone porcelain. He, in turn, was succeeded by Seth Pennington, famous for the production of punch-bowls and excellent imitations of oriental ware. Other well-known china makers at this time were Samuel Gilbody and William Reid who had works on 'Brounlee Hill'. After 1800, the industry rapidly declined and the Shaw Brow site was turned over to other industrial uses including a soap works, grinding mills, a large coach factory, and wheelwrights' and builders' yards.

A parallel development of technological significance was also taking place in Liverpool at this time. This was the process of print-ing on pottery, discovered by John Sadler and his partner, Guy Green, at their works in Harrington Street. The first printed pots and jugs were made about 1752; their quality so impressed Josiah Wedgwood that he later entered into an agreement with Sadler to have his famous Queen's ware printed in Liverpool. Ultimately, the whole process was transferred to Staffordshire, Sadler having retired sometime before 1781, though Guy Green carried on the business until the end of the century.

Perhaps it is relevant here to make a brief mention of a third and overlapping interest in the making of pottery on the south shore of the river. A site at Toxteth had been purchased by Charles Roe in 1772 where, in order to promote his industrial interests, a small copper works was erected. It is believed (though there is no exact proof) that Messrs Abbey and Graham purchased the site in 1794 for the purpose of making pottery. Two years later, a joint stock company was created by Messrs Worthington, Holland and others, under the title of the Herculaneum Pottery Co. It is of interest to note that many of the operatives were drawn from Staffordshire and also from the various works in the centre of Liverpool. The first production was a printed ware; china-ware was undertaken in 1800. The growing competition from the Potteries and pressure to acquire the site for timber-yards and shipbuilding interests, however, under-mined the trade of these works and in 1833 the site was sold. Though manufacture continued for a few years after the sale, the land eventually became part of Liverpool's extending dock system.[26]

Liverpool's second craft industry, that of clock- and watch-making, was an offshoot of the Prescot industry, which for more than a century had maintained itself with a high reputation for quality and excellence of workmanship.[27] The craft was brought to Liverpool by John Wyke, who was a native of Prescot. In this house, complete with court and garden, off Dale Street which he built in 1764–5, he established himself as a well-known clock-, watch-, and watch-tool maker. His expertise lay in the cutting of toothed wheels, chains, and mainsprings, as well as in the construction of clocks. Peter Litherland carried on Wyke's work. In 1794 he invented the rack lever escapement, and Robert Roskell, who adopted this invention, expanded the watch-making business by entering the export trade. It is reported that he sold more than 30,000 watches to South American markets alone. He started business in Byrom Street some time about 1800 and moved in 1803 to premises in Church Street where he and successive generations continued the manufacture.[28]

The constantly changing pattern of Liverpool's industrial history during the middle years of the eighteenth century was an adjunct of a more dynamic expansion in overseas trade. If one is tempted to ask why this industrial enterprise ceased to maintain itself after 1800, the answer must lie in the nature of Liverpool's needs which, in turn, promoted Liverpool's growth. The mercantile interests in the port were the primary sources of wealth. These interests required increasing quantities of low-priced manufactured goods. As communications with the hinterland increased, the flood of such goods poured into Liverpool from the factories of Lancashire, Cheshire, Staffordshire, and the Midlands. Thus the demands for cargo, which no longer could be satisfied from the resources of Liverpool's own industrial capital, were increasingly supplied at highly competitive rates from outside. In this way Liverpool's needs as a port turned her into a commercial rather than into an industrial centre.

V

What was the effect of this growing enterprise upon the physical environment of Liverpool itself? In the first first place, there was a changing emphasis in the pattern of land ownership. As outlined in Chapter 1, the Corporation had acquired a lease of 1,000 years on heathlands and wastelands south of the Pool. In 1777, the purchase of the reversion of this lease was made for the sum of £2,250. This gave the Corporation control over areas which were later to include Lime Street, William Brown Street, and London Road as far east as Crown Street and as far south as Parliament Street. In other words, rights had been established over land on which the central area of the town could be built and also over the southern shore of the river, where the future dock system or at least a good part of it could be extended. This must surely have been an example of one of the most profitable investments on record.

In the second place, the impact of industrial and commercial expansion on the growth of the town was impressive. By the middle of the eighteenth century, the number of streets, lanes and alleys in the town was 222. There were now four churches, St Nicholas's, St Peter's, St George's, and St Thomas's, and in addition to these Anglican churches, there was the old Presbyterian chapel in Quay Street, the new Presbyterian chapel in Benn's Gardens, the old Anabaptist chapel at the bottom of Dale Street, the Quaker Meeting House in Hackins Hey, a Roman Catholic chapel in Lombard Street and a Jewish synagogue in Stanley Street, from which it may be observed that Liverpool was becoming possessed of a shrewd and diversified religious conscience, since all these buildings had been raised by public subscription.

The commercial buildings of the town were, in some cases, as imposing as the ecclesiastical architecture though, more often than not, business was transacted in private houses and shops. The Exchange and Town Hall were then rebuilding; the Customs House was at the side of the Old dock; the Stamp Offices were, however, at 'Mr Williamsons and Mr Fleetwoods, booksellers'; the Excise office 'kept by Mr Johnson' was in Paradise Street; the Salt office 'kept by Mr Greenwood' was in Princes Square; the Dock office 'kept by Joseph Valens' was in Brook Square, the Sun Fire office 'kept by Mr William Powell' was in Fenwick Street and the Post Office 'kept by Samuel Street' was at the Woolpack Inn, near the Exchange. All this suggests a fairly high concentration of commercial activity in both public and private buildings and a narrow confinement of business in the streets, alleys and courts of the old town.

If Liverpool's citizens and merchants were engrossed in business and in the making of money, however, one must add in fairness to them that they were generous in its expenditure. The Bluecoat School was testimony to the liberality of Bryan Blundell and his friends; the Infirmary, opened in 1749, was founded and supported by public subscription; the Work and Poor House in Hanover Street, the Sick and Lame Hospital in Shaw's Brow, the Sailors' Sixpenny Hospital, were all in some measure or other the objectives of charitable enterprise. In addition, there were sets of alms-houses in Dale Street, Hanover Street and on the Heath, together with the Free School, founded by John Crosse at the time of the Reformation and subject to endowment under the wills of William Clayton and Richard Houghton and many other benefactors.[29] In the field of amusement, there was the Playhouse in Drury Lane. The more famous Theatre Royal in Williamson Square was not opened until 1772. There was a tennis court in Dale Street and two bowling greens, one situated a little beyond Salthouse dock and the other near present-day Lewis's store and the Adelphi hotel. There was an assembly room within the somewhat forbidding exterior of the Tower; a room not far removed from the other part of the building then used as the common gaol. In all respects, Liverpool must have been a noisy, dirty, busy community, keenly conscious of religious scruples, moral standards and generous action. It was a strong and vital society, but as yet it lacked direction in economic affairs and leadership in cultural and social endeavour. Such leadership was to come from a variety of sources within the following fifty years of the eighteenth century.

From the reign of Queen Anne onwards, therefore, Liverpool had not only acquired the attributes of a port, but had secured the men with ideas and initiative to make her a factor of importance in that upsurge of promotional activity called the Industrial Revolution. The French economic historian, Paul Mantoux, stated that in order to understand the importance of Liverpool in the eighteenth century, it is necessary to comprehend that its growth was progressing faster than that of local industry. 'It seems to be bound up with the general trade of the country and to run parallel with it', he wrote, '. . . it may be said that the history of Liverpool illustrates during nearly all the years of the eighteenth century the history of English trade.'[30] This view gives great weight to external influences and is, perhaps, somewhat biased in favour of trade. The general thesis is correct, but the time-scale given by Mantoux needs some re-appraisal. If one takes the tonnage of shipping entering and clearing the port between 1716 and 1744, there is a surprisingly low annual average rate of growth of 0·7 per cent. Between 1744 and 1851, the rate is at a phenomenally high level of 4·9 per cent per annum. After 1750, however, the growth of a large import trade, coupled with improved communications with the expanding industrial activity in the hinterland, led to a re-adjustment of motivating influences. There was an inherent driving force activating new trades and new markets which, in accordance with Mantoux's thesis, made the port a vital and strategic element in the nation's economic growth. The significant point, however, is that this did not take place until the period 1744–1850.

CHAPTER THREE

The Growth of Liverpool's Trade, 1700–1835

I

Tobacco, Sugar, Salt & Coal.

The effectiveness of Liverpool's expansion as a trading centre lay in the growing power of merchant capital. From 1700 onwards, the profitability of merchant voyages saw a net return of double and, more often than not, treble the original outlay of capital. Yet, despite this, only a comparatively few Liverpool merchants left large estates on death. Of some 60 wills examined (1770–1810), 28 well-known merchants left £5,000 or less, 7 left between £5,000 and £10,000, 2 between £10,000 and £20,000, 4 left upwards of £20,000 and only one as much as £100,000.[1] These figures relate only to personal estates. Undoubtedly much capital went in the purchase of land; but for the most part the evidence suggests that increasing resources were ploughed back into trade, the expansive nature of which demanded a constant replenishment of funds. Some eighteenth-century merchants lived in a style becoming their wealth. Already, by 1750, their fine new Georgian houses were being built along Duke Street, Park Lane, Great George Street and some as far away as Everton Brow, but the majority were content to live (even as late as 1770) over their counting-houses in the narrow alleys and streets of the business quarter. The making of money was a full-time occupation, not as yet identifiable with luxurious living standards and the more refined pursuits of a leisured class.

To some extent the image of the Liverpool merchant in the eighteenth century has been distorted by his association (very often quite erroneously) with the slave trade. It is true that this trade absorbed a substantial part of the port's shipping from time to time, but not all Liverpool merchants were slave traders. What cash benefits accrued from the direct trade in the carriage of negroes were, perhaps, of less importance to the growth of Liverpool than the more indirect effects of the stimulation which this trade provided in the form of new markets overseas. If the African trade as such is put into a proper relationship with the West Indian and Virginian trades, it will be seen that its influence has been overemphasised. Of greater importance is the effect of this stimulation on the existing traditional pattern of trade and the effects of this influence on an already expanding economy.

Let it be said at once that long before Liverpool men became actively engaged in the transportation of negroes, the two most important commodities in the port's import trade were tobacco and sugar. Between 1704 and 1711, the imports of tobacco increased from approximately 600 tons to just short of 1,600 tons, an increase of virtually 250 per cent in seven years.[2] Within the same period, the import of raw sugar rose from 760 tons to 1,120 tons, an increase of nearly 50 per cent.[3] The measure of Liverpool's involvement in these trades can be judged by a comparison with the figures of imported sugar and tobacco at the end of the eighteenth century. Between 1785 and 1810, annual imports of sugar rose from 16,600 to 46,000 tons, and those of tobacco from 2,500 tons to 8,400 tons.[4] To this extent, Liverpool merchants and Liverpool ships helped to meet an increasing demand and, in this process, the resources derived from the slave trade were undoubtedly used in both a promotional and a financial sense. It will be shown hereafter how this happened.

As far as Liverpool's traditional interest in tobacco was concerned, the importation of this commodity is said to have begun with a cargo, in 1648, ordered from London by James Jenkinson.[5] It was not until the 1660s that Liverpool ships made direct voyages to Virginia. Both tobacco and sugar were commodities with a moisture content and were therefore difficult to assess by weight for the purpose of levying Customs' dues. While the local administration for Customs' returns was at Chester, Liverpool merchants could, either by fraudulent returns or by open bribery, escape payment of import dues. But after 1700, when Liverpool had its own Custom House, the efficiency of local officers on the spot created consternation. The battle royal which developed in 1702 between the Customs officials and the tobacco importers (represented by Thomas Johnson, Peter Hall, Richard Norris, and John Pemberton) has often been quoted. It is sufficient here to state that attitudes towards the payment of Customs dues in the early part of the eighteenth century were no whit less liberal than they are today. Writing to Norris on 26 March

1702, Johnson recorded a conversation he had held with William Clayton who was then Member of Parliament for Liverpool. Referring to the frauds on the Customs, Clayton said 'I am sure it would be better were there no such practices'. Johnson was staggered by this extraordinary point of view. 'It was', he protested, 'the usual thing. It was practised by the whole town.' This incident shows that the administration of the port needed to be brought under regulation and a due discipline created. The protracted negotiations which followed did much to bring about an ordered system of Customs administration. However, the extent of Johnson's own indebtedness was never satisfactorily assessed and, at his death, it is believed that a considerable sum was outstanding and had to be left unpaid.

The trade in sugar from the Barbados was not at first extensive. It started in real earnest after the 1680s, consequent upon the establishment of refineries in the town by Danvers and Smith. There is, however, evidence that ships were being sent, possibly one or two each year from 1665 onwards, to bring back sugar cargoes. In the letters of William Blundell there is a record of the *Antelope* returning with sugar, a venture in which Blundell invested £40 and on the successful conclusion of which he more than doubled his outlay.[6] Generally speaking, however, the rapid increase in this trade did not take place until Liverpool's closer association with the West Indies was established through its interconnection with the African trade.

If, therefore, the pattern of Liverpool's growth was being determined by an initial employment of resources in traditional import trades, it is equally true that an even greater measure of expansion was resulting from the export trades of coal and salt. These two trades not only brought increasing returns, but stimulated the flow of capital outwards from Liverpool to the Cheshire salt mines and to the West Lancashire coalfield. This in turn led to the improvement of communications between the port and its hinterland. As a result there followed a greater employment of shipping, both coastwise and overseas. The economic importance of salt had been recognised by Liverpool merchants as early as the first half of the seventeenth century. 'The Salt Trade', wrote John Holt, 'is generally acknowledged to have been the Nursing Mother and to have contributed more to the first rise, gradual increase, and present flourishing state of the Town of Liverpool than any other article of commerce.'[7] The interconnections of the trade grew rapidly. Besides being an ideal ballast for ships, salt was an essential commodity for the

Newfoundland cod fisheries. The salted fish was taken to the West Indies or the Mediterranean and there sold or exchanged for sugar, coffee, wine, or fruit. In the coastal trade, salt was also of great importance; it was taken to Cornwall whence, in return, came china clay for the pottery industry of Staffordshire and, later, for Liverpool's own pottery industry. In the cross-channel trade to Ireland salt was also carried for agricultural purposes although, in this market, Liverpool salt, taxed in the interests of the native Irish industry and for revenue purposes, had to compete with duty-free salt from Spain and Portugal. Liverpool's own industries also needed salt in increasing quantities. The metal-working and glass industries used it as a flux; the pottery industry used it for glazing, and later it became an essential ingredient in the manufacture of soda, which was basic to the growth of the chemical and soap industries.

As we have already stated, there are records of the manufacture of salt in Liverpool from the beginning of the seventeenth century.[8] At the end of that century, the names of Thomas Johnson and John Blackburne are associated with the refining of rock salt.[9] Blackburne's refinery was near to the second wet dock, opened in 1753, and called the Salthouse dock. This refinery competed with the brine boilers of Cheshire and, for a period after 1702 when an Act was passed closing the industry to all newcomers, it enjoyed a privileged position which allowed a rapid expansion of production. The brine boilers of Cheshire also took advantage of the Act and entered the business of refining rock salt, sending their shipments via the Weaver and the Mersey for exportation overseas. The volume of fine white salt began to increase rapidly. Between 1732 and 1752, annual quantities shipped down the Weaver increased from 7,954 tons (14,000 tons if rock salt be added) to 14,359 tons.[10] By 1770, exports of white and rock salt from Liverpool had reached 48,000 tons, most of it going to America and Ireland.[11] The trade continued to increase and the magnitude of it in the nineteenth century may be judged from a Liverpool memorial in 1861 which claimed that salt 'exceeded the export of coal and iron together, being one-half of the loaded tonnage cleared at the Port of Liverpool'.

All this increase in the salt trade would have been impossible without a corresponding increase in the coal trade. The growing activities of metal works, iron foundries, salt refiners and glass-makers increased the pressure of demand for more coal from the collieries of south-west Lancashire.[12] Despite some improvements in communication,[13] the carriage of coal into Liverpool continued to be subject to hazards and impediments. A crisis was reached in 1753 when the Prescot Hall mine, which had a virtual monopoly in the supply of coal by land to Liverpool, raised prices.[14] There was an immediate outcry from the consumers and the agitation which followed was sufficiently powerful to induce the Common Council of Liverpool to consider plans for the improvement of communications between the town and the source of supply. This was not so much a decision to offset the harmful effects of rising costs as a realisation that Liverpool's future prosperity depended upon the rapid improvement of her links with south-west Lancashire, Cheshire, and the Midlands. The first step towards the fulfilment of this realisation had already been taken by turnpiking the road to Prescot and later, in 1749, extending it to St Helens. But in spite of this the surface was not sufficiently durable to withstand the wear and tear of the increasing carriage of coal to Liverpool. In 1753, the Trustees were empowered to extend the turnpike to Warrington and from St Helens to Ashton.[15] The additional tolls levied to meet the cost of these extensions raised the price of coal still higher to consumers in Liverpool.[16] Again the Common Council of the town took action in the economic interests of its citizens by initiating, in 1754, a scheme for the improvement of the Sankey navigation.[17] This scheme served two purposes. In the first place, it opened up a rich new coalfield to Liverpool, east of Prescot, which could act as a rival to the Prescot Hall mine; in the second place, it offered an alternative means of communication to the turnpike road and so helped, by increasing supplies and by making transport more efficient, to ensure adequate supplies of coal to Liverpool. On petition from certain Liverpool merchants,[18] a Bill was introduced into Parliament on 20 March 1755. It became law 'for making navigable the river or brook called Sankey and the three several branches thereof'.

The effects of this enterprise upon the trade of Liverpool were soon felt. Sarah Clayton, a well-known Liverpool personality, was encouraged to open the coal pits on her land at Parr[19] and by 1769 the rich coal-bearing field around St Helens was being exploited. By 1771, 90,000 tons of coal were being carried down the canal annually, 45,000 tons to Liverpool and 45,000 tons to Warrington, Northwich and elsewhere.[20] In 1773, the Duke of Bridgewater's canal was connected with the Mersey and a small dock was built at Liverpool to

accommodate the Bridgewater coal flats (or barges).[21] The following year saw the opening of the Leeds, Liverpool canal and the
inauguration by this route of supplies of coal from the Wigan field.
Thus, by the mid-1770s, Liverpool had the means to satisfy her demand for fuel. Henceforth there were adequate supplies to satisfy
domestic and industrial requirements and a surplus for export. In
1770, these exports amounted to 8,500 tons, of which 3,500 tons
went to Ireland and 1,500 tons to the American colonies.[22] Troughton records that by 1791 the export of coal from Liverpool amounted
to no less than 79,000 tons, 57,000 tons going to foreign ports and
the remainder by coastwise shipping.[23] Equally remarkable was the
increase in the production of salt—a natural consequence of the expansion of the trade in coal and in the rapid development of Liverpool's overseas' trade. Shipments of white salt down the Weaver
increased from 14,000 tons in 1752 to 40,000 tons by 1782-3.[24] In
addition equivalent amounts of rock salt were also shipped. These
shipments, together with the surplus from Liverpool's own refineries, were not sufficient, however, to meet the needs of Liverpool's expanding markets abroad. The consequence of this was that
Liverpool merchants were forced to acquire brine pits at or near
Winsford in Cheshire and work them.[25] This new investment
(estimated at £12,000) produced an immediate increase in production. By 1796, 100,000 tons of salt were being unloaded in Liverpool
and 186,000 tons by 1820.[26] In this year, 58,500 tons of rock salt were
exported from Liverpool to markets overseas. The salt barges returned up the Mersey to the Sankey canal where they were loaded
with coal as back freight.

    Thus it was that the traditionally established trades of sugar and
tobacco in imports, and coal and salt in exports, stimulated the
growth of Liverpool's contacts with Newfoundland, Virginia, and
the West Indies, and promoted the flow of resources into the development of communications between the port and sources of supply
in south-west Lancashire, Yorkshire, and Cheshire. All this activity
was largely distinct from other factors which widened the scope of
the port's trade such as, for example, the investment of merchant
capital in the African trade. As we shall see, however, the interaction
of the trade in slaves led not only to a variety of new import trades,
but to the promotion of commercial activity through the establishment of banking and insurance facilities and through a more closely-
knit identity of interests in the ordering of these new trades under

regulation from trade associations. In other words, the port of Liverpool was assuming international status and was in process of creating a trading and an institutional framework to protect, encourage and enlarge its economic potentialities.

II

Slaves.

The introduction of a whole series of new products into Liverpool's import trade was, at one and the same time, the result of new demands and the entry of merchants and seamen into the African and West Indian trade. As we have seen, the establishment of sugar refineries had led to the growth of contacts between Liverpool and the West Indies. In the early years of the eighteenth century, as an adjunct to the sugar trade, Liverpool merchants had engaged in a fairly extensive contraband trade in Lancashire cloth with Spanish traders in Kingston, Jamaica. This trade, however, was prohibited in Parliament in 1747 as an infringement of the Navigation Laws, and the merchants so engaged had to transfer their resources. More often than not they were drawn into the African trade.[27]

There are known records of the carriage of negroes in Liverpool ships from Africa to the West Indies as early as 1700.[28] Probably there were voyages before this date, but it was not until after 1740 that a great expansion took place. Before 1740 the profitability of the trade to Liverpool merchants was curtailed by the fact that it was dominated by their rivals in London and Bristol. By the middle years of the century the Bristol merchants were beginning to compete on favourable terms with London merchants. After 1760, however, the Liverpool venturers, partly by reason of improved ship design and partly because of commercial acumen, were selling negroes in the West Indies at much cheaper rates than those offered by the London or Bristol men.[29] This enabled Liverpool, in a comparatively short time, to acquire a large share of the trade. Its importance was recognised by the Corporation who petitioned Parliament in 1788 against abolition proposals 'which so essentially concern the welfare of the Town and Port of Liverpool'.

Such new enterprise, morally indefensible and—let it be stated—odious in the eyes of the majority of Liverpool's most prominent citizens, was undertaken by comparatively few men as a regular business. Chief among them (for which records are extant) were the

Davenports, the Leylands, the Earles, the Backhouses, and the Tarletons, while many others, such as the brothers Arthur and Benjamin Heywood, engaged in single or a limited number of ventures purely as a speculation. In the cold light of financial gain, the business was far less remunerative than has generally been supposed. Net returns on individual voyages fluctuated between 500 per cent and total loss.[30] By its very nature it was hazardous and uncertain and even though it was highly organised, average returns remained low. It was above all a highly speculative trade and rested upon the availability of credit from the merchant to the planter.[31] Indirectly, however, it was a source of profit to the town and to the hinterland of Liverpool inasmuch as it needed supplies of cheap goods to maintain it, and was a ready source for the supply of food such as sugar and raw materials such as cotton. As far as Liverpool merchants were concerned the nature of the so-called triangular trade was not simply that of a ratio between outward cargoes, negroes or returning West Indian or American produce; it had grown out of older trades in which cloth and salt had mainly been exchanged for sugar and tobacco. It stimulated a commercial mechanism which embraced the exchange of any variety of products which could be bought and sold at a profit. Not invariably did Liverpool ships bring back West Indian or American cargoes. Of 110 ships' voyages examined by the author, only 15 brought back produce to the venturers.[32] The remaining 95 returned either in ballast or with small freights for other merchants. The proceeds from the sale of slaves were remitted in the form of bills. These bills were discounted in Liverpool and elsewhere and the balances thus created against the planters enabled other merchants, with ships better adapted than the slave ships for the carriage of produce, to engage directly in the transport of cotton, coffee, cocoa, rum, sugar, dyewood, and tobacco. In this way a stimulus was given to the creation of banking facilities; one such resultant creation being Heywood's bank. Another direct effect was seen in the employment of resources in shipbuilding. William Fisher was a chief supplier of hulls to slave traders. The process was relatively simple. The hull would be fitted and rigged and her holds filled with outward cargo at the expense of the company of venturers. The voyage completed, the ship as often as not was sold and a profit declared on the undertaking as a whole. The next cargo would start *ab initio*. After 1780, however, companies began to be formed for the sailing of fleets of vessels, demands for ships increased and shortages of shipping space occurred. It was at one such juncture that the Rathbones, a family violently opposed to the slave trade, found their legitimate business of importing timber impeded. They thereupon took the decision to enter the ship-building business and supply their own needs.

The profitability of the Liverpool slave trade has been the subject of much speculation.[33] It must be remembered that, for a large part of the time when Liverpool merchants were engaged in the trade, this country was at war. Privateering was a recognised form of activity and many a group of Liverpool merchants profited from it; but they were equally the victims of privateering. The risks in the African trade were great and for this reason, if for no other, a high return was expected from it. It is true that after 1775 some voyages realised as much as 500 per cent. More often than not, however, the return was less than 15 per cent, and many a voyage returned less than this. Sometimes a loss on the sale of negroes could be offset by the sale of gold dust and ivory from the West African coast.[34] If conditions were unfavourable in the West Indies, a ship's captain might have to dispose of his human cargo at prices far below a remunerative level. Against the proceeds from the sale of negroes had to be set a whole series of fixed charges, including not only wages to the crew and commissions to the captain and agents, but privileges to the captain, mate and other members of the ship's company on the number of negroes sold, very often amounting to as much as one-third of the aggregate proceeds. When the final balance was cast, an individual merchant might have cause to complain that, in view of the hazards of the trade, and the high rate of the depreciation of his ships, his return on capital was not overlarge. If the return to the individual was not so great as some historians would have us believe, there can be no doubt that the economic advantages accruing to Liverpool from the slave trade were inherently bound up with the port's growing prosperity. The 42 principal African traders left a total personal estate valued at £342,000.[35] In terms of hard cash this represented an average of £8,143, but if the value of land and other property were added the total would have been in excess of £550,000 with an average value of resources at approximately £13,000. The real point at issue is not the size of the individual or the aggregate amount, but the fact that a considerable sum was continuously available in the port for the promotion of trade and the stimulation of demand. In this respect, it is of relevance to know that at the height of the slave trade in 1790, 138 Liverpool ships were engaged with a tonnage of 24,530, employing 3,716 seamen. The total value of outfits amounted to £357,000 and the capital employed was £1·04 million.[36]

By 1770, the imports of West Indian and American products had reached high levels: sugar 8,250 tons, cotton 1,510 tons, rum 186,750 gallons and tobacco 4,000 tons.[37] Forty years later, in 1810, the figures show that a tremendous expansion had taken place. That this should have been so is to some extent remarkable, as the commercial climate was not invariably propitious. Although the planter, ship-owner, and manufacturer had been able to build up a considerable trade behind the shelter of the free port system[38] and the Navigation Laws, the incidence of war, and finally the abolition of the slave trade itself, had a depressive influence. Furthermore, the state of Britain's internal economy could on occasion cause contraction in demand for overseas products; the financial crisis of 1793 and the commodity crisis of 1797 exemplified this. Nevertheless, despite crises and a growing volume of bankruptcies among merchants, money-lenders, and bankers, the volume of West Indian-type products continued to increase. Of the 24 principal commodities imported from the West Indies, cocoa, coffee, dyewood, sugar, and rum were the most valuable. Between 1785 and 1810, imports of cocoa into Liverpool rose from 25 tons to 550 tons. Up to 1800, the West Indian source supplied the whole of Liverpool's needs but thereafter the bulk of the imports of this commodity came from Central and South America. In much the same way, coffee (1,295 tons in 1785; 4,626 tons in 1810) was originally almost wholly imported from the West Indies but, after 1800, imports began to arrive in increasing quantities from South America and after 1810 more than 50 per cent came from this source. The most important commodity, cotton, rising from just under 2,000 tons in 1785 to 40,000 tons in 1810, was subject to constantly changing sources of supply. Up to 1801, the West Indies had been the chief source with substantial shipments from the Mediterranean in particular years. Thereafter the United States was the principal source of raw cotton. By 1810, the West Indies was supplying only 6 per cent and the United States' total had risen to well over 50 per cent. This dominant position was maintained throughout the nineteenth century. Imports of sugar (rising from 16,600 tons in 1785 to 46,000 tons in 1810) were, as one would expect, wholly a West Indian commodity. In fact, until 1805, all sugar imported into Liverpool came from the West Indies; after that date, however, the United States and South America began to encroach upon this monopoly and by 1835 the Islands were supplying only 50 per cent of Liverpool's needs. In this latter year, a significant new source was opened up, the East Indies supplying some 16 per cent of total imports. This was a reflection of the cessation of the East India Company's monopoly and the bringing of the Far East within the acquisitive grasp of Liverpool's merchants and ship-owners. The import of rum followed the same pattern of growth and differentiation of source, increasing from 396,000 gallons in 1785 to 578,000 gallons in 1810. This commodity was almost wholly imported from the West Indies until 1815. Thereafter, the percentage fell and, by the middle of the 1820s, Liverpool was importing half her total supplies from Central and South America. The same process of diversification can be found in the substitution of Baltic and Canadian timber for West Indian logwood; Mediterranean and Far Eastern fruit, ginger, and pepper also began to replace West Indian supplies. In short, there was a shift away from markets which had served Liverpool's needs for more than a century to the widening horizon of new markets in all parts of the world.[39]

What had caused these changes? One prime factor influencing the scope of trading activity sprang from 21 years of war with continental Europe and, in 1812, with the United States of America. The impact of the Continental System, Milan Decrees, embargoes and other dislocations to the normal flow of trade, led to diversions of resources into new and, more often than not, equally profitable avenues of trade. There was, however, a secondary factor which has not been generally noticed and which is remarkably substantiated by the figures quoted above. This was the mounting strength of the move-ment, actively promoted in Liverpool by William Roscoe and William Rathbone, for the abolition of the slave trade. Feeling the growing strength of opposition, the more actively engaged slave traders (who were, if nothing else, shrewd business men) started as early as 1795 to hedge their risks. This took the form of widening the scope of their trade with new markets (particularly those in Central and South America) so that, in the event of a curtailment of the African trade, their capital could still find profitable employment elsewhere. The net result of this was that as one source of wealth was closed, many more were created. In this way Liverpool's merchants and seamen were given a new and more dynamic interest in the development of trade with the whole world—the keynote of Liverpool's strength and prosperity in the nineteenth century.

III

Although the trade of Liverpool was fast assuming an expansive character, it was subject to degrees of fluctuation which, over short periods, were catastrophic in their effect. Such fluctuations were caused by the impact of war, by overspeculation in commodities or by shortage of funds in the hands of bankers and merchants, coupled with too great an extension of credit. This was also an over-riding fact after 1780; thereafter trade came increasingly under the influence of cyclical movements. This fact, in particular application to Liverpool, was of major importance to the pattern of expansion. The economy of the town had become firmly linked with the textile industry in Lancashire and Cheshire as well as with the producers of many primary products overseas. Thus any adverse set of conditions affecting the one or the other was bound to act in a double sense on the prosperity of Liverpool.

The crises of 1793, 1797 and (to a lesser extent) 1813, were examples of the growing sensitivity of the port's commercial mechanism to economic fluctuations in the world at large. A high level of speculation in foreign produce in 1792, followed by a short fall in commodity prices coupled with uncertainty over the political situation, led to lack of confidence and restriction of credit.[40] Unfavourable conditions induced a number of bankruptcies among importing merchant firms and there followed a run on the banks as confidence began to wane. The crisis broke in March and reached its peak in June, sweeping away in its course one of the town's largest banking houses, Charles Caldwell & Company. The contraction of credit arising from this crisis amounted, in Liverpool alone, to three-quarters of a million pounds. This had restrictive effects on large numbers of small merchants with relatively large commitments for the supply of piece-goods outwards to foreign markets. They found themselves suddenly unable to meet calls upon them. As a consequence, the import of raw cotton fell from 35,000,000 lb in 1792 to 19,000,000 lb in 1793.[41] Faced with the prospect of widespread ruin, the Common Council, on petition from 112 merchants, made representations to Parliament and secured the passage of a local Act enabling them to issue Corporation notes up to a given amount. A Loan Office was set up and, against due security, notes were issued in 1793. The effect of this action was almost instantaneous. The pressure upon the banks was relieved, bankruptcies ceased and trade began to revive. The Corporation had once again demonstrated its authority and, by its intervention, had helped to sustain the prosperity of the port. On this occasion it may also have prevented a prolongation of industrial depression in the textile areas of Lancashire and Cheshire.

The crises of 1797 and 1813 were caused by a different set of circumstances, though the results were similar, arising from a restriction of cash and a curtailment of credit facilities. The initial causes of the crisis in 1797 sprang from an external drain on resources largely brought about by the restoration of a gold standard in France. This in turn led to a restriction of cash payments. The effects of the crisis can be seen, particularly in the decline of figures for exports of piece-goods, imports of raw cotton and output of Yorkshire woollens. Employment in shipping fell sharply and even the iron trade, which had been generally prosperous throughout the war, was adversely affected.[42] The impact of all this on Liverpool was serious and far-reaching. As trade declined, forward commitments were cancelled, credit contracted and merchants, speculating on a rising market in commodities, were over-extended and forced into bankruptcy. The resultant ruin to trade, shipbuilding, sailmaking, rope-making and allied occupations was as great as the crisis of 1793 had been to the smaller cotton merchants.

The dislocation in the pattern of Liverpool's trade between 1812 and 1813 was due less to economic than political events. The prologue to the war of 1812 with the United States has to be set against the background of the Napoleonic Wars, against attempts to stifle trade by means of Decrees and Orders in Council. From the point of view of growth, the measures promulgated by the British and French governments did not seem seriously to affect Liverpool's progressive development. The same, however, cannot be said of the worsening of relations with the United States, though the actual effects of the war itself on the fortunes of merchants trading with America were far less serious than has been hitherto supposed.[43] What did cause havoc, however, was the uncertainty which preceded the war and the chaos following the passage of the Non-Importation Act. As in earlier crises, the small men suffered the most. The earnings of shipwrights, carpenters, chandlers and other tradesmen were affected by the absence of American shipping, a situation which did not improve until 1813 when ships began to arrive from Brazil and the West Indian trade started to show signs of revival. The six months of trade with the United States which ensued after the Orders in Council had been repealed enabled merchants to clear stocks but the returns from this trade in the form of commissions were insufficient for them to meet commitments, especially if they had extended credit to their American customers.[44] Funds normally transmitted from European sales of American produce were not forthcoming during 1811 and 1812, because of the general economic depression, it was impossible for merchants to recoup their losses by selling American produce at high prices on the home market. There is no doubt that the war of 1812 seriously affected the promotion of Liverpool's trade, but there is ample evidence to show that those who suffered most were the speculators in produce rather than the legitimate merchants. This was especially the case with those who expected to profit from a shortage in cotton. Thus the phenomena, associated with cyclical fluctuations and now inherent in Liverpool's economy when aggravated by war, privateering and seasonal variations in supply, caused widespread damage and hardship to merchants and craftsmen alike. The rise and fall in shipping and in shipbuilding activity was a corollary of these fluctuations.

IV

The over-all increase in the volume of trade in the period 1750 to 1835 was, apart from the years of crisis already referred to, reflected in the general level of production in shipbuilding in Liverpool. As one might expect, there was a great increase in the volume of tonnage entering and clearing the port. Not only was there a substantial rise in the number of foreign ships, in particular, from the United States, but up to 1800 there was an extensive increase in the number of British owned ships; an increasing proportion of the latter being Liverpool built.

 There had been shipbuilders in Liverpool from early times. The builders had slipways along the shore before 1700. During the eighteenth century a great stimulus was given to the establishment of shipbuilding firms, partly because of a growing demand for ships, partly because supplies of English oak were becoming exhausted and the port was receiving increasing supplies of African, American, and Baltic timber and also because, in time of war, it was stated that the route to and from Liverpool via the Irish sea was a comparatively safe one.[45] Between 1700 and 1750, there are records of 144 shipwrights and allied workers in Liverpool. By the end of the century the figure had increased to 600.[46] Not all of these may have been continuously employed in shipbuilding, but in 1804, an account of employment for the merchant yards of Great Britain returned a figure of 487 for Liverpool. At that time the most important shipbuilding firms were Humble & Hurry, Rathbone & Co., Fisher & Co., Leather & Co., Hind & Son, Peter Quirk and William Quirk. In the period 1789 to 1808, Liverpool built 155 ships, more than half of which were between 100 and 200 tons and only two were over 800 tons. By comparison with this, if one examines the shipbuilding activity in Liverpool during the twenty years from 1815 to 1835, the following pattern is made clear; 51 ships of between 100 and 200 tons were built, 48 between 200 and 300 tons, 34 between 300 and 400 tons, 10 between 400 and 500 tons, 3 between 500 and 600 tons, and only 2 between 600 and 700 tons.[47]

The inference is that Liverpool's shipbuilding activities had suffered a relative decline following the ending of the Napoleonic Wars, and that the magnitude of operations (as indicated by the size of ship built) had scarcely increased over a period of 50 years. This is surprising when one remembers the vast increase which took place in these years in the volume of Liverpool's trade. One possible answer is that Liverpool merchant capital (which provided roughly 80 per cent of the funds for shipbuilding) sought other cheaper sources of supply after 1815. The Liverpool Registers of Merchant Ships confirm this. East coast ports such as Hull, Whitby, and Scarborough, were receiving orders from Liverpool merchants for ships of a larger tonnage at a lower cost per ton than those being produced in Liverpool yards. Also, the impact of Canadian tonnage in filling Liverpool's needs was increasingly apparent after 1815. In 1825 it was estimated that a 300-ton ship cost approximately 95 dollars per ton in Canada and 110 dollars per ton in Britain.[48] The consequences of this cost differentiation can be judged from the figures of external purchases. By 1835, roughly half the ships being used by Liverpool merchants had been built either in Canada or in other British ports.

During the first half of the nineteenth century, the same dynamic influence in the pattern and growth of Liverpool's trade is discernible as that in the eighteenth century. There was, however, the significant difference that new industrial processes added new products to the cargoes carried, new and more efficient means of transport increased the profitability of trade and added to the wealth of the port's merchant class. In general terms, however, Liverpool continued to control the export trade for coal, salt and manufactured goods, produced within a radius of one hundred miles, in return for food and raw materials. The magnitude of the expansion involved a vast outpouring of capital from the port into the financing of new trades, new markets and new means of communication.

Against this background the relentless pressure for coal and salt continued. For a period of more than a century and a half, by a process of ruthless rationalisation, the organisation of these two trades had reached a high stage of efficiency. The production of rock salt and white salt was raised from 150,000 tons in 1800 to 500,000 tons in 1840 and to 1,000,000 tons in 1870.[49] Of these amounts, Liverpool was exporting 452,000 tons overseas by 1852 and 116,000 tons coastwise and to Ireland.[50] As the old craft industries, such as watch-making and clock-making, glass and pottery, declined in the face of growing competition from Switzerland, America, St Helens, and Staffordshire, they were replaced by new ones. In this context, the fundamental nature of the old internal coal-salt triangle is again forced upon our attention in that it created ideal conditions for the manufacture of chemicals. The successful introduction of the Leblanc process by Muspratt at his Vauxhall Road works in the 1820s laid the foundations of the heavy chemical industry in south-west Lancashire. His work promoted the establishment of soda factories in the St Helens, Widnes and Runcorn areas and, later, with the adoption of the ammonia-soda process, in the Cheshire salt fields. The alkali, bleaching powders, and other chemicals were not only absorbed in large quantities by the textile industry, but became the basis of a new trade with the United States. The production of soda also stimulated the manufacture of soap and glass. It enabled the soap boilers of Merseyside to utilise the cheap and plentiful supplies of palm oil from West Africa instead of more expensive fats. It was the foundation on which St Helens built up its plate, window and bottle glass industries.[51] By 1857, Liverpool was exporting 33,000 tons of soda mostly to the United States—and all the soap to Ireland as well as four-fifths of the total British exports of this commodity.[52] Exports of glass of all descriptions had, by the same year, reached 11,000 tons. In the traditional trades, a phenomenal expansion had taken place during the first half of the nineteenth century. Imports of raw cotton into Liverpool increased from 40,000 tons in 1810 to just under 360,000 tons in 1850; American wheat from just over 8,000 tons to nearly 75,000 tons; flour from 900 tons to 103,000 tons; sugar from 46,000 tons to 52,000 tons; rum from 578,000 gallons to 726,000 gallons. Tobacco alone of the imported commodities showed a decrease from 8,400 tons in 1810 to just over 7,000 tons in 1850.

Exports, no less than imports, provided evidence of a rapid rate of expansion. By 1852, the port was shipping well over 1,000 million yards of piece-goods to all parts of the world; well over a quarter of a million tons of coal; 315,000 tons of iron bars, rails, hoops, rods, and pigs; 25,000 tons of linen; 8,000 tons of manufactured goods; 54,000 tons of pottery and 5,600 tons of manufactured copper. The total value of Liverpool's exports, in 1857, amounted to £55 million of which 42 per cent consisted of cotton yarns and goods, 21 per cent of other textiles and 20 per cent of metals, cutlery, hardware, and machinery.

An analysis of the causes contributing to this expansion shows that they were widespread and diverse in character. First and foremost, Liverpool's growing prosperity was simply a reflection of the rising industrial productivity and growth of effective demand in the country as a whole. Secondly, her trades had become organised and institutionalised. The West Indian and West African Associations of Liverpool merchants were principal agents in the maintenance of trade and, through their political influence and links with the Treasury, enabled loans to be raised for the financing of trade.[53] Thirdly, the old restrictive system imposed by the Navigation Laws was relaxed in 1787. Thereafter, Spanish and French colonial ships could call at certain free ports in the West Indies and a new and lucrative trade was thus opened up between the Islands and South America. There was also participation by Liverpool ships southwards from Brazilian ports in the seal and whaling fisheries of the south Shetlands.[54] Fourthly, trade with the United States, already increasing after 1790, was given great impetus after the war of 1812 and showed a phenomenal increase in volume. In this process (apart from the difficult years between 1811 and 1813) the American Chamber of Commerce, founded in 1801 in Liverpool, did much to foster better relations and promote trading contacts.[55] Fifthly, new markets were added to Liverpool's list and came within her commercial orbit for the first time. Her merchants had long since agitated for the breaking of the East India Company's monopoly with the Far East. The Indian trade was thrown open in 1813; that with China in 1833. This enabled merchants, in particular John Gladstone and William Rathbone, to develop new enterprises and trade in new commodities and with the coming of the steamship it enabled shipowners such as Alfred Holt, Thomas and James Harrison, John Swire, the Rathbones and others, to open up the Pacific to Liverpool capital.

It was, above all, the accumulation and promotional use of capital which gave some Liverpool men and Liverpool ships the means, not only of realising, but of providing employment for new ideas. In part, this took the form of creating a more efficient system of communication between the port and markets, both for raw materials and finished goods in Lancashire, Yorkshire, the Midlands, and the Black Country. Starting with the opening of the Liverpool and Manchester railway in 1830 (in which Liverpool corn merchants had a lively interest[56]) a vast railway network was created, thus augmenting the geographical importance of Liverpool and stimulating the expansion of trade after 1830. In part also and as correlative to the building of railways, it led to the promotion of new capital works such as docks, quays, warehouses and port facilities necessary for the accommodation of the increasing volume of goods to be handled. Finally it provided for a relatively swift transfer from sail to steam, to the rise of the Liverpool steamship owner and to the amalgamation of engineering know-how, seamanship and commercial skill which gave Liverpool a dominant position in the British economy during a period of forty-odd years from 1870 to 1914.

CHAPTER FOUR

Shipping and Commercial Organisation, 1800-1900

I

As material prosperity increased, the Liverpool of the eighteenth and early nineteenth centuries acquired new physical features which were, in both style and taste, the essence of a growing spirit of enlightenment. Liverpool men and Liverpool ships had done much through the media of wood and sail to stamp the imprint of their ideas upon a relatively small part of the world. With the transformation to iron and steam their grasp of commercial potentiality brought the oceans and ports of the whole globe under their influence. As a result, Liverpool merchants and shipowners, endowed with great wealth, began to live in a style befitting their influence, and their fine town houses became the centres of gracious living.

To some extent, the process of acquiring the art and culture of a gentleman can be traced back to an *élite* of Liverpool merchants, whose views and cultural standards did much to alter the character of the town itself and, by example, to enliven the minds of its citizens. Among this group were to be found John Gladstone, William Rathbone, Jonas Bold, Samuel Hope, Nicholas Waterhouse, Benjamin Heywood and, a little later, George Holt and William Brown. But of them all, by far the most influential by virtue of the width and variety of his interests, was William Roscoe; so much so, that if a description of the spirit of Liverpool between 1790 and 1820 were to be sought, it could not be better designated than by the term 'Roscoe's Liverpool'.

William Roscoe was undoubtedly the product of his age. As a banker, he was fully engaged in the commercial life of the port. As a man of liberal political and social ideals, he was wholeheartedly against many of the practices engendered by greed and lust for power, in particular the slave trade, which he abhorred, doing so much to effect its abolition. As a scholar, he was a first-class botanist and his book on the classification of species had a lasting effect on the future development of botanical work in this country. As a biographer, his volumes on the lives of Lorenzo de Medici (1795) and Leo X (1805) had distinctive literary quality. His general ideas on education were ahead of his time. He was active as chairman of the General Committee for the establishment of the Liverpool Royal Institution in 1817 and became its first President in 1822.[1] His library, which contained many first editions of seventeenth-century poets, was the envy of his contemporaries, and his paintings, including a fine set of Italian Primitives, eventually became the basis of the city collection in the Walker Art Gallery.[2] His interest in architecture was equally perceptive. He took a prominent part in designing the outward features of the town's public buildings and helped to finance the construction of one of the town's best-known streets of Georgian houses, Rodney Street. His comprehensive faculties were freely put at the service of his fellow citizens as banker, as Member of Parliament for Liverpool and as a general committee man. In short, the spirit of Roscoe's genius communicated new standards of taste and basic principles of humanitarianism to his contemporaries and, as a consequence, the materialistic and acquisitive instinct of an earlier period was given new perspective and new direction.

In physical terms, this new spirit was manifest in the improvement of the town's public and domestic architecture. A fine new Town Hall was built from designs by John Wood in 1754, replacing the earlier Exchange and Council Hall dating from 1673. When the roof, dome and interior were destroyed by fire in 1795, John Gladstone, as prime mover, secured the necessary funds to rebuild it in the form which has lasted down to the present day.[3] Castle Street was widened in 1786 and the old clutter of mediaeval houses backing on to it was demolished to make room for new commercial buildings.[4] The old Castle, previously dismantled, was finally removed and St George's, a fine new church, constructed on the site. Thus the business quarter of the town had been partially replanned by the end of the eighteenth century. Meanwhile, on the outskirts, the semi-circular belt of Georgian streets from the river continued its progress; Rodney Street, Hope Street, Catherine Street, and Parliament Street were all part of this development and during the 1820s and 1830s the Abercromby Square area, following the draining of the old peat moss, was in process of completion. The march of bricks and mortar, however, was not purely of a domestic character; hospitals, churches, and schools came within the programme. A fine concert hall was opened in Bold Street and a music room in Myrtle Street, adjacent to the site which later housed the Philharmonic Hall. There were theatres in Williamson Square and Queen's Square, the Lyceum library in Ranelagh Street and the Athenaeum library and newsroom in School Lane. In form, therefore, the town began to assume a more gracious and elegant aspect and its physical features were conforming to the wealth and taste of its principal inhabitants.

A subtle change, however, was soon to take place in the composition of Liverpool Society. The powerfully-knit commercial families, who as freemen formed the governing body of the Corporation, had begun to widen its membership. The newer men, many of whom derived their wealth from trade, had purchased blocks of land in the outlying areas of Liverpool around Gateacre, Kirkdale, West Derby and in the intervening spaces of Edge Lane and Wavertree. Some of these men were agents or solicitors to the Earls of Sefton and Derby. John Leigh and John Shaw Leigh, for example, had acquired land at Edgehill and were *rentiers* in the Lovat, Troughton and Cardwell street development. Richard Earle, another of Lord Derby's agents, also owned land in this area and he and the Leighs amassed considerable fortunes, particularly from sales of land to the railway companies after 1830. Very often, the acquisition of this land had begun as a speculation on credit; other land, however, such as that owned by the Durning family in the Edge Lane-Wavertree neighbourhood, was directly purchased out of the profits from trade. The changing system of land ownership can be traced on Charles Eyes' *Plan of the Town and Township of Liverpool 1796*, and Jonathan Bennison's *Plan of the Town and Port of Liverpool 1835 and 1841*. These men of real estate, the Hollingshead, Drinkwaters, Harpers, Cases, Aspinalls, Clarkes, and Branckers, were acceptable within the closed system of social status. They were an intermediate class between the older Liverpool hierarchy and the future merchanting, steamship-owning families of the latter half of the nineteenth century. For the most part, the outlying suburban areas of Everton, Kirkdale, West Derby, and Toxteth were still within the possession of the noble families of Derby and Sefton. They were joined by another noble house. In 1821, the Marquis of Salisbury married the daughter of Bamber Gascoyne and granddaughter of Isaac Green, a Liverpool and Prescot attorney. Through his wife, the Marquis inherited the manors of Everton, West Derby, Childwall and Wavertree, and thus established his family as a considerable owner of land on the outskirts of Liverpool. These estates, together with those in Kirkdale owned by the Derbys and those in Toxteth owned by the Seftons, formed a strategic ring. They were in a fairly continuous state of development from 1830 onwards, for the building of streets, and through sale (as we shall see later) to the railway companies whose extending lines of communication had to pass through them. In the process, the wealth of the landowner was augmented and through this his influence in the life of the town and port was, in both a political and social sense, increased. By contrast, the poverty of the mass of Liverpool's population (aggravated by the flood of Irish and Welsh immigrants) was to be seen in the overcrowded courts and cellar dwellings of the old town. The distinction between rich and poor was thus giving the town both a new aspect and a social problem of considerable magnitude.

II

The lure of Liverpool, both as a source of livelihood and prospective fortune and as a centre where education and culture could be acquired, was undoubtedly great. Young men of ability began to leave the farms and fields of their ancestors and seek new careers in shipping, merchanting or shipbuilding. John Swire came from Halifax in 1812; George Holt from Rochdale (with a 'guinea in his pocket') in 1807; the Brocklebanks and Booths at an earlier period from Whitehaven and Orford respectively; the Ismays from Maryport and the Inmans from Silverdale; the brothers Thomas and James Harrison from Garstang; William Wheelwright even came over from the United States. Of them all, the most flamboyant and, in some respects, the most successful was a young Welshman from Caermarthen named Alfred Jones. These new men, among others, provided a galaxy of talent which when allied to the experience of the established families, the Rathbones, the Fishers, the Gladstones, the Claytons and the Williamsons, was to provide the resources, the energy and the explosive ideas necessary for the transformation of Liverpool into a steamship port during the second half of the nineteenth century. This was not all. Their individual talents and specialisms created an amalgam of knowledge of engineering know-how, of commercial enterprise, of administrative efficiency and of practical experience unrivalled in any other port at that time.

It is, perhaps, true that the founders of Liverpool's largest shipping companies were pioneers in the management and running of steamships. Nevertheless, shipping enterprise was in constant process of promotion, capital resources were built up and shipping lines, engaged in a variety of new trades, were established. Some firms, such as Bahr-Behrend & Co and Brocklebanks, had their origins in the eighteenth century, but of the principal promoters after 1800 the most prominent were John Bibby, James Moss, the Papayanni brothers, John Glynn, William Lamport, George Holt, Charles McIver, Robert Alexander, Donald Currie, James Baines, James Beazley, John Pilkington, Henry Threlfall Wilson, and James Dowie.

Some of these men began their careers as shipowners in a very small way. James Moss took shares in a ship and gradually built up his capital stock before launching his company of sailing ships to the Mediterranean; John Bibby began by running a small fleet of packet ships between Parkgate and Dublin before establishing his service to Alexandria and, later, to the north Atlantic. After 1869, much of the success of this line was due to Frederick Leyland. By means of shrewd investment in ships and with the help of friends, Leyland accumulated sufficient capital to be able to purchase the Bibby line in 1873. John Glynn founded his company largely from his own resources in 1811. Charles McIver started his connection with the Mediterranean in 1851 with one ship. He was so successful that Samuel Cunard and George Burns joined him. Thus was created the Cunard service to the Levant. William Lamport and George Holt founded their firm in 1845 partly by capital from friends and associates and partly from inherited wealth. They were in association with James Moss in running ships to the eastern Mediterranean, but shortly afterwards established a more lasting connection in the River Plate trade. The ships of all these companies not only maintained and increased Liverpool's trading relationship with traditional eighteenth-century markets, but developed sources of supply (particularly after the repeal of the Corn Laws) for grain from Russia and the Balkans and, during the cotton famine in the 1860s, for cotton from Alexandria.

On the north Atlantic, apart from the Liverpool-based companies which will be considered later, there was considerable activity from American companies using Liverpool as a terminal port. The regular sailing-ship schedules of the Black Ball line were part of the general pattern; the Diamond line, founded by Enoch Train in 1839 traded between Liverpool and Boston. During the American Civil War George Warren, who had come to Liverpool in 1853 to manage the Liverpool office, gained control of the line and transferred the ships to the British flag, making Liverpool the headquarters of the company. Although continuing to use sailing ships until 1877, the Warren line had begun the transformation to steam as early as 1863.

In the early trade between Liverpool, India, and Australia (apart from the Brocklebanks, Harrisons, Clans and others) the names of Robert Alexander, Donald Currie, James Beazley, John Pilkington, Henry Threlfall Wilson, and James Baines, need a brief mention. Alexander, in conjunction with Liston, Young & Co of London, had started a sailing-ship service with India and Australia in 1864. He went into steamships in 1871 and eventually created the Sun Steam Ship Co which, in turn, became operational as the Hall line. Donald Currie, a former Cunard employee, founded the Castle line to trade with Calcutta, but was drawn into the South African trade and later his line became part of the Union Castle organisation. In the Australian trade, Liverpool became a rival to London for the carriage of emigrants, particularly during the period of the Australian gold-rush. Most of the companies engaged in this trade, however, did not long survive the search for gold. Baines's Black Ball line which, in 1860, had 86 ships employing 4,000 men, was driven into bankruptcy; Wilson and Pilkington started as ship-brokers in 1845 and their first White Star ship sailed in 1849. In 1867, however, the flag and goodwill were sold to T. H. Ismay.[5] James Beazley's company with 28 sailing ships was one of the few Australian services to survive, though in 1864, with the re-organisation of his resources in the British Shipowners Co, both sailing and steamships were henceforth used. Subsequently, this company came under the management of Gracie Beazley and Co.

Enough has been said to demonstrate the intensity of Liverpool's shipping enterprise between 1815 and 1870. By the middle of the nineteenth century, the relative importance of Liverpool's overseas markets, measured in terms of tonnage cleared, was as follows; to the United States, 852.6 thousand tons; to Canada, 187.5; to the West Indies, 71.1; to Brazil and the River Plate, 76.1; to the Mediterranean and the Black Sea, 153.4; to Africa and the Cape of Good Hope, 44.4; to Australia, 23.3; to the Baltic, 14.0; to France 34.8

The Mersey and the Dee: the Collins' chart of 1689

Liverpool's waterfront in 1650

TO

RICHARD STATHAM, ESQ., TOWN CLERK,

THIS VIEW OF LIVERPOOL, AS IT APPEARED IN 1650,

From a Painting in the Possession of Ralph Peters, Esq.

IS HUMBLY INSCRIBED, BY HIS OBEDIENT SERVANT,

and to Spain and Portugal, 25·8.[6] It is clear from this that while she was still maintaining such traditional markets as the Baltic and the Mediterranean with degrees of importance, Liverpool's main sources of livelihood from shipping were being derived from the cross-Atlantic trades. This reflected the growing preponderance of primary products such as cotton, sugar, coffee, rubber, timber and grain, in import cargoes, and of the increasing flood of emigrants and textiles outwards. It was not a true balance, but it is signficant in the light of the eventual changes which were soon to be made by the advent of the steamship, changes not only in the relative importance of cargoes, but in the differential pattern of new markets opened up and served.

It is estimated that nearly £2 million was accumulated in the creation and operation of sailing ship lines. Much of this capital was, by 1860–70, being re-organised in the formation of steamship services; but perhaps the most important contribution which such companies made sprang from the service to markets and the commercial organisation which was established in ports all over the world. This was the linking period between the eighteenth century when Liverpool's trade was based primarily on the produce of plantation economies, and the steamship trade of the later nineteenth century based on continental demands for manufactured goods.[7] This change in emphasis meant also changes in products and in sources of supply. It was the forerunner of Australian and South African wool; of New Zealand and Argentinian meat; of Canadian, Argentinian, and Australian wheat; of South African, Brazilian, and Mediterranean fruit; of Indian tea and rice. In return for these products, Merseyside was to exchange cotton piece-goods, engineering goods, machinery, chemicals, and railway equipment. In other words, the enterprise of the latter-day sailing-ship men created and maintained preconditions essential for the rapid expansion which was to come after 1870.

Before the efforts of the steamship men could be brought to fruition, however, the whole question of the merits of iron and steam over those of wood and sail in the composition of Liverpool's mercantile marine had to be solved. It is not necessary to go into details of a controversy which raged intermittently over a period of three decades. It was hard to convince Liverpool's merchants and shipowners that a steamship could be made a more economical form of transport than the graceful clipper ship. Even as late as 1857/8 the voyage of the Harrison ship *Admiral Grenfell* to the China coast seemed to prove the arguments of the clipper men.[8] She not only sailed in waters far beyond the reach of any steamship, but made a net profit to her owners on this voyage alone of £20,000. Yet within four years the Harrisons were building steamships and Alfred Holt was establishing his steamship service to the West Indies, preparatory to his greater undertaking of sending steamships to China and Singapore.

What was the link between the 1830s when sailing ships were predominant and the 1860s when they were being replaced by the steamship? For the first part of the answer to this question, we must turn to the aspirations and work of another Liverpool immigrant, William Laird, who came from Scotland in 1810 and established an ironworks on the Birkenhead side of the river in 1824.[9] As we shall see later, his plans included not only the building of an up-to-date, well-designed town to house his workmen, but also a dock system with canal communication to the shipping roads at Hoyle Lake which might, in time, rival Liverpool as a port. It was but a short step for Laird, with his engineering skill, to progress from the manufacture of iron to the construction of iron ships. In this he was encouraged by his son John, who had been trained as a solicitor, but abandoned that career to join his father's business in 1828. In that same year the first order for an iron ship was received from the Irish Inland Steam Navigation Co. The vessel in question was a 60-foot iron lighter. Two further orders for similar vessels followed and in 1830 a fourth order was placed which, as events proved, was greatly to enhance the reputation of the Lairds as shipbuilders. This was for a paddle steamer called *Lady Lansdowne*. She was 133 feet long and, at William Laird's suggestion, was equipped with watertight bulkheads.[10] By 1838, the yard had built 17 ships, among them the *Rainbow*, at that time the largest iron ship to have been constructed, and the *Robert F. Stockton*, their first screw-driven ship.

As we have seen, Liverpool's shipbuilding industry, owing to the shortage of British timber, was having to rely more and more on imported supplies. This raised costs and led merchants and ship-owners to seek cheaper construction in the east-coast yards and in Canada. The new product, iron, now being fashioned into ships on Liverpool's very doorstep seemed to provide a solution to the problems causing decline in output from Liverpool yards. Laird's iron ships had a much lower unit cost of construction than wooden sailing ships, and it seemed that it was only a matter of time before a more efficient engine would be fitted to supply motive power. Unfortunately, however, the depressed years of the 1840s slowed down progress; orders for ships at the Laird works fell off and experiments could not be resumed until the following decade. By that time, elements in the problem of producing an efficient iron steamship capable of making oceanic voyages had changed, and the initiative in their solution passed from the Lairds to other hands.

The second part of the answer to the question posed above is to be found (as far as Liverpool is concerned) in the career of Alfred Holt.[11] This young man, son of George Holt, started life as an engineer, being apprenticed at an early age to the chief engineer of the Liverpool and Manchester Railway. His subsequent association as consultant to the shipping firm of Langport & Holt (in which his brother Philip had an interest) engaged his attention on problems concerned with ship design and motive power. Lamport & Holt had been interested, among other things, in sending sailing ships to the eastern Mediterranean to take part in the Alexandria trade. In conjunction with James Moss & Co, they were beginning in the early 1850s to replace sailing ships with small steamships. In July 1851 their second steamship, *Orontes*, built by Alexander Denny of Dumbarton, was lying in Liverpool awaiting her engines from the makers, Messrs Hicks of Bolton. In August, Holt sailed on this ship as supernumerary engineer, and as he himself said afterwards, this voyage gave him his first taste for marine engineering.

Alfred Holt had not been unaware of the improvements in design and motive power which the Lairds had made in the construction of iron ships. In particular he accepted the principle of the screw propeller and his first ships incorporated this method of propulsion. To have started as a ship designer in this way was no fortuitous event. Profitable employment for iron ocean-going steamships was uncertain. It is true that Tod & McGregor had launched the *City of Glasgow* and that this ship, in her short life, had acted as pioneer to the first line of Atlantic-run iron steamships owned by the Liverpool, New York & Philadelphia Steam Ship Co, founded by William Inman. It is also true that the Cunard Company were laying down iron ships with screw propellers towards the end of the 1850s. By this time the Harrisons were extending their European coastal services by the use of screw-driven iron ships and in 1866 inaugurated a Liverpool–New Orleans service with one of their most famous early steamships, the *Fire Queen*.[12] At an even earlier date William Wheelwright's Pacific Steam Navigation Company was using iron screw steamships powered by Elder's compound engine on the service between Liverpool and the western coast of South America.[13] Apart from these few isolated efforts which were largely confined to the Atlantic trade and the coastwise coal trades, iron screw steamships had made very little impression on the seagoing traffic of these Islands before 1865. By the end of the 1850s, the problems of coaling, boiler pressure, safety of the engine, propeller-shafting and overall construction of the ship were as yet too imperfectly understood to allow long-range voyages to be made.[14]

It was to these problems that Alfred Holt addressed himself. In 1852, the main sources of contention centred round the screw propeller, the tensile strength of iron and the compound engine. Holt's training as a railway engineer had endowed him with a knowledge of steam propulsion, boiler pressures and shafting. In applying this knowledge to ships, he became one of the first men to combine the features of iron, screw and engine to the transformation of our cargo carriers. The principles were incorporated into a ship with a length of $8\frac{1}{2}$ beams, depth about three-quarters thereof and powered by a compound engine. Three such ships were put into service by Holt between Liverpool and the West Indies. Although moderately successful, Holt found that the high coal consumption incurred a high cost and also that the relatively large bunkering space cut down that used for the carriage of cargo—the earning space in the ship. The final problem to be solved, therefore, was that of making the ship pay its way. This involved improvements to the engine with a view to reducing coal consumption and bunkering space. In a series of experiments on the *Cleator*, in which Holt perfected his idea of a tandem compound engine (in which high and low pressure cylinders were arranged in tandem fashion), the outcome was so successful that coal consumption was reduced to $2\frac{1}{4}$ lb per indicated hp per hour. This not only meant that the steamship could be worked at a profit, but that on long ocean voyages, such a ship, proceeding by a providentially arranged system of coaling stations would henceforth have a winning advantage over the sailing ship. It was a breakthrough which enabled Holt to start his Far Eastern service with the first three ships—*Agamemnon*, *Ajax* and *Achilles*—of his newly-established Ocean Steam Ship Company. These advances in technology enabled the Harrison brothers to rebuild the fleet of their Charente Steam Ship company, linking Liverpool with the Gulf ports, with Mexico, the West Indies, Central and South America, and India; they were instrumental in the development of Alfred Booth's line to South America; they provided Alfred Jones with the means of opening up West Africa through the African Steam Ship Company and the British & African Steam Navigation Company, and they gave to Inman and Ismay the chance to create profitable services across the Atlantic.[15]

There was, however, a counterbalancing influence to the opening up of the Far East to cargo liners, an influence which sprang from the career of Samuel Cunard and the development of North Atlantic passenger services. Cunard had been born in Halifax, Nova Scotia, in 1787. After serving with a firm of Boston shipbrokers, he started business as a trader. He and his father eventually became shipowners and secured the mail contract to carry between Newfoundland, Halifax, Boston, and Bermuda.[16] Twenty years later, when Samuel was 43, he was controlling a sailing fleet of nearly 40 ships. In 1831, Cunard and his brothers took a financial interest in a steamship, the *Royal William*, which went into service on the Halifax–Quebec route. She was a paddle steamer which in 1833 made a successful crossing of the Atlantic from Pictou to London. The advent of steamships on the Atlantic, especially with the crossings of the *Sirius* and the Great Western, fired Cunard's imagination. In 1839 he came to England, secured a contract for the carriage of mails across the Atlantic and entered into an agreement with Robert Napier to build four steamships for the new venture.

While visiting Glasgow to make final arrangements about the ships, Cunard first met George Burns, who had built up a successful line of steamships sailing between Glasgow, Belfast and Liverpool.[17] He had Liverpool connections through the McIver family who acted as his agents. Burns and David McIver agreed to provide financial support for Cunard's new service and, within a short time, 32 business men of George Burns's acquaintance had raised £270,000,[18] more than enough capital to build the four ships, float the company and set up port and sales organisations. Cunard guaranteed £55,000 (later £67,500), Napier, £6,000, Burns, £5,000, David McIver and his brother Charles, £4,000 each. Thus was established the British & North American Royal Mail Steam Packet Company, the designation by which the Cunard Company was first known. The first four ships were of 1,100 tons and were powered by engines of

420 hp; *Britannia* was the first, followed by *Acadia, Caledonia* and *Columbia*. Cunard returned to Halifax to build up the Halifax–Boston end of the line; Burns undertook administration in Britain, particularly with matters calling for negotiations with the Government; and David and Charles McIver built up the terminal organisation in Liverpool. Cunard returned to take up permanent residence in England in 1847 and died in 1878. Following his death a joint stock company was created with a capital of £2,000,000, under the title of the Cunard Steam Ship Company. Two years later, the organisation became a public company. As the prospectus stated, the needs of trans-Atlantic trade demanded ships of size and power which only a large public company could provide. We shall deal with some of the more relevant details of the operations of these ships in subsequent sections of this book.

Thus, by the end of the 1860s, Liverpool men, by experiment, had successfully put their ideas to the test. Working in the new media of iron and steam they had launched upon the world a series of new shipping companies whose operations, by the end of the century, were to embrace the five continents and most of the shipping lanes of the oceans. As a result, Liverpool ships traded in every port and brought back to the docks and warehouses of Liverpool the wealth flowing from a new commercial enterprise. It was one thing to have conquered the elements and to have brought the whole world within measure of Liverpool's grasp through the use of iron and steam; it was another matter to expand the resources, the administrative efficiency and the commercial system necessary for the exploitation of technical innovation. How this was done forms part of the second of Liverpool's revolutionary inspirations in the sphere of shipping and trade.

III

The immediate result of the effective emergence of the steamship as a potentially viable ocean carrier was a steamship building boom. In Liverpool large blocks of capital (estimated at something just under £7 million between 1869 and 1875) were invested in ships, and the number of shipping companies increased rapidly. In fact, many of these companies were single-ship companies, so organised because of the investment holding of shares and, one presumes, in order to limit liability.[19] The prospect of intense competition from home-based companies, therefore, was imminent, apart from that which would undoubtedly arise from foreign firms.

In this context, the more substantially capitalised companies sought as a primary objective the safeguarding of their financial position. This could only be done initially by breaking into established trades and by maintaining regular and efficient services. In terms of trade it meant the concentration by Liverpool shipowners on the export of coal, salt and Manchester piece-goods in return for imports of China tea, American wheat and cotton, African palm oil, Indian jute and linseed, Brazilian cotton, hides, coffee and tanning materials and West Indian sugar and cocoa. The process of establishment was not an easy one, for primary commodities were seasonal in character and accordingly in order to secure the best possible economic advantage, shipowners had to engage in a complex logistical operation. It required the right number of ships to be at the right place at the right time, with a reasonably flexible system of freight rates to meet competition from other shipowners engaged in the same trade. It also required an efficiently organised system of agents on the spot, capable of securing forward cargoes at agreed rates. In both these respects, Liverpool shipowners were highly successful. By improving the speed of his ships, Alfred Holt not only won the China tea-race by 1870, but earned as much as £100,000 from the freight on this one commodity. In this he was helped by the initiative and resource of his principal agents, Butterfield & Swire in Shanghai and Mansfield & Co in Singapore.[20] In much the same way Harrisons broke into the cotton and wheat trade of the Mississippi basin through their New Orleans agent Alfred Le Blanc & Co[21] and into the tea and linseed trade from Calcutta through Hoare, Miller & Co. In the West African trade, there was a slight difference, the flow of commodities being first in the hands of Messrs Fletcher & Parr of Liverpool and, secondly, under the guidance of Elder Dempster & Co. Working through branch houses on the Coast Alfred Jones was able to control both the carriage and a major part of the commodity trade and, in this way, to neutralise the activities of the principal merchants who might have otherwise competed with him on favourable terms.[22] The same story can be given a parallel in the Brazilian trade through the agencies of Saunders Bros & Co and in the Mexican trade through Garcia & Co of Vera Cruz.[23] In fact, wherever Liverpool steamships carried bulk commodities, men were sought with the requisite ability to serve them as agents. This by itself constitutes no new phenomenon in the relationship of the shipowner and his source of supply; the new element in this organisation lay in the initiative and financial promotion of trade which the new type of agent exercised. How then was trade financed under this system?

Perhaps the greatest difference between the old and the new-style agents lay in the fact that the new companies were highly capitalised undertakings, very often with steamship fleets of their own or under their management, and trading in a wide variety of products over a considerable part of the world. In the days of the sailing ship, merchanting had been in the hands of foreign correspondents or agencies working on a commission basis. These firms also entered into joint-account arrangements with English and American merchants, each taking a share in a particular venture. This type of arrangement was frequently used by Rathbone Bros & Co in their trade in American breadstuffs and China tea.[24] Finally, the agents bought and sold produce on their own behalf as speculators, sending goods back to England in return for shipments of manufactured Manchester cottons or Yorkshire cloth and Sheffield cutlery. The agency houses also dealt with such things as shipping and insurance for their United Kingdom correspondents, sending home detailed reports of market conditions and advising on freights and other relevant matters.

Usually the remittance of proceeds on the sale of British produce abroad was in the form of bills, drawn by the local firms on their correspondents in Britain or bought locally, or by direct purchases of such articles as cotton, tea, silk, wheat or coffee which were then sent back to be sold in Liverpool or London. Sometimes, when bills and currency were scarce (as in the China trade in the 1850s) barter arrangements were made. Very often, however, British firms might wish to import commodities without sending out export goods to cover such purchases. In this case, the transactions were financed in a variety of ways. In the cotton and tea trades, for example, letters of credit were sent to American and China firms allowing them to draw upon Liverpool houses or banks. It was quite frequently the case that credits sent out covered only a part of the cost of the goods bought; the balance was made up by a marginal credit on a specified bank. Having drawn the bills under a credit, the American, Brazilian, China, Indian or other foreign firms had to discount the bills in order to obtain currency to pay for the commodities. The usual procedure was to discount the bills with local banks or with other merchant houses requiring bills for remittances which they then had to send back to Britain.[25] Deals of this kind would normally present little difficulty; it was only when uncertainty about future trading prospects (such as that in China in the 1850s and in America during and after the Civil War) created lack of confidence, that this kind of financial structure ceased to operate efficiently.

IV

The new steamship agents performed all the functions hitherto undertaken, but they exercised greater control and, in financial matters, were generally more independent of their principals. Being broadly based in their activities they were able to offset the harmful effects of depression or shortage of funds much more effectively than the older type and more narrowly based firms. This was especially the case in the Far Eastern, Gulf, Mexican, West Indian, Brazilian, and West African trades.

In China, the growth of Indian business had, during the 1840s and 1850s, become part of a triangular pattern of settlement between Britain, India and China. The opium trade, a main item in this structure, was a lucrative one and a considerable volume of bills, used for the financing of China's trade, found its way into the hands of Indian agents.[26] Many of the older-established merchant houses in China, such as Dent & Co, Birley & Co, Jardine, Matheson & Co, had to choose between accepting bills on opium shipments or carrying an outstandingly large burden of obligations from Chinese merchants. This very often proved to be a burden which, in time of crisis, threatened their own financial stability. The new steamship men of Liverpool were men of scruples. Neither the Rathbones nor the Holts wished to become involved in any trade financed from the receipts on the sale of opium, yet, without some form of reliable commercial paper, it would have been impossible to secure cargoes and conduct a successful shipping business.

At this juncture, the forceful personality of John Samuel Swire makes a contribution. He was the son of John Swire, a Liverpool merchant who, in partnership with Jonathan Roose, had traded during the first half of the nineteenth century very much in the style of Defoe's 'universal merchant' with all parts of the world.[27] After John Swire's death in 1847, his two sons, William Hudson and John Samuel, had carried on the family business. In the 1850s, however, William left for the United States, where he started a branch house in New York; John Samuel went off to Australia, successively to work in the gold-fields and on a sheep station. He also founded a further branch house in Melbourne. In 1867, having been attracted into the China trade, he formed with R. S. Butterfield the firm of Butterfield & Swire in Shanghai. It was perhaps fortuitous that the opening of this firm was coincident with the arrival of Holt's first steamship in Chinese waters, but it is no accident that on grounds of moral scruples and business foresight Alfred Holt should have chosen Swire to be his principal agent on the China coast.[28] In Singapore, Holt chose the equally newly-established firm of Mansfields to act for him.[29] These were significant and important appointments, not only for the Holt organisation, but for Liverpool shipping generally. This was so, as we shall see later, in particular relation to the threat of growing competition from British, American, and Dutch rival companies trading in Far Eastern waters.

The principal distinction of these new agencies lay in the width and diversity of their interests. This in turn presupposed a solid capital structure capable of withstanding periods of trade fluctuations. In 1872, Swire had built up a small fleet of river ships and coast boats under the title of the China Navigation Company, capitalised at £360,000.[30] The small ships of this company sailed up the Yangtze and along the coast, collecting cargoes and storing them on the wharves in Shanghai, where they were eventually loaded on to the Holt main line ships. In Holts' interests, Swire made concessionary arrangements with tea producers and, by a regulated system of freight rates, did much to alleviate steamship competition from other British, American and Chinese companies on the Yangtze river. In much the same way, Mansfields were eventually to perform similar functions at Singapore through the medium of the East India Ocean Steam Ship Company. As the name implies, this company (with a fleet largely composed of Holt ships and Mansfield-owned ships) collected cargoes from the East Indian Islands.

In the West African trade, there was also the growth of large unit organisation though with significant differences of detail from that operating in the Far East. It was largely through the activities of the

Lairds of Birkenhead that Liverpool's interest in West Africa was once again revived following the decline in contacts after the abolition of the slave trade. McGregor Laird, subsequent to the exploration of the Niger delta by the Lander brothers, led an ill-fated expedition up the river, in 1832, to see how far it was possible to penetrate into the interior of Africa. The commercial possibilities of such a venture were obvious. Unfortunately, most of the members were wiped out by jungle fever. McGregor Laird, one of the few survivors, returned impaired in health to Birkenhead where, after convalescence, he joined his brother John in the shipbuilding firm. During the 1830s and 1840s, trade between Liverpool and West Africa had been reduced to a few items such as palm oil, ivory, gold dust and an occasional cargo of palm kernels. Divorced from its connection with the West Indian trade and cut off from the promotional finance from the slave trade, the commerce and shipping to and from the West African coast had become stereotyped and static. The potentialities for growth were there for men who were prepared to risk capital in the exploitation of vast natural resources. The steamship was the key to a new system of sea communication; the capital of shipping lines and merchants was the answer to the development of commercial facilities both on the coast and at the centres of distribution in the interior.

The dream of opening up West Africa to Liverpool had continued to influence the thoughts and actions of McGregor Laird. In 1852 he, together with other Liverpool and London men, formed the African Steam Ship Company with a direct service between Britain and ports on the West African coast. The small steamships for this company were built by Lairds. A Charter was granted giving the directors rights and privileges in the development of their trading connections and a mail contract was also negotiated.[31] At first, the company achieved a moderate success, the prospects were excellent, so much so that in 1869 there seemed to be good grounds for the creation of a competitive line. Accordingly, in that year, the British & African Steam Navigation Company was formed. Although the firm originated in Glasgow, its vessels sailed from Liverpool from the start. Thus Liverpool once again became involved directly in the organisation of West African trade and, through this, indirectly in the political and economic policies of the region as a whole.

Messrs Fletcher & Parr had been the agents for the African Steam Ship Company. In 1861, they had four young employees: Alfred

Jones, John Holt, Alexander Elder, and John Dempster, four men who not only undertook the day-to-day business of the firm, but who were all conversant with the commercial details and many of the more important problems of the trade. With the creation of the British & African Steam Navigation Company, Elder and Dempster formed a partnership to act as agents for the new company. John Holt, seeking a more active participation in the trade, had already gone to Fernando Po to learn the business on the spot. Here, after an initial struggle, he built up a large merchanting business under the title John Holt and Co. Making Fernando Po his base, he used small sailing schooners to supply the West Arican ports with cloth, hardware and other industrial products in exchange for palm oil, palm kernels, coffee and other oilseeds.[32] For the carriage of his cargoes to and from the United Kingdom he mainly relied on the steamships of the two Liverpool lines though he chartered ships whenever it was expedient to do so. Meanwhile, back in Liverpool, Alfred Jones had joined Elder and Dempster in 1879 and was busy first in building up trade for the firm and secondly in creating for himself a dominating position in that trade. By 1884, he had succeeded in becoming the controlling partner in the firm, Elder and Dempster having 'retired' in that year. Thus it happened that Holt became the principal Liverpool personality as merchant on the Coast and Alfred Jones, as agent and later as shipowner, as protagonist in Liverpool. The latter's career as a shipowner in control of the two West African lines will be referred to in a subsequent chapter; all that need be said here is that he created a monopolistic situation which went far beyond his interests in shipping and, in doing this, he tied the economy of the West African region inextricably to the growing prosperity of Liverpool.

In the Atlantic cargo trades there was some differentiation of function caused mainly by the technological and industrial nature of the markets served. By the 1860s, Rathbones had a well-organised system of purchase arrangements for American wheat with a monthly (and later a quarterly) limit; they also had joint-account transactions with the Liverpool firm Ross T. Smyth & Co. In the cotton trade, there was a growing tendency by American producers to ship 'on consignment to order' and so by-pass the normal function of the export agent.[33] The Harrison brothers, however, established their own agency in New Orleans under Alfred Le Blanc. He appointed representatives in the cotton belt and in the wheatlands of the mid-western States to negotiate the purchase of cotton and wheat at concessionary rates and ship consignments on through-freight agreement via the railroad system direct to shipside at New Orleans.[34] In Brazil, the firm of Saunders Bros & Co (and later Julius von Sohsten) performed a similar service for shipments of cotton from Pernambuco. These agents, however, were not inhibited in using their initiative nor, as was very often the case, in employing their own resources in ventures outside their normal terms of reference. Two examples of this are to be seen in Alfred Le Blanc's entry into the Mexican fruit trade. This was a very useful source of supplementary cargo at times when cotton shipments were small. The second was the entry into the Brazilian flour and coffee trades, as supplementary cargoes for ships diverted from the West Indies to Brazil at times when seasonal scarcity of West Indian produce caused short cargoes. In their Indian trade (at first largely tea and linseed) Harrisons used rather more conservative and traditional procedures, using the services first of Peel, Bellaine & Co and, after 1891, Hoare, Miller & Co. The Calcutta trade was subject to strict Conference arrangements; cargoes were strictly allocated and freight charges agreed between the various shipping lines.[35] On the western shores of South America the Pacific Steam Navigation Co was equally well served by the firm of Noel West.

A final assessment of the economic function of the early steamship agents, such as those described above, is that the commissions which they earned from the business conducted for the shipping companies were relatively small in relation to total receipts. In times of depression they were often less than that required to cover overheads. The relationship between the Liverpool steamship owners and their new agents must be considered as something more powerful than considerations of profit and loss. They had a common identity of purpose and the driving force was that of mutual well-being. This was a new concept in commercial organisation and was, in the 1860s and 1870s, peculiar to Liverpool.

<h1 style="text-align:center">V</h1>

The rapid growth from 1865 to 1875 of steamship building and steamship owning on Merseyside argues a high degree of capital accumulation and capital concentration. In 1870, the ten principal shipping lines in Liverpool had an employed (as distinct from nominal) capital of £3·5 million. By 1875, this had increased to £4·8 million and by 1880 to £5·6 million. One measure of this high concentration of capital can be made from the claim of the Liverpool Steam Ship Owners' Association (founded in 1858) that it represented some 30 per cent of British steam tonnage at the end of the 1870s.[36]

How had this happened? In the first place, one must accept that because we have been mainly interested in the growth of Liverpool's trade, the emphasis has been laid on the creation and working of cargo-liner companies; but there was an equally important flow of capital into passenger-liner companies, in general, on the transatlantic route and, in particular, on the carriage of emigrants from Europe to the United States and Canada (widely designated the Atlantic Ferry). Cunard had been a pioneer in this service, but by the 1850s and 1860s, competition from two other major Liverpool lines began to affect Cunard's position. The Inman line had been founded in 1850.[37] At first it did not offer direct competition on the New York run, making Philadelphia its terminal, but in 1856 this was changed to New York. The second Liverpool company to offer direct competition to the Cunarders was that of T. H. Ismay's White Star line, a line which had originally been established by Wilson and Pilkington to operate packets to Boston and, later, to Australia. Shortly after the purchase, Ismay raised £400,000 for the creation of a new line of ships sailing between Liverpool and ports in the United States. This was the Oceanic Steam Navigation Co, founded in 1869 and known by the old title of the Wilson and Pilkington ships as the White Star Line.[38] The competition from this company compelled Cunard and Inman to find fresh capital and build new fleets, principally of steamships.

In the second place, there were diverse ways by which Liverpool men built up resources. The Holt brothers used inherited capital as a basis and augmented this from the profits of their own enterprise and subscriptions from a small group of close personal friends. The Harrisons began by investing small sums in ships' shares, gradually bringing in members of their family until they owned a fleet of sufficient size and capability to start oceanic services. At this point they founded their steamship company. The Rathbones financed their steamship enterprise from the profits of their timber business and produce trades; the Swires from merchanting, agency work, direct participation in produce, having originally created assets from Australian gold, sheep and other activities, all this being finally supplemented by help from friends. The Inmans and Ismays began with small investments in ships and enlarged their holdings into a company structure. Wheelwright promoted his company by personal contacts and floatations on the open market. Alfred Jones alone seems to have been an exception. He allowed others to create the shipping lines and subsequently took them over from the profits of his own resourcefulness. The general pattern of structure in Liverpool was the creation of a management company with a controlling interest in the capital stock of the shipping company. Thus, Alfred Holt & Co became the managers of the Ocean Steam Ship Co; T. and J. Harrison the managers of the Charente Steam Ship Co; and Elder Dempsters the managers of the African Steam and the British & African Steam Navigation Companies. Such was the progress that before long these steamship organisations became virtually self-financing. They bore their own risks, they embarked on rebuilding programmes and paid for them out of reserve funds; they financed companies ancillary to their shipping business such as, for example, lighterage companies; they built and owned docks, warehouses (and in Swire's case, a sugar refinery), stevedoring companies and collieries. They spread their wealth widely in helping to found schools and universities, and they added generally to the social and physical well-being of the ports which they served through the creation of clubs and recreational facilities of all descriptions. Sometimes, as in the case of the Rathbones, the Holts and the Harrisons, the members of their numerous families were instrumental, through the pursuit of philanthropic work, in bringing about social reforms which had lasting benefit for sections of the community at large. These Liverpool Forsytes were in process not only of changing Liverpool, but in so doing were changing or were about to change large areas of the world as well.

In the field of general economic policy these men and the body of merchants in Liverpool had welcomed and supported the movements towards a liberalisation of trade. It was Liverpool's own Member of Parliament, William Huskisson, who in the 1820s relaxed the more inhibitive restrictions of the old Navigation Laws, arranged reciprocity trade agreements and codified and simplified the tariff structure. It was William Ewart Gladstone, a native son of Liverpool following Peel's budgetary reforms, who brought in a virtual abolition of duties apart from those for purely revenue purposes. With his budget and commercial treaty with France in 1860, the way was opened up for a general free trade system.[39] This freedom came at the right moment for Liverpool's steamship owners; it freed them from restrictions on shipping and it enabled a rapid expansion to take place in primary commodity trades and in the export of manufactured goods. The interests of the Liverpool men were therefore well served in Parliament. As if to emphasise the importance of the link between Liverpool and Westminster, a London Parliament Office (as we have seen) had been established for the purpose of keeping shipowners and merchants informed about government policy and, conversely, of acquainting Members of Parliament with the views and needs of Liverpool's commercial interests.[40] This was undoubtedly a powerful lobby, a fact which goes some way towards explaining why sanction was generously granted for the flow of funds into ships, docks and other port facilities during the middle years of the nineteenth century.

VI

If the Liverpool of the early nineteenth century can be aptly described as Roscoe's Liverpool, that of the 1870s cannot be given an adequate nomenclature. The shipping magnates and merchant princes built new houses, imposing in size but often in execrable taste, around Sefton and Princes Parks, at Greenbank, Allerton, Mossley Hill, and Aigburth. Some bought estates in Wirral and other parts of Cheshire, while others immured themselves in the fastnesses of North Wales. On the whole, however, despite the outward signs of vast wealth, they lived simple lives. They were pious, earnest men, mostly staunch Unitarians or Presbyterians. Apart from one or two notable exceptions, their impact on the life of Liverpool was far less effective than it had been in Roscoe's day, partly because they had become remote from it and partly because Liverpool itself had burst the physical limits of a compact community.

As opportunities for employment increased, the population had grown rapidly. Of two eighteenth-century estimates, the first in 1773[41] gave a total of 34,400 and the second in 1790[42] provided a figure of 53,853. Although certain categories of person were excluded

(*above*) The Prince's Dock in 1821; (*below*) The old dock and the
Custom House

(*above*) Aerial view of Albert Dock, showing Dingle oil jetties and south docks; (*below*) Aerial view of the north docks to Gladstone

from these counts, the magnitude of the increase coincided with the trend observable in the census returns from 1801 to 1821. By the turn of the nineteenth century, population and building had spilled over the borough boundaries into Everton, into Toxteth park and into the inner portion of West Derby. On Wirral, the only town of any size, apart from the market town of Neston, was Tranmere. Here the countryside had a scattering of villages and hamlets with a low density population. By 1841, however, the population map of Merseyside had been radically altered. Liverpool township had increased its number of inhabitants from 77,600 in 1801 to 223,000, the congested inner wards of Howard Street, Dale Street and Thomas Street, with their back-to-back houses and crowded courts being at peak density. Migrants were flooding in from all parts of Britain, not least from Ireland. The process of spilling over into Toxteth in the south and into West Derby and Kirkdale to the north was stimulated by the extension of the dock system. There were also subsidiary effects on population growth, as already stated, in the riverside townships of Bootle, Seaforth, Waterloo and Garston.[43] Thus, the elongated plan of Liverpool's built-up area, closely related to the line of the estuary, was already taking shape. Indeed, this growth was reflected in the rapid increase of Woolton and Wavertree, both old agricultural villages.

From an analysis of baptismal registers and other sources, as R. Lawton has shown, it is clear that the growth of population, between 1801 and 1841, was caused by a high rate of natural increase and by a large inward balance of migration. After 1861, the pattern of migrational settlement becomes plainly discernible with movements outwards from the overcrowded core. The Irish immigrants moved into the Scotland Road area which was primarily Catholic, while Ulster Protestants lived on the fringes in Kirkdale: Welsh immigrants settled in Everton, Toxteth, and Wavertree. In the general employment of these immigrants, the Irishmen worked mainly in the docks, while the Welshmen established themselves in the retail trades of dairying and drapery and in building and constructional work. Thus, in outline, the main characteristics of Liverpool's physical development had taken place and by 1911 most of the townships, in an arc from Waterloo to Garston, had come within a high density category.

In the period 1850 to 1900, terraced houses, hideous in the yellow brick of the Welsh building contractor, had topped the sandstone ridge and were engulfing Everton and Wavertree. Long ribbons were stretching out across the fields and heathlands to West Derby, Childwall, Gateacre and towards the pleasant 1820 resort of Waterloo; and as the demand for ships increased so too did the demand for docks. Northwards and southwards from the original eighteenth-century dock system new wharves and quays, new wet-docks and dry-docks appeared. Behind them rows of mean streets, housing dock workers, were already engulfing the once pleasant villages of Bootle and Seaforth to the north and St Michael's hamlet, Toxteth, and Dingle to the south. Liverpool had extended her influence to the far ends of the earth, she had amassed vast wealth, but she had become ugly in the process.

Such a generalisation, however, must have its qualification. Civic pride eventually began to express itself in the form of a well-laid out area, graced by imposing public buildings in classical style. This area was that bounded by Shaw's Brow to the north, Queen's Square to the south, the old Haymarket to the west and Lime Street to the east. In 1745, the Corporation gave land running down from Lime Street for the building of an Infirmary. This was opened in 1749 at a cost of £2,648. Three years later, two detached wings were added to form a Seamen's Hospital at an additional cost of £1,500. In 1789 a lunatic asylum was built in the gardens behind the Infirmary. These buildings were demolished in 1826, the new Infirmary having been built in Brownlow Street. The new lunatic asylum was built in 1835 in Ashton Street, on the site of what is now the University's old quadrangle.

The need for an orchestral hall and music centre had been apparent for some time. In 1836, therefore, subscriptions were raised for this purpose, amounting to £23,350. The design of the new building to be built on the site of the old Infirmary and called St George's Hall, was thrown open to public competition. Harvey Lonsdale Elmes was the successful architect and the first stone was laid in 1838, the whole massive structure being completed in 1854. This hall was an imposing addition to Liverpool's public buildings and exemplified the spirit of achievement in the minds of her citizens. Unfortunately, the prospect of this building was marred, for many years, by the close proximity of St John's church, built in 1783 and, according to contemporary opinion, not in aesthetic harmony with the new surroundings. Meanwhile, the old clutter of industrial buildings on Shaw's Brow was being cleared, largely owing to a bequest from Sir William Brown (founder of Brown Shipley & Co) and a large public library and museum were opened in 1857. Thus Liverpool was given the semblance of a civic centre where music, art, and scholarship could flourish.

A general impression that Liverpool's growth was the result of purely materialistic pressures, therefore, needs some qualification. Despite the widening gaps in the social structure between vast wealth on the one hand and poverty on the other, the general conscience could be stirred to make provision for non-material and enlightened action. In one respect, namely that of the health of an expanding population, the town government can be said to have given a lead to the world. Following the ravages of cholera and smallpox epidemics in the early 1840s, there was an urgently expressed demand for a better system of health adminstration. Accordingly, under the provisions of a local Act regulating sewerage, drainage and housing conditions within the borough, W. H. Duncan, physician to the Infirmary, was created the first Medical Officer of Health on 1 January 1847. If Liverpool had established the means of acquiring wealth, prestige and power, in material terms, its citizens had not neglected the needs of poverty. In this aspect of the town's consciousness, at least, there was a corporate sense of responsibility which had its roots in the peculiar nature of Liverpool herself.

CHAPTER FIVE

The Physical Attributes of the Port, 1700-1858

I

We must now return to the eighteenth century in order to pick up the threads of other important physical developments in the growth of the port. These were largely associated with, and parallel to, the growth of shipping, trade and commercial organisation. In form, they are concerned with the building of docks to accommodate, not only an increasing volume, but also an increasing size of ship, and the provision of adequate port facilities in the shape of quays and warehouses for the handling and storage of cargoes. In this the links between the various systems of communication from the dockside via railway, canal, and road, assumes a rightful place. Finally, one must be concerned with the overall administration of the docks and the relationship between dock and town development. In such inter-action of promotional and administrative function, the port itself emerges as a Merseyside rather than as a purely Liverpool entity, embracing dock and port installations on both sides of the river.

Today, one does not perhaps appreciate the immense difficulty of making a dock system in the eighteenth century. Apart from the physical hazards arising from a strong 30-foot tide-race in the estuary, there were frequent and annoying delays in progress and completion owing to shortage of funds. Furthermore, because of the rights of property owners leasing land from the Corporation, land for dock construction was not easily acquired and, when acquired, not always accessible on the landward side. These facts explain the long periods of time which invariably elapsed between the passing of an Act authorising construction and the actual date on which the dock was opened to shipping.

We have seen how the burst of enterprise at the beginning of the eighteenth century led, among other things, to the building of the first wet dock in Liverpool (see pp 13–14). The work on this first dock had proceeded very slowly under the direction of Thomas Steers, partly because of the difficulties encountered in sinking the brick walls through soft mud to the underlying rock and partly because of lack of finance. By 1717, the funds initially voted had been exhausted. In addition to the £6,000 which the Corporation had been authorised to borrow (and which had been borrowed and spent) they had expended £5,000 of their own money. Some £4,000 was still required to complete the work. Accordingly, another Act was sought (3 Geo I, c 1) authorising the trustees to borrow that sum on security of the rates. The dues which were to be levied on ships using the dock were 4d a ton on coasters, but more on vessels engaged overseas; the latter were to pay rates based on the 'medium' of the imports and exports of the preceding three years. It was estimated that these dues would yield £600 a year. The accounts of the dock trust were placed under the inspection of nine commissioners, three to be appointed by the Mayor and Corporation, three by the Justices of the County Palatine of Lancaster and three by the Justices of the County Palatine of Chester.[1]

In form, this first dock system consisted of a narrow gut from the river into a small octagonal tidal basin. This, in turn, led into the main wet dock of some three acres in extent made out of the Pool. To the north of the tidal basin was a small dry dock. There was, however, a basic flaw in such a layout. In bad weather ships crowded into the tiny tidal basin and blocked the entrance to the wet dock. Thus by 1737 there was, in the words of the Town Council 'an absolute necessity for an addition to be made to the present dock or basin . . . and also for a convenient pier to be erected in the open harbour on the north side of the entrance into the present dock . . . for the safety of all ships when ready to sail from the port, to lie till a fair wind happens, which very often are prevented when in the wet dock by other ships lying at the entrance and are all pressing to get out before them'[2] (Minutes of Council, 11 January 1737).

In pursuance of an Act of 1738 (11 Geo II, c 32) work began immediately on improving the tidal basin, which was enlarged to just over four acres and the 'dry' pier—that is, the sea wall of the tidal basin—was ready for use in 1743. It took another ten years to implement the other provisions of the 1738 Act authorising the building of a second dock. This dock, designed by Thomas Steers (though probably finished by Henry Berry) was opened in 1753 at a cost of

£21,000. This second or 'south' dock was eventually renamed Salthouse, receiving this name from Blackburne's salt works at the eastern end of it. The shape of the dock was irregular, being confined by, and having to be adapted to, the configuration of the streeets surrounding it. Salthouse became the depot for Irish ships laden with agricultural produce and for the smaller class of French and Mediterranean ships bringing back wine, brandy, and fruit. To some extent, therefore, this second dock sees the beginning of a geographical specialisation in the system. The reconstructed tidal basin, known locally as the 'dry dock'[3] because it had no flood gates and was, therefore, empty at low water, was converted into a wet dock (renamed Canning dock) in 1829, shortly after the old dock was closed and filled in.

The rapid increase in the volume of shipping using the port after 1750 created such pressure on the space in the two docks, that it became necessary for the Corporation to seek new powers for an extension of the wet dock area. Accordingly, in 1762, another application was made to Parliament for such powers. The preamble of the Act (2 George III, c 86) recited that 'the trade and shipping of the town and port of late years is greatly increased, and the ships and vessels are more numerous and of larger dimensions, and require a greater draught of water than heretofore'; 'that the two wet docks and dry pier, already constructed, are not sufficient for the reception of the ships resorting hereto; that vessels, especially His Majesty's ships of war, stationed at the port, are obliged to lie in the open harbour, exposed to the rage of tempestuous weather and of rapid tides and currents in imminent danger of shipwreck'.

Work on the new dock (contemporaneously called North Dock but later renamed Georges Dock) was begun in 1762 under the direction of Henry Berry, who had succeeded Thomas Steers as dock engineer in that year. This change of direction coincided with far-reaching changes in the regulation of the dock system as a whole. Under the provisions of the 1762 Act, all the property in all the docks, piers, buoys, landmarks, beacons and lighthouses 'formed under it or under former Acts, was vested in the Mayor, Bailiffs and Common Council of Liverpool as Trustees.'[4] It empowered them to bring actions or prefer bills of indictment by the name and style of the Trustees of the Harbour and Docks of Liverpool.

Unfortunately dock-building did not proceed smoothly. In October 1762 a violent hurricane 'so beat up the waters in the river that a large part of the newly-built wall on the eastern side was destroyed'.[5] This disaster led to protracted delays and the resumption of work did not take place until 1767, the first stone being laid on 1 April 'by Mr Thomas Johnson, Mayor'.[6] The cost was estimated at £21,000 and the new three-acre dock opened in 1771 provided ample and safe anchorage for West Indiamen and American ships for forty years. Extensive alterations were made to George's dock under the authorisation of an Act of 1799, though as we shall see, a period of twenty-three years was to elapse before the new works were completed. In its final reconstruction some 21½ yards were added to its width and a large tidal basin was attached to it. From George's pier, ferry boats and packet ships (some belonging to the Black Ball line) took their departure.

Mention must be made of the construction of a small, but highly important dock called the Duke's dock. This extended from the Mersey to Wapping and was between the Salthouse dock and what was later the King's dock. It was built by the Duke of Bridgewater for the reception of his coal flats which, as we have seen, brought fuel for the glass, iron and salt works in the industrial area of Liverpool. These flats came from Manchester via the Bridgewater canal and were sailed down river from the junction of the canal with the Mersey to this dock. The Duke also erected a spacious warehouse on the dockside 'for the security of goods'. The dock itself was subsequently enlarged by the formation of a short branch or cut from the south side of it and carried underneath a large block of warehouses. Close by there was an open space which was turned into a yard housing a depot for the disposal of cargoes.

With the ending of the war of American Independence, a post-war boom in trade led to a 'press of ships in the harbour' and it was generally agreed by merchants and shipbuilders that increased wet-dock space was urgently needed. Accordingly yet another Act was sought in 1785, the preamble to which contained the oft-repeated plea that ships 'for want of an additional dock and being obliged to lie in an open harbour, are exposed to the rage of tempestuous weather and the rapid tide or current, and are in imminent danger of shipwreck'.[7] The seven-acre King's dock was completed by 1788, at a cost of £25,000, but the six-acre Queen's dock, having encountered difficulty in the layout of the site, was not finished until 1796; though smaller than King's dock, it cost £35,000. A further degree of specialisation was added to the port's operations by the building of a tobacco warehouse at King's dock. This provided storage space for a rapidly expanding trade and helped to supply an extensive tobacco manufacturing industry in the town.

One interesting point connected with the extension of docks southwards from the old dock is that encroachments had to be made on the land used by ironmasters, shipwrights, and shipbuilders. The building of the first dock had, long before, moved the shipbuilders from the shore just south of the castle, but they had not moved very far. A print published in 1728 shows a ship under construction just below where the castle had stood; further building is shown to the south beyond the old dock entrance. To the north, George's dock had also eliminated the more important of the traditional building sites. After 1765, therefore, the shipbuilders found themselves restricted to a small area between the Salthouse dock and the river and to one or two plots on the shore to the south. With the acquisition of land for the laying out of the King's and Queen's docks after 1785, ship-building activity was driven still further southward to sites which eventually proved to be inconvenient and unremunerative. This process continued during the first quarter of the nineteenth century and, coupled with a decline in orders after 1830, the Liverpool ship-building industry which had been so vital to the port was superseded by the Lairds on the Birkenhead side of the river.

The momentum in the construction of docks slackened after 1796. This was caused by a number of factors, some peculiar to Liverpool and others resulting from the national involvement in war. Henry Berry, whose forceful enterprise had contributed so much to the promotion and execution of dock schemes for about forty years, was succeeded as dock engineer by Thomas Morris in 1789.[8] Morris, whose experience had been largely gained outside Liverpool, was called upon to supervise and complete Queen's dock, but thereafter his services were not in demand; in fact, by the time the next dock was built he had been succeeded by John Foster. In fairness, how-ever, one cannot blame Morris for the delay in implementing new schemes. Despite the fact that trade and shipping continued to expand with great rapidity during the Revolutionary and Napoleonic wars, the inhibition on development was primarily that of shortage of funds. As we have seen, the succesive crises after 1793 led through lack of confidence to scarcity of cash for the normal transactions of trade and once a crisis had passed, pressure on the allocation of resources assumed a different emphasis. In the years from 1796 to

1816, this emphasis would appear to have been directed away from the physical development of port facilities into that of the promotion and maintenance of trade.

Nevertheless, in 1799, another Act was passed giving powers to the trustees to build two further docks as need arose during the next twenty years. The uncertainties of the time, however, made them reluctant to build. As demands for shipping space grew they were accused (a little unjustly perhaps) of pandering to local landowners. The West India Association and the American Chamber of Commerce demanded that the Trust should be reformed to include representatives of merchants and shipowners. On application to the King's Bench for a mandamus to compel the trustees to build another dock, they secured a degree of initiative and a legal sanction to enforce their views. As a result, another Act was passed in 1811, containing the necessary authority, and work began almost immediately on two projects; the first was the construction of a small wet-dock called Union (afterwards enlarged into Coburg) of some two-and three-quarter acres; the second and more important was that of Prince's Dock. Other necessary improvements were also put in hand, a further four acres being added to Queen's dock in 1816 and a further two acres to George's dock in 1822–5. Prince's dock was completed in 1821. The largest yet built, it originally contained a water area of eleven acres and cost £650,000. It was entered by means of two locks, each 45 feet wide, leading from its own four and a half-acre basin to the north and to the George's dock basin to the south. The entrance was modernised in 1868 and again in 1949. At the time of its opening, this dock provided sufficient accommodation for vessels 'trading to all parts of the world'. This, at least, was the generally expressed view reflecting the euphoria of the time.

Meanwhile, the provision of dry dock space had not been forgotten. The most important services of repair and maintenance had, over the years, grown in proportion to the needs for loading and discharge. As part of the general scheme of improvement since 1737, three graving docks had been built, opening on the west side of the tidal basin to the Old dock.[9] Enfield mentions several small docks 'called graving docks which are formed with flood gates to admit or exclude water at pleasure. These admit two or three vessels at one time for the purpose of repairing them.' As new extensions were authorised in the years ahead, graving docks were included as part of the new works. They were essential elements in the provision of port services and added considerably to Liverpool's potentialities as a shipping and commercial centre.

Between 1811 and 1825, the dock water space was increased by approximately 80 per cent. This fact is perhaps indicative of the new and insistent pressure on the Corporation to provide berths for a rapidly increasing tonnage both coastwise and overseas, in the latter category especially from America. It is also a measure of the growth of technology and of resources. During the eighteenth century, five wet-docks (excluding Duke's) had been constructed at a cost of roughly £150,000. This was a formidable sum of money to have expended. In physical terms of labour and technological innovation it was an even more formidable task to have accomplished. Yet during the first quarter of the nineteenth century, or more precisely in the fourteen years from 1811 to 1825, such progress had been made and such capital ready for investment, that the work of fourteen years was able to achieve practically the same result as a previous century of effort. As in the case of so many other aspects of Liverpool's development, the tempo was changing. The century-old industrial entrepreneurship was beginning to decline in the face of more more urgent needs from commerce and, in this context, the rapid construction of docks assumes priority.

In the process of decision-taking, there seems to have been a fairly straightforward division of function. In the eighteenth century, power for the acquisition of land and for the raising and use of resources was vested in the dock Trustees by successive Acts of Parliament. The spur to endeavour, however, was usually initiated as a result of representation from shipowners, shipbuilders, and merchants. The dock engineers were responsible to the dock Trustees or an appropriate committee for the formulation of schemes and these, when approved, were carried out under their supervision. By the end of the eighteenth century, however, the power of the trustees, as representative of Corporation authority, was beginning to be challenged by vested interests, but even so the control of an established oligarchy was difficult to break. Thus, though the Act of 1811 created a committee of twenty-one members, they were all of the Corporation 'subject to the control of the Trustees in Council assembled' to exercise power over the docks. The organisation of control was closely knit and it was not until 1825 that any breach of the system was effected. By a further Act of that year the constitution of the dock committee was altered. Provision was made for eight of the twenty-one members to be elected by the dock ratepayers, the Corporation still continuing to act as trustees and to have power of veto.[10] Stemming from this Act was the authority to extend the docks northwards from the orginal basins near what is now Pier Head; it was the starting point for the work of one of Liverpool's most famous dock engineers, Jesse Hartley. It was, in truth, the beginning of a new era in dock construction on the Liverpool shore of the Mersey.

II

- 60

For a period of thirty-six years from 1824, the expansion of Liverpool's dock system was under the control, sometimes despotic in character, of that genius of granite cyclopean structure, Jesse Hartley. Hartley's ambitious and monumental ideas continuously outstripped available resources. Although the Act of 1825 had given wide powers to the trustees for the raising of funds, a succession of enabling Acts had to be sought in 1828, 1830, 1841, 1844 and 1846–7, to cover both excess of expenditure over estimates and plans for future construction.[11]

At first, Hartley was not too exuberant. His scheme for the Brunswick dock, opened in 1832 on the south side, involved a ramped quay suitable for the unloading of timber. The dock contained a water area of some twelve acres with a half-tide basin attached to it with an additional area of one and a half acres. Two large graving docks opened out from its southern extremity; the old tide-mill called Jackson's dam being absorbed into the dock and lands belonging to the Corporation forming part of the site.[12] At the same time, works at the north end were pushed ahead and Clarence dock, intended for the berthing of steamships and placed at some distance northward to avoid risk of fire, was opened in 1830. This, together with Waterloo (opened 1834), Trafalgar and Victoria docks (opened 1836), was on the site of land owned by the Corporation and, with their quays and basins, covered some fifty-six acres. The Brunswick dock had cost £438,000, while the land and building of the Clarence, Trafalgar, Waterloo and Victoria systems amounted to £795,000. It is not surprising, therefore, that the preamble to the 1828 Act should have stated that 'the purchase under the authority of the preceding Act had exceeded the estimates but, as the trade of the port was increasing so rapidly, the utmost expedition was required to accommodate it'. Power was therefore taken to increase the debt by £200,000. This was to be a recurrent theme of the Hartley administration, so much so that by 1847 the bonded debt stood at £4,784,000.

It would not be relevant in this present volume to embark upon the details of each dock built by Hartley. He certainly showed great skill and constructive ability in planning his works, making the best use of the land available with rectangular docks and branches wherever possible. This involved the building of the dock basin in the shape of a parallelogram with the short end abutting on the river. Accordingly, many more docks could be allocated to a given length of river frontage and also provided with a vastly increased linear space for quays and berths. The first dock of this kind was the Waterloo, opened in 1834, and followed two years later by Victoria and Trafalgar, the latter dock being allocated as an addition to the Clarence dock for the use of steamships. Hartley also extended the building of enclosed docks complete with their own warehouses. This was not a new idea, for as early as 1805 Liverpool had been put on the same terms as the port of London with regard to its warehousing system, and in 1810 a plan for enclosed docks and warehouses had been sanctioned by the Corporation. This plan, however, was rejected by Parliament, largely owing to pressure of the vested interests from private warehouse owners. Accordingly, during the 1820s and 1830s, capital had flowed into the building of warehouses and storage depots in the streets and open spaces behind the docks themselves. For the most part, this caused higgledy-piggledy development and was relatively inefficient in operation. In 1839, Hartley produced a scheme for a new dock on the western side of the old Salthouse dock. It was to be equipped with warehouses on the grandest scale and have the latest hydraulic machinery to control the gates. The plan was carried against vehement opposition and the Act, authorising the work, was passed in 1841. This enterprise was to be given the name of Albert and, on 30 July 1845, the Prince himself came to Liverpool to open it. It covered about seven and a half acres and had cost (together with the land and warehouses) £721,736. The Prince was greatly impressed 'and showed an astonishing acquaintance with the principles of hydraulics'; but he apparently did not comment on the warehouses. It was left to Picton to do this. 'The works for strength and durability were unsurpassable', he wrote, 'but it is regrettable that no attention whatsoever has been paid to beauty, as well as to strength. The enormous pile of warehouses which looms so large upon the river and in its vastness surpasses the pyramid of Cheops, is simply a hideous pile of naked brickwork.'

The dock-warehouse system, thus inaugurated, was found to be an efficient adjunct to the commercial facilities of the port. Plans, incorporating this principle, were soon in train to extend the dock area to both the northward and southward. In 1843, land was purchased from the Earl of Derby giving 1,000 yards of river frontage in the township of Kirkdale beyond the old boundary of the borough. At the south end, similar purchases were made of land between the Brunswick dock and the Herculaneum pottery works. This latter area had been intended for development by a private company, the Harrington Dock Co. The work was authorised and exemptions were granted by Parliament from certain port charges to vessels using these docks. The Harrington Company spent about £50,000 in clearing the ground and in the construction of two small inlets for river craft. It was obvious that developments on the scale now required for the shipping of the port was far beyond the scope and capacity of private sources of capital. The Harrington Dock Company were unable to proceed with their works and in 1843, against bitter opposition, their property and land passed into the possession of the Liverpool Dock Trustees for the price of £253,000. The acquisition of sites and renewed authorisation under the provisions of an Act of 1844, gave Jesse Hartley and his engineers the chance to build dock-warehouse systems and earn for themselves an unassailable reputation.

The new docks included those on the Harrington site as well as five spacious ones at the north end, forming a complete system and a junction with the Leeds and Liverpool canal by means of a short cut and locks (to which the Canal Company contributed £50,000). These docks consisted of the Salisbury, Collingwood, Stanley, Nelson, and Bramley Moore, the latter named after the Chairman of the Dock Committee. They were opened in 1848 and added some thirty-three acres of water and two miles of quay to the dock estate. Hartley had not only employed his two main principles but had extended and improved on them. The arrangement was admirable for inter-communication. Space fronting the river was economised and tidal basins, so long a feature of the old system, were altogether eliminated. Instead of an outer basin, the Salisbury dock with two entrances from the river gave adequate opportunity for docking and departing long before and after full flood tide to the other docks in which it was in connection. The Wellington dock and half-tide basin, covering an area of approximately eleven acres, was added to the system and opened in 1849.

This incredible activity, spurred on by Hartley's enthusiasm, continued into the 1850s. To the south, the Wapping dock was built and joined to the Salthouse by a cut. This proved to be a costly operation as it involved the acquisition and the demolition of a large area of property, the purchase of which cost £377,000. The drain on land and resources was never-ending, and signs of strain were beginning to show during the early 1850s. In fact, the Wapping dock with its fine range of warehouses took a considerable time to complete. It was not opened until 1858, having been upwards of ten years under construction. The simultaneous demands for labour, materials, sites, and money undoubtedly had a multiplier effect on Liverpool's internal economy. The vastness of the enterprise was matched only by the earning capacity of the ships using the harbour; increasing wealth from shipping was, therefore, the resource maintaining and underpinning the whole structure.

The Sandon (opened 1851) with a further 10 acres, the Huskisson (opened 1852) with 14·1 acres, were the next two docks to be added. The latter was originally intended for the berthing of timber ships, but it was extended by a 7·1 acres cut eastwards in 1860 and became available for the general use of large ocean-going ships. Mention of the timber trade (particularly with British North America) in this context underlines an important new development in the 1850s. Hitherto, as we have seen, the discharge of timber had been traditionally located in the south docks. By the end of the 1840s, however, storage facilities for timber were becoming limited and expensive. It was therefore proposed to construct a timber dock at the north end and to transfer the bulk of the timber trade there. The proposal was implemented by the construction of the Canada dock with an extent of nearly 18 acres, opened in 1859.[13]

We have already referred to the land purchased from the Harrington Company at the southern end of the dock system. For many years it constituted a rather derelict area of waste ground, but at length a small dock and two extensive graving docks were built. These were opened in 1864, the floating dock being called

Herculaneum, containing about three and a half acres and opening directly from the river by two pairs of entrance gates. By this time, however, Hartley was dead and the administration of his docks and quays had passed from the hands of the trustees to a new form of organisation, the Mersey Docks and Harbour Board which was henceforth to be responsible for the systems on both sides of the river.

Any assessment of Jesse Hartley's contribution to Liverpool's expansion from 1824 to 1860 must necessarily contain an appraisal of his skill as an engineer. We are not competent to do this. It is perhaps only necessary here to make a simple calculation to judge the significance of this man's work. In 1872, the total wet dock area amounted to 255½ acres with 18¼ miles of quay space. This included the docks built before 1824 and after 1860. Jesse Hartley's contribution to the total was 140 acres of wet docks and approximately ten miles of quay space. In other words, his energy and foresight had been responsible, in a short period of thirty-six years, for the provision of more than half of Liverpool's dock area. In financial terms, the Hartley works, including land, dock and warehouse construction, alterations and improvements, cost something less than £5¼ million. This, on all counts, was a superlative achievement and testimony, not merely to Hartley's skill and initiative but also to the vision of those members of the Dock Committee and other interests who supported him.

III

Meanwhile, on the Birkenhead side of the river a series of attempts, some not very successful, had been made to construct a dock system. It had long been a cherished idea of the Lairds (and indeed of some Liverpool merchants) to establish Birkenhead as a port with facilities of such magnitude and efficiency that it might one day rival Liverpool. This was a foolish aspiration in view of the strength of Liverpool's enterprise and, until the Birkenhead docks and dock promotion were taken over by the Mersey Docks and Harbour Board in 1857, the story is an unhappy one of financial mismanagement and inefficient skill on the technical side in coping with the engineering problems of the site. Yet, despite this, Birkenhead possessed 165 acres of dock space and 9 miles of quays by 1872; and though much of this construction had been inspired and carried out after 1857 by the new Mersey Docks and Harbour Board, the achievement was considerable, and Birkenhead could claim to be a port in its own right.

The most obvious starting point had been (as on the Liverpool side) the deepening and walling-in of a large marshy inlet known as Wallasey Pool. As early as the 1820s Telford had been retained to draw plans for the development of a dock system.[14] This, however, was an academic exercise; the times were not propitious and nothing of a practical nature was done. Sometime before 1828, however, Sir John Tobin, a prominent member of Liverpool Corporation (and descendant of a slave-trading family), William Laird, founder of the Birkenhead iron works and John Askew, harbour master of the port, among others, bought tracts of land on the margin of the Pool and announced their intention of building docks. The plan was well based. By virtue of its geographical position, Birkenhead could be made accessible by railway to the Midlands and via Chester to the North Wales coalfield. By a prospective use of railway links such docks could be given shorter lines of communication with the industrial areas of the Midlands, the Black Country and Shropshire and could, therefore, compete on favourable terms with Liverpool. Moreover, Laird was in process of laying out Birkenhead on a fine plan, centred upon Hamilton Square, with spacious houses for his iron-workers, the streets and public buildings illuminated by an entirely new principle and using gas. In short, Birkenhead was not only becoming an important new town on Merseyside; it had prospects of a growing trade and industrial development. There were therefore grounds for the alarm expressed by Liverpool Corporation, as dock Trustees, at the activities of Tobin, Laird, and Askew. They began negotiations for the purchase of the land in question and finally acquired 206 acres at a cost of £180,264. Notice was given that a bill would be sought to construct docks on the pool. To this, however, the Liverpool Dock Committee objected on the grounds that the proposals for new dock construction on the Liverpool side would provide ample service for increasing tonnage in the Mersey. One cannot avoid the suspicion that Liverpool was exercising monopoly rights to suppress developments at Birkenhead. Be that as it may, nothing further was done until 1843 when fresh promotion was sought with the aid of external sources of capital (notably from Joseph Bailey and Sir Isaac Lyon Goldsmidt). A company was formed under the title, the Birkenhead Dock Co, and J. M. Rendel was appointed as chief surveyor and engineer. The whole scheme had been kept secret as, indeed, Rendel's plans for the building of docks on the Pool had been. Application was made to Liverpool Corporation in the names of individual persons for the purchase of the land on the water's edge. The Council discussed the application at some length, but in the end agreed to sell for £330,000. They were somewhat incredulously surprised when the new dock company began to develop the site and the works proceeded against a background of bitter recrimination.

An Act was passed in 1844 making provision for Commissioners of the Birkenhead docks to embark upon the task of raising funds and building the docks and quays. They were to 'form, maintain and repair a sea wall along the eastern limit of Wallesey Pool between Seacombe and Woodside ferries, and also construct an embankment from Bridge End in Birkenhead to the opposite side of the Pool, for penning up the water of the said Pool'.[15] Despite engineering difficulties (some of which were the result of Rendel's lack of foresight) and despite shortage of funds, the first two docks, Egerton and Morpeth, were opened in 1847. In June of the same year, new commissioners were elected and, with new men in charge of administration, it was discovered that the old commissioners had spent all the available cash and had undertaken work without proper authority. After making an unsuccessful appeal to Liverpool for financial help, negotiations were started with the Commissioners of Woods and Forests to take the frontage lands, build the river wall and complete the dam on the line of the present four bridges. The impact of this sorry state of affairs on the town of Birkenhead was far-reaching; employment on the docks had ceased and this, coupled with a decline in shipbuilding orders at Laird's works, caused widespread unemployment and distress. Many skilled operatives left the town to find work either on the Liverpool side of the river or in the workshops of the Midlands. 'Birkenhead', it was stated in 1847, 'was a splendid ruin.'

Work on the dock site was not resumed until March 1849; Rendel, who had been the subject of bitter criticism for failure to maintain the impetus of the work, resigned his post in July. Not much progress was made until 1850 when James Abernethy was appointed engineer. Then, the dam was built 'in a temporary manner'. As things went from bad to worse, the cost began to be counted. The Parliamentary estimates for the building of the Woodside basin,

Egerton and Morpeth docks, the Great Culvert, river walls, the Great Float as laid down in the first Act was £400,000. The extra cost of additional work up to 1848 was approximately £170,000. The actual cost up to 1846 was £205,155 with an estimated cost of finishing the proposed work at £416,820. Deducting the amount of stock standing at £44,091, the total cost of completed and proposed work thus amounted to £577,884. The Parliamentary sanction for £400,000 was increased by a further £169,941, totalling £569,941. Excess of actual cost over approved estimates, therefore, amounted to £7,943.[16]

According to Rendel's estimate the total amount which had already been spent was £225,000 and the cost of completion would be £342,400,[17] a figure which can be compared with an independent estimate by Robert Stephenson of £345,500.[18] Thus, assuming that the plant was saleable, the total cost of the works could be estimated at £570,000. This was about £20,000 above the original estimate. Again, these figures do not exactly agree with other estimates that were put forward at the Enquiry of 1848. The total on this occasion was £582,175. Actual cost amounted to £591,553, giving a deficit of £9,378.[19] Compared with the vast activity and the financial stability on the Liverpool side, the achievement in Birkenhead was far from propitious. All that had been accomplished in three years was a mere seven and half acres of dock space, for the most part badly constructed and fraught with financial uncertainty.

In the years following, confusion became worse confounded. By the end of 1847, it had become apparent that local support for the dock scheme had seriously diminished, and it had been decided to wind up the affairs of the Dock Company. This, however, was not implemented. In fact, the company was rehabilitated and, in 1848, under the authority of a new Act (11 & 12 Vic, c 42), they agreed to purchase the Herculaneum dock site on the Liverpool side. Within a few months, however, the commissioners were approaching the Liverpool Dock Committee to take over the whole of their under- taking at cost price; but this offer was declined. Yet another Act was passed in 1850 authorising additional capital to the extent of £50,000 and work was begun once again. Political manoeuvres behind the scenes secured the reinstatement of Rendel and induced the Com- missioners of Crown Lands, who exercised rights over reclaimed land totalling 120 acres from the foreshore in two reserves north and south of the low water basin, to remove their interest in the south reserve by giving to the trustees all the land which they owned there. In addition, they agreed to pay for the building of the quay walls adjoining this and and to pay the trustees £22,000 which had already been spent on them. The latter were also permitted to raise a further £50,000 to complete the walls on their side of the Pool. Other provisions required the Crown to build a permanent road across the dam between Birkenhead and Seacombe and to enable the Birkenhead, Lancashire and Cheshire Junction Railway to make a track across the temporary dam. Work on the Great Float (ie the open area of the Pool) was given new impetus and, on 31 March 1851 about forty acres of this water area were opened. Prospects were further improved when the line of the Birkenhead, Lancashire and Cheshire Junction Railway was extended to Warrington giving hope of attracting trade from Manchester.

In 1850, Thomas Brassey, the rising contractor, agreed to complete the works under the revised Rendel plan for £500,000.[20] For a time thereafter the financial situation improved. The government had established an emigrant depot in Birkenhead and sailings were beginning to increase. Negotiations were also pending for the South American and General Steam Navigation Co to start a line from Birkenhead to Brazil. Shipping dues began to increase as firms became confident that the new docks could provide a relatively cheap and easy service for their ships.

Brassey had close connections with Birkenhead, having begun in business there and having lived there for eight or nine years as a land surveyor, brick and lime maker. He subsequently became a contractor for a number of local railways: Grand Junction in 1835; Chester–Crewe, 1839; Lancashire–Carlisle 1844; Chester–Holyhead, 1845. He also acted with Rendel as engineer for the Birkenhead and Chester Junction Railway in 1847 and for the Victoria Docks and Warehouses in 1852. Brassey had already worked on one major dock scheme, that of Greenock Harbour in 1845, and was later to be responsible for Barrow dock in 1863. As far as the works at Birkenhead were concerned, Brassey began by tackling the problem of building a temporary dam at the mouth of the Pool, to enable the tidal basin and graving docks to be constructed. To help finance this scheme, he used the £22,000 paid over by the Commissioners of Crown Lands, for the walling of their North Reserve by the Dock Trustees. It was, perhaps, too auspicious a start. The dam collapsed on 14 March 1854 just as it was nearing completion.[21] Brassey agreed to restore it at his own expense by August of that year, but on more careful investigation, it was apparent that the cost would far exceed his means. This fact, together with the disappointingly small rate of return on his dock bonds, induced him to revoke his previous undertaking and insist on cash in order to continue the work. He was reasonably sure such an ultimation could not be accepted and, when the Committee rejected his proposal, he threw in his hand and withdrew from the project.[22]

The early history of the Birkenhead dock project is therefore an unedifying story. It is in part the record of supineness, bad faith, incompetent engineering and unwise business decisions. Too little was done too late. It was, however, also the medium by which resentment and jealousy were kindled between Liverpool and Birkenhead. In wider political terms, it also involved Manchester. This thriving cotton metropolis, intent on pursuing free trade policies, had become resentful of the monopoly exercised by the Liverpool Dock Trustees. By making capital out of the quarrel between Liverpool and Birkenhead, Manchester and, on occasion, Parliament itself, put pressure on the Liverpool Corporation to effect a liberalisation of dock and town dues. With regard to the economic effects of the latter, the controversy was heightened in various Parliamentary Committees of 1855, in the Commission on Dock Charges in 1853 and the Select Committee on Local Charges upon Shipping of 1856. The pressures thus created were in all probability of importance in bringing the whole dock system of the Mersey under a public body in 1858.

IV

So far, the physical attributes of the port, as represented by its dock system, had perpetuated privilege in the continuance of Town Dues and had, by a closed-dock arrangement, created a monopolistic structure. It may be arguable that complete autonomy was essential in the interests of Liverpool's prosperity; but in a period which witnessed the growing liberalisation of trade, the activities of the Dock Committee were bound to arouse anger and resentment. The whole episode of Liverpool's opposition to the Birkenhead dock scheme was seen as evidence of a determination to stifle competition. In particular, Manchester, in their struggle to obtain supplies of cheap raw materials, regarded the monopoly control of Liverpool over its docks (on which they were almost wholly dependent) as objectionable and counter to their own economic interests. They regarded the scale on which dues were levied as a tax on imports of raw materials and on exports of finished products. Further resentment was caused by the fact that out of these dock dues an annual payment (averaging £120,000), known as Town Dues, was made to the Corporation of Liverpool. This levy was used to lighten the incidence of local rates.

Through the formation of the Mersey Docks and Harbour Board in 1858, it was anticipated that the more serious objections would be overcome. The Town Dues were converted to a lump sum of £1,500,000 and paid to the Corporation of Liverpool. The new Board took over the management of the docks on both sides of the river with an agreement to complete Rendel's plan for rail links with the Birkenhead docks.[23] It was, however, a hollow victory for the Manchester men. The dock dues were not substantially reduced nor was railway access carried out on anything like the scale contemplated. For the next twenty-five years the impact of port charges as an element in the cost of raw material supplies, was softened by the reduction in prime costs which were effected by the operation of steamship companies; but the controversy was renewed in the 1880s and it was left to that generation to establish a competitive alternative, by making Manchester itself into a port with access to the sea via the Manchester Ship Canal.

The new Dock Board, however, gave promotional focus to the development of the port. Of the twenty-eight original members, twenty-four were elected by the Dock Ratepayers and four were nominated by the Conservancy Commissioners. This membership comprised a fair cross-section of those using the port and normally included many who were shipowners. Apart from the powers conferred upon the Board for the day-to-day working of the dock system, specific functions were vested in the Board for the seeking of Parliamentary sanction under Dock Acts, for the raising of funds for the new dock schemes. The initiative for such action by the Board usually came from outside pressures. Ideas were brought to the Board for discussion and these, if considered worthwhile, were then pursued and brought to realisation. It goes without saying that many ideas were discussed at the behest of ship owners, the long controversy concerning the size and depth of docks to accommodate larger passenger liners being an example. There were occasions, however, when the forceful persuasion of a single individual effected lasting and beneficial change: in this connection one can cite T. H. Ismay's insistent effort to dredge and deepen the Bar at the mouth of the Mersey, and Sir Richard Holt's initiatory proposals for the Langton entrances. Thus, although the Board was the ultimate source of promotional power, the exercise of decision-taking was open to procedure from a wide range of interests. If monopoly had been created, it was a monopoly not impervious to new ideas.

Parallel to the growth of monopoly in the dock system, there was a similar development in the other major physical attributes of Liverpool's growth, namely, in the lines of communication with the hinterland. To some extent, Liverpool had always been at the mercy of river navigation and canal companies, particularly in the matter of rates charged on the carriage of goods. For this reason and chiefly as a countervailing influence, coastwise shipping had been given an impetus. By the middle years of the nineteenth century, however, the problem had been given a new order of magnitude through the service of a rapidly expanding railway network.

In order to understand the impact of railways upon the progress and prosperity of Liverpool as a port, one has to unravel a number of threads in an otherwise complicated pattern. There is the involvement of Liverpool capital in the early railway promotions; long-established trading connection between Liverpool and Manchester; the elimination of competition through amalgamation and the creation of a railway monopoly; the interaction of dock and railway monopoly; and, finally, Liverpool's peculiar position as a vast transit depot at the terminus of a railway system.

Despite the initial opposition and obstruction offered by local landowners to the early railway schemes, it soon became obvious that there was a potentially high development value in land on the outskirts of the town. This fact was given greater emphasis as the number of railway promotions increased and the prospect of alternative and competing routes was proposed. Landowners suddenly found new and lucrative opportunities to swell their bank balances. By allowing inroads to be made into their estates, they built up large sums on call and thereby went some way towards solving the problems of liquidity which even the largest of landowners experienced from time to time. John Shaw Leigh obtained £250,000 from the Liverpool & Bury Railway Co for the ownership of passage rights over his estates in north Liverpool,[24] the Earl of Derby nearly £500,000,[25] the Earl of Sefton upwards of £100,000[26] and the Marquis of Salisbury £170,000.[27] More often than not considerable sums for the purchase of land were taken in blocks of railway stock and this, when added to the rapidly increasing capital investment from multitudes of small units, represented a considerable flow of local resources into this new form of transport. By 1850, it was estimated that £0·8 million had been invested by Liverpool alone in the railways serving the port.[28] Thereafter, a new and important source was added to the list of investors. The new steamship companies, in the process of building up reserves, bought railway shares on an extensive scale. By 1875, the fifteen largest Liverpool cargo-companies had a total railway holding of £1·7 million, of which approximately half was in United Kingdom companies.

The flow of local resources into railways had been originally attracted in an endeavour to improve communications and facilitate the flow of goods between Liverpool and Manchester. Although the prosperity of both towns was based upon mutual dependence, a spirit of rivalry was engendered and this, as the nineteenth century advanced, turned into what can only be described in modern terminology as a love-hate relationship. The distinction between the Liverpool gentleman and the Manchester man is, perhaps, symptomatic of this. Nevertheless hard economic facts could not be gainsaid. By 1851, Braithwaite Poole, the London & North Western Railway goods manager, estimated that 125,000 tons of goods passed from Liverpool to Manchester in a single year, as compared with 26,000 tons to Birmingham and 35,000 tons to the Black Country, 29,000 tons to Sheffield, and 27,000 tons to London. Thus, Manchester took 52 per cent of Liverpool's outgoing railway traffic and, of this, 70 per cent consisted of cotton.[29] After 1860, grain joined cotton as a principal import commodity and, as we shall see later, put an increased strain on the railway facilities provided.

To a large extent the annoyance arising from the monopolistic nature of Liverpool's railway network, was a concomitant of the technical difficulty of bringing railways into the centre of Liverpool, and partly of the way in which amalgamations had taken place in the 1830s and 1840s. The eastern approach which had been planned for the Liverpool & Manchester railway had to pierce the sandstone ridge, and this involved the construction of costly cuttings and tunnels. At first, the line had its terminus at Crown Street, the carriages being winched up a steep incline to Edgehill by means of cables. Crown Street, however, was an inconvenient site and a further tunnel was built to the more central situation of Lime Street where a new terminus was opened in 1836. Any alternative competing line wishing for cheaper construction had the choice of one of two approaches. The first, skirting the northern end of the ridge where only a comparatively short tunnelling was necessary, ran along the shore into Tithebarn Street. This was the route followed by the Liverpool & Bury railway across John Shaw Leigh's estate to Exchange Station, opened in 1850. The other was along the south shore from Garston. During the 1860s the Manchester, Sheffield & Lincolnshire railway, in association with the Cheshire Lines Committee, extended their track from Garston; but the link-up with the centre of Liverpool to the terminus at Central Station was delayed by expensive land purchase and difficult tunnelling, and the through-line to Central Station was not completed until 1874.

Meanwhile, as a result of a series of amalgamations, the two other main lines serving Liverpool had strengthened their respective positions. The advent in 1837 of the Grand Junction Railway, linking Manchester and Birmingham via Crewe, and Birmingham and Liverpool via Warrington and Newton-le-Willows, was the first step in the transformation of the port's goods traffic.[30] The costly intrusion of the Cheshire Lines Committee in the 1870s did not fulfil the promise of a competitive goods service and, accordingly, shipowners, merchants, and agents became disproportionately dependent on one railway system for their needs. Consequently, the growing controversy about the provision of facilities and the charging of excessive rates developed into a struggle between the Dock Committee, representing shipowners and merchants, and the LNWR goods department. This in turn became centred on two personalities, Bramley Moore, the chairman of the Dock Committee, and Braithwaite Poole, the railway goods manager. The first shots in the battle, however, were fired by the newly constituted Chamber of Commerce founded in 1850. They made representation that the rapidly growing trade of the port seemed to be in danger of constriction, because of the scale of railway charges and the inadequate provision of wagons in the dock area. At a heated meeting in 1853, Braithwaite Poole sought to put the responsibility for lack of facilities at the dockside on the dock administration itself, the congestion, in his view, being caused by the 4,000 carts belonging to dock users, and occupying an inordinate amount of waterfront space. To this, Bramley Moore somewhat tartly retorted that every shipowner had the right to complain of the facilities provided by the railway companies. He also made a bitter attack upon the practice of the railway companies in charging differential rates and, in so doing, of discriminating against the true interests of the port. If the LNWR, he concluded, would carry goods at the same mileage rate from Liverpool to Manchester as that charged from Manchester to London, they would give practical proof of a desire to increase the commercial potentialities of Liverpool.[31]

The question of monopoly and discriminatory rates was a bone of contention for many years. In one sense it was a case of the biter being bit, as dock charges for the Manchester merchant were themselves monopoly rates, and this merchant saw no reason why the railway rates on his goods going to other parts of the country, should not be to his particular advantage as compared with those which had to be paid on raw materials from Liverpool. The issue took a more serious turn in the 1860s, the whole controversy being heightened not merely by the growing flood of imports, but more particularly by the expansion of one commodity, namely grain. John Patterson, representing the Liverpool corn merchants, gave evidence before a Royal Commission in 1867 and stressed the inconvenience of the restrictions felt by corn dealers, stating that the high railway charges forced trade out of its natural channels.[32] He further accused the railway companies of offering bounties to divert the trade into channels through which it would otherwise not flow. In fact, the flow of traffic was so great that the railways were often in difficulty in trying to cope with it, and took an easy way out by charging high rates. The argument continued into the 1870s and 1880s. W. B. (later Sir William) Forwood declared in 1872 that 'by manipulating terminal charges and by using the leeway of maximum charges allowed under statute, railway companies were free to turn the steamer traffic over to such portions of their systems which they might elect';[33] such policy was, perhaps, more in the interests of the railway shareholders than in those of the port. As we shall see later, the outcome of this controversy caused such annoyance and suspicion that the trade of Liverpool was directly and adversely affected.

Finally, one must attempt an explanation of this failure to secure a reliable and efficient railway communication based on a competitive network of routes. The failure was partly owing to accidents in the timing and promotion of schemes, resulting, as J. R. Kellett has pointed out, in a complementary rather than a competitive system; and partly owing to Liverpool's peculiar position in the railway network itself. Liverpool was, as Wilfred Smith has stressed,[34] a vast trans-shipment point at the end of a railway system. It was not, as in the case of Manchester or Crewe, a link in a railway trunk system. There was, therefore, a certain discontinuity in the flow of traffic, a fact which might help to explain the relative absence of trunk route rivalry. When all factors are assessed, however, it becomes difficult to avoid the conclusion that one of the chief causes of the port's failure to obtain a satisfactory solution of its railway problems, was the relationship between a dock monopoly and a railway monopoly. These two structures, very often for valid economic reasons, pulled in different directions. Implicit in this statement was the privileged position which a closed dock system with its vast array of bonded warehouses gave to the port. Anything which threatened this privilege, such as the building of docks at Birkenhead or the intrusion of railways into the dock area with separate and distinct administrative control, was a threat to be resisted. In short, although Liverpool could build up an effective autonomy in the handling and carriage of goods by sea, it could not exercise that same degree of autonomy over the collection and distribution of goods by land. As will be seen in a later chapter, the continued refusal to accept the realities of the situation led eventually to the establishment of both canal and railway schemes to bypass the port and these schemes, pursued with energetic foresight, limited the extent of Liverpool's dock monopoly and made serious encroachments into her overseas trade.

CHAPTER SIX

The Growth of Merseyside's Trade and Shipping, 1865-1914

I

From 1830 onwards, Liverpool's docks were being used by a growing volume of steamship tonnage. Up to 1860, however, this tonnage was principally engaged in coastal and cross-channel services, the oceanic trades being still very much in the control of sailing ship companies. In fact, sail died a hard and lingering death. Even as late as 1912, some docks on both sides of the river Mersey were at times crowded with barques and schooners, cheek by jowl with the iron and steel steamships. By that time, however, the sailing ship was performing a specialised and distinctive function, mainly carrying grain and bulk cargoes over long sea routes between Australia, the West Coast of America, and Britain. Nevertheless, the traditions of sail persisted despite improvements to the safety and reliability of steam propulsion. Holts' early steamships to the Far East all carried sail, and, as late as 1880, Harrisons were using iron sailing ships for the indentured labour trade between India and South America. In the West African trade, too, the African Steamship and the British & African Steam Navigation Companies used sail, chiefly on the outward voyage; so did Booths in their voyages to Brazil, relying on the steam engine to a minimum. In overall economic terms, steam may have conquered sail, but in practice it was not for another two generations that sail ceased to function.

Undoubtedly one of the more important stimuli effecting the change from sail to steam was the opening of the Suez Canal in 1869. Apart from the obvious advantage of providing a shorter route to India and the Far East, it was from the start a most convenient steamship highway. At the then current stage of steamship technology, it gave to the British shipowner a cost advantage on long oceanic voyages. Consequently, the Canal became a predominantly

British route, some 75 per cent of all ships passing through being sailed under the British flag. There were, however, wider implications for the steamship in the use of the Suez route. As D. A. Farnie has shown in his study of the Canal,[1] the opening of this waterway had a profound effect upon the balance of trades, first, with the Mediterranean and, secondly, at a later date, with India and the Far East. It brought a flood of British shipping into the Bombay freight market and started the transfer of that port's trade from sail to steam.[2] It revived the long cherished hope that India might provide an alternative source of supply to the United States for the import of raw cotton; it gave Brindisi an advantage over Marseilles, especially as the former port had been connected by rail through the Mont Cenis tunnel with Central Europe. Nevertheless, Marseilles was opened up to trade in cheaper Indian cotton and even Liverpool began to import this cotton in the spring and early autumn 'so placing it in competition with the cream of the American crop'.[3] Though India did not eventually become a rival source of supply for cotton, Bombay and Calcutta were opened up to Liverpool steamships. At least, until 1876, 'Liverpool exported more Indian cotton to Europe than the Continent imported direct from India'.[4] Within the context of rapidly-changing patterns of trade, therefore, the Canal became identified with Liverpool's steamship development.

II

The following figures of net registered tonnage of shipping using the port after the establishment of the Mersey Docks and Harbour Board show a consistent rise:

Net Registered Tons—million

1858	4·4	1890	9·6
1860	4·7	1900	12·3
1870	5·7	1910	16·6
1880	7·5	1914	19·0

These tonnages are drawn from dues paid and, as only one charge was made for both inward and outward berthing and clearance, the entries and clearances amounted roughly to double those given.[5] Within this framework, however, there were certain important fluctuations. Between 1862 and 1865, there was a levelling-off in the upward trend. This was largely caused by the decrease in the volume of cotton supplied from the United States during the Civil War. There was a further rise in 1866 to 5.5 million tons but again a check until 1871. This static situation, though perhaps explicable in relation to general economic factors, is less so when one takes into account the rapid establishment of new steamship routes which Liverpool firms started in this period; those, for example, which opened up trade with Malaya and China, India, Brazil and the Southern United States—all of which were distinct from the increasing volume of emigrant traffic. The stable figure between 1877 and 1879 of 7 million tons must have been caused mainly by considerations other than the onset of depression because there seems to be little correlation between the volume of shipping using the port and cyclical fluctuations in output. There was, however, some correlation with the trade cycle during the years from 1885 to 1887, but throughout the 1890s there was a continuous and rapid increase coinciding with the rebuilding programmes of nearly all the large Liverpool-owned steamship companies. From 1900 to 1914, apart from 1910 which showed a decrease over the previous year, the annual increase was substantial, amounting over the period as a whole to well over 50 per cent. In general, these mounting tonnages reflect two things; the first was that Liverpool was sharing in the expansion of world trade after 1880, a fact which, as far as Liverpool herself was concerned, was a corollary of the opening up of new markets by her own steamship companies; the second was the relative position of Liverpool as a United Kingdom port. In 1857, Liverpool's export trade, by value, amounted to approximately 45 per cent of the United Kingdom's total; this compared more than favourably with London's 23 per cent, Hull's 13 per cent, Glasgow's 4 per cent and Southampton's 1.6 per cent. In the following half century, Liverpool's share fell to about 36 per cent, and we shall examine the causes of this decline in a later chapter. In the import trade, the port handled approximately one third of the United Kingdom total, a figure which also declined to just under one quarter by 1914.[6]

A second indicator of the port's growing activity, during the period from 1870 to 1914, is to be found in the volume of goods imported and exported within a constantly changing pattern of trade. In the latter half of the nineteenth century, King Cotton reigned supreme in Liverpool. The steamships brought in a flood of supplies, the tall warehouses stored it, the Cotton Exchange regulated prices and ensured future deliveries. The resultant manufacturing processes produced millions of yards of fine and coarse piece-goods which, as exports, were carried in Liverpool ships to all parts of the world. It was a complete cycle. As an import, cotton was by far Liverpool's most important commodity. In 1820, it amounted to about 111,000 tons; by 1850, the figure had risen to 360,000 tons. This volume was never less than 80 per cent of the United Kingdom's total importation and, in many years, it accounted for nearly 90 per cent. If supplies failed in one part of the world, alternative sources could usually be found, and although American cotton continued to dominate the market, the growing importance of Egyptian and East Indian cottons (particularly after 1840) must not be overlooked. Many Liverpool merchants, believing that too great a dependence on United States' sources might be dangerous, sought to widen the area of supply by bringing in Brazilian cotton. Their fears were more than justified in the 1860s when, as a consequence of the American Civil War, cotton imports from the Southern States were virtually cut off and famine, which not even Liverpool's warehouse stocks could alleviate, was the result.[7] The dislocation was not easily remedied; even by 1870, the import of American cotton had only reached some 66 per cent of the 1860 figure. Nevertheless, during the last quarter of the century, the upward trend had been resumed. During the 1880s the annual average was just over 450,000 tons; this increased during the 1890s to just under 660,000 tons and was stabilised in the years from 1910 to 1913 at 690,000 tons.[8]

An extraordinary change, however, had taken place between 1850 and 1913 in the composition of Liverpool's import trade. Although the volume of cotton imports had increased and although Liverpool still accounted for between 70 and 80 per cent of all cotton imported into the United Kingdom, the cotton as a percentage of Liverpool's total imports, at current values, decreased from just over 40 per cent in the early 1850s to 30 per cent by 1913. Similarly, in the traditional trades in sugar and tobacco, volumes rose absolutely, but fell relative to Liverpool's total import trade; for example, an average of 355,000 tons of sugar (as compared with 62,000 tons in 1850) was imported in the three years before 1914, but the share of Liverpool's total imports, at current values, was only 2·4 per cent; that of tobacco with a volume of 40,220 tons (7,000 tons in 1850) also stood at 2·4 per cent by value. Obviously other newer commodities had helped to swell the list and increase the aggregate. Of these, grain of all descriptions was the most important. Wheat for the same period averaged 1,180,000 tons (121,000 tons in 1852); barley, at 41,000 tons (9,600 tons in 1852), oats, at 65,000 tons (34,600 tons in 1852), and maize, at 185,000 tons, together accounted for 8 per cent of total imports by volume. Rubber, a highly important new commodity, amounted to an average of 5·2 per cent, copper to 2·4 per cent, tin to 1·5 per cent and wool to 4·4 per cent. Finally, of the new or nearly new commodities, hides and rice were the most significant and amounted to 2·5 per cent of total imports. Timber alone of the older-type commodities had an average annual import value of £4·4 million and a share percentage of 2·5. Thus, by 1914, from an import list consisting of a few major items and a large number of smaller items, it can be concluded that the decline in the share of the traditional commodities had been offset by new ones, amounting in total to approximately one quarter of total imports by value.[9]

In Liverpool's export trade, by far the most important items were cotton yarn, piece-goods and other cotton textiles. These amounted to approximately half of total exports (by current value) in 1901; by 1905, this share had fallen to 47 per cent and by 1913 to 41·6 per cent. Although there was a decline in the exports of yarn after 1905, the volume of piece-goods exported rose from 3,812 million linear yards in 1901 to 4,720 million yards in 1913. This latter increase was very largely the result of rising demand from India. The reflection of outward cargoes of heavy engineering and railway equipment to India, South America, Mexico and South Africa is shown in the figures for these exports. They rose from £15·1 million in 1901 to £19·0 million in 1905 and £34·7 million by 1913, representing 16·7 per cent of total exports in 1901 and 20·4 per cent in 1913. One other major export needs to be mentioned. This was wool and woollen and worsted piece-goods; these items rose from £5·4 million in 1901 to £10·1 million in 1913 and represented, in this latter year approximately 6 per cent of Liverpool's total exports. One further point of particular interest is to be found in Liverpool's re-export trade. During the early 1900s it was of negligible proportions, but in 1911 there was a considerable increase, amounting to

£27·2 million. This figure increased to £30·3 million in 1912 but fell to £25·1 million in 1913. This trade was principally with European countries and was, as we shall see later, of considerable importance to Liverpool as an exporting port in the years from 1920 to 1939.[10]

If we take a reasonably broad view of Liverpool's trade between 1850 and 1913, it is possible to draw the general conclusion that imports trebled in value at current prices, but that volumes increased between three and four times. Exports increased nearly fourfold in value and nearly fivefold in volume. This is substantiated by the rise in the tonnages entering and clearing the port and fully justifies, if indeed justification were needed, the heavy investment in docks, warehouses and port facilities, and also the flow of resources into the establishment of steamship companies. In short, Liverpool not only provided herself with the means of carrying a vast increase of imports and exports, but acquired the port facilities to handle, store, and despatch these volumes of goods and commodities both inwards and outwards. If one needed an example of Victorian initiative and foresight, the port of Liverpool must surely be that example *par excellence*.

III

A third, though perhaps less reliable, indicator of the port's well-being is to be found in the level of earnings of her shipping lines. In the main, these earnings were affected by three factors: the general level of demand, the incidence of competition over particular sea routes, and the facility by which shipping companies, through technical innovation, could provide cheap and efficient services in the carriage of a constantly changing composition of cargoes.

In the forty years after 1870, the freight rates on most of Liverpool's imported commodities fell by an average of 60 per cent, and those on exports by just over 50 per cent.[11] These reductions were obviously caused by the operation of the steamship and by the magnitude of the scale on which goods were carried. At the same time, there were a succession of technical improvements to the steamship itself including, for example, the use of steel, the improvement of ventilation, the change-over from compound to triple-expansion engines and the use of electricity. One of the most practical improvements came from the inventiveness of Alfred Holt. By the introduction of steel girders to support the upper deck, he was able to dispense with the rows of pillars in the hold and so give greater freedom for the storage of cargo, particularly the awkward bulky packages of heavy engineering equipment which became a staple of Liverpool's export trade after 1885.[12] These technical devices meant more efficient ships, and they were also incorporated into bigger ships; the average size of the Liverpool steamship increased from 2,500–3,000 tons deadweight to an average of 10,000 tons deadweight in the period under review. The combination of these two factors had the effect of achieving economies of scale and thus reducing the cost per ton-mile. After 1890, Holts reduced these costs by as much as 50 per cent[13] and Harrisons by nearly 55 per cent.[14] In other words, technical improvements had virtually kept pace with, and had been one of the causes of, decreasing freight rates. On the other hand, though receipts on a unit of cargo had fallen, the unit cost had also fallen. Bigger ships and an increasing voyage pattern, however, enabled a vastly increased volume to be carried.[15] Accordingly the net earnings of shipping companies were, in bad years, at least maintained and, in good years, substantially increased. By way of illustration, the following comparison of net profits per voyage is relevant.

The decline in average net profits per voyage after 1871 reflects the general fall in freight rates, but the general stability after 1900, as expressed in terms of net earnings per gross ton, incorporates the effectiveness of reduced costs in the sailing of the ships. The very low earnings of 1891–2 for all companies were primarily the result of increased and intense competition from both home and foreign rivals and illustrates, with a degree of emphasis, the third factor mentioned above affecting the earnings of shipping companies. In Holt's case the fall in receipts in this year was caused by intense competition from the Dutch in the Far East and from a bitter struggle at home with the China Mutual Steam Navigation Co, founded in 1882. Harrisons' falling receipts can be explained as the outcome of a fierce rate-cutting war with Brocklebanks and the Indian Mutual in their Indian trade, and with the Leyland Line and the West Indian & Pacific Steam Ship Company in their New Orleans and West Indian trades. Elder Dempsters' West African trade (included in the ten other companies) was also assailed by the inroads of a powerful German group under the title of the Woer-

Average net profit per voyage 1871–1913

Year	Far Eastern and Australian Trades	West Indian, Gulf Indian and South African Trades	South American and Australian Trades
	(in £000)		
1871	5·1	3·2	4·1
1881	4·7	3·9	3·8
1885	1·57	0·44	—
1890	0·73	1·20	—
1891	0·62	1·12	1·6
1892	0·37	0·59	—
1893	0·71	0·79	—
1894	1·63	0·91	—
1895	1·90	0·76	—
1896	0·85	1·07	—
1897	1·56	1·27	—
1898	2·68	1·98	—
1899	4·50	1·84	—
1900	4·03	3·20	—
1901	2·70	1·81	2·4
1902	2·95	1·47	—
1903	2·10	1·30	—
1904	3·15	1·24	—
1905	4·29	1·21	—
1906	3·94	1·09	—
1907	3·12	1·31	—
1908	2·93	0·93	—
1909	2·83	1·14	—
1910	3·94	1·74	—
1911	5·22	2·18	4·9
1912	5·50	3·29	—
1913	7·06	3·55	—

Source: Compilation from *Royal Commission of Shipping Rings* (1909), and shipping accounts of Holts, Harrisons, Pacific Steam Navigation Co. and other Liverpool shipping companies.

Average net earnings per gross ton 1898–1914

	(in £) Harrisons	Holts
1898	2·4	
1899	1·9	
1900	3·0	
1901	1·5	
1902	1·1	
1903	1·1	
1904	1·2	
1905	1·1	
1906	0·9	
1907	1·2	
1908	0·7	
1909	0·9	0·7
1910	1·3	0·9
1911	1·4	1·2
1912	2·3	1·2
1913	2·4	1·4
1914	1·9	1·0

Source: Holt and Harrison MSS voyage accounts.

mann Line. It is, therefore, of interest to see how Liverpool shipping companies attempted to overcome these threats to their earning capacity, and to make an assessment of their success or otherwise in their efforts to maintain trade between foreign markets and their home port.

IV

In the newly established Far Eastern steamship trade, the threat to earning capacity from uncontrolled competition came from two sources. The first was from home-based shipping companies with new, fast, technically-improved ships; the second was from entrenched foreign shipping companies, particularly Dutch and American, whose hold on the river trade in China and the Island trade of the Archipelago was difficult to dislodge. In their efforts to maintain a competitive position, the Holts were advised, directed and sometimes browbeaten by the forceful genius of John Samuel Swire.[16] As we have seen, Swire's own shipping activities on the Yangtze and along the China Coast had been subjected to annoying interference from the British firm of Jardine Matheson, the American firm of Russell & Co, and the China Merchants Navigation Co. As early as 1872, Swire had established a pooling agreement, a system which ensured all companies of a reasonable share of available cargoes.[17] This was not the first time such a scheme had been applied; the Moss shipping interests had entered into proto-conference agreements in the Levant trades in the 1860s and, as will be shown later, there was a combination in the Brazilian trade in 1870–1. Nevertheless, the particular principles which Swire had worked out were introduced into the Calcutta Conference of 1875 and into the first China Conference of 1879. This latter Conference, under Swire's chairmanship, brought together all the principal firms (such as the Shire, Castle, P & O, Messageries Maritimes, Glens and Holts) engaged in the China trade under one umbrella. They all agreed to a classified list of freight charges and offered merchants a deferred rebate as an inducement to securing loyalty to Conference ships. In return, the shipowners promised regularity of service and prompt delivery of cargo. This Conference, if it achieved nothing else, brought a degree of order to the trade, increased the commercial tempo and, by maintaining levels of receipts, helped in safeguarding the growing capital resources of the shipping lines.[18]

Such safeguards, however, were no reason for complacency. Within a Conference system there was still room for degrees of competition, and the most efficiently managed firm with the most up-to-date ships made the greatest profit. By the mid-1880s, Holts' iron compound-engined ships, once so revolutionary in design and speed, were being outclassed by new steel ships of the Shire, Glen and Castle lines, powered by triple-expansion engines. Despite Swire's fulminations, Alfred Holt stubbornly refused to alter the material, the design or the motive power. Consequently, the competitive advantage passed from Holts' hands and profits began to fall. In addition to this threat to Holts' technical supremacy, there was an even greater threat to their trading position through the creation of a new, powerful rival company in Liverpool, the China Mutual. This latter company was equipped with fast, modern ships and though, at first, it was a member of the China Conference, it was strong enough by 1886 to offer a direct challenge to Holts and the other China companies. The China Mutual left the Conference in 1887 and allied itself with the Mogul shipping interests. A fierce rate-cutting war followed, virtually to the financial ruin of both groups. Holts' average annual net earnings fell from £175,000 to £35,000 (for the periods 1883–6 and 1887–91).[19] It was not until the 1890s, when new management instituted a complete rebuilding of the fleet, that Holts could claim that they had overcome the damaging effects of a conservative management, which had brought them to the verge of destruction. The China Mutual never really recovered. Although readmitted to the Conference, the company's economic position had been severely undermined, and in 1902 Holts acquired a controlling interest. Both companies, each with their separate managements, became one organisation.[20]

Meanwhile, in the Far East, the course of events was also taking a less propitious turn. The trade in China tea, the great staple of the 1870s, was beginning to decline in the 1880s. This commodity was being replaced in the British market by cheaper and more strongly flavoured Indian teas. The fall in the value of homeward cargoes was, however, offset (at least to some extent) by changes in outward cargoes. By the 1890s railway and heavy engineering equipment became the new staples.[21] Nevertheless the loss of the tea trade made it all the more imperative for Holts to find new sources of supply for homeward cargoes. The most lucrative prospects seemed to lie in Sumatran tobacco, Javanese sugar and other East Indian bulk commodities. In the Islands, however, the Dutch held a monopoly position. Like Holts, the Dutch main line companies, the Nederland and the Rotterdam Lloyd, had created feeder services from the Islands to Batavia, such trade being confined to ships under the Dutch flag. As a means of breaking into this trade, Holts created a Netherlands Ocean Steam Ship Co in 1891. This enabled them to operate in the East Indian ports on equal terms with their Dutch rivals, a move which was so successful that it made the services of the East Indian Ocean Steam Ship Co redundant. In 1899, therefore, this latter company, started by Mansfield, was sold to Norddeutscher Lloyd.

As a further extension of their interests in the Pacific, Holts had always cherished the idea of a transocean route. This had been partially achieved by the opening of a service between north China and the west coast ports of America, but their ultimate aim had been to link Australasia with China and Malaya. At first a small service was started between Singapore and Western Australia. In 1901, however, a direct line was started from Glasgow to Sydney and Melbourne. This was not particularly lucrative; in fact, for the first few years the ships operated at a loss.[22] Nevertheless, by 1914, conditions had begun to improve and the Holt organisation can be said, by that date, to have created a truly Far Eastern and trans-Pacific shipping line, linking Liverpool with a wide variety of markets. As a further cover for the employment of resources in these new trades, they extended protection outwards from the China Conference to other agreements including the Straits Settlements' Conference and the Principals' and Agents' Conference. Through such agreements the disruptive tendencies of local shippers were neutralised, volumes of cargo were kept high and the resultant receipts maintained and, in good years, swelled the levels of earnings.

There was a similar pattern of expansion and protection of Liverpool's trade with India. When Harrisons sent their pioneer steamship, the *Fire Queen*, through the newly-opened Suez Canal to Bombay in the early months of 1870, they were adding merely a technological dimension to a long-established and traditional Liverpool trade. The Rathbones and the Brocklebanks had already gained experience of the Indian primary commodity trades through the provision of well-ordered services, but it was the steamship which was henceforth to foster the commercial potentialities of the trade. At first, however, competition was severe; Indian ports became choked with steamships following the shipbuilding boom of the early 1870s. As a consequence, Liverpool companies were signatories to the Calcutta Conference but there continued to be, despite Conference agreements, a good deal of savage in-fighting. Rathbones were not strong enough to withstand the damaging effects of vicious competition and were forced to sell their steamships to Harrisons. Thus, after a century of shipowning in Liverpool, this firm fell victim to the pressures of the steamship age. For the Harrisons, the purchase of the Rathbone ships and berthing rights gave them an entry into the Indian tea trade. The competitive struggle was intensified. The receipts from voyages fell, and it was only by using the remnants of their old sailing fleet in the carriage of Indian indentured labour to the sugar plantations of Brazil and the West Indies, that the profitability of ships in their Indian account could be assured. In the late 1880s, Brocklebanks and the

Anchor line left the Calcutta Conference and joined with the Indian Mutual in a free market. The ensuing rate-cutting war brought injury rather than gain to all companies. When peace was restored in 1892 and Brocklebanks and the Anchor line were re-admitted to the Conference, a new basis for agreement had been negotiated. Henceforth, the Indian market was shared out among the shipping companies by an agreed voyage allocation. It brought Harrisons, Brocklebanks and their principal external rivals, the Clan, Anchor and City lines, into a more harmonious relationship and provided a workable system which lasted without interruption until 1914.[23]

V

By contrast with the Indian and Pacific trades, Liverpool's new connection with West Africa was organised within the framework of a quasi-monopoly. As we have seen, Alfred Jones had joined Elder Dempster in 1879 and had acquired a dominant position in West African trade. When in 1884 both Elder and Dempster 'retired', Jones was left as head of the firm in a position of power. By virtue of that position he was agent for, and manager of, the African Steam Ship Co. It was a comparatively short step from this to the acquisition of a similar controlling interest in the rival firm, the British and African Steam Navigation Co. According to legend (which has much to support it in fact) Jones accomplished this end by means of the banana. Visiting the Canaries, he was impressed by the excellent quality of the fruit and decided to introduce it to the British market. He bought land, started plantations and financed an export company. The venture succeeded, and with the profits he began to buy up the shares of the British and African Steam Navigation Company. By 1890, he had a controlling interest and thus found himself in a position to determine the course, direction and policy of Liverpool's trade with West Africa.[24]

Like Alfred Holt in the Far Eastern trades and the brothers Harrison in the Indian and American trades, Jones was confronted by the strength of competition, in this case particularly from foreign shipping companies. Having secured his domination of British lines, he had now to face encroachment into the West African trade from the powerful German Woermann line. In 1895, after a somewhat cursory rate war, he managed to persuade the Woermann line to join with their two British rivals in the establishment of a West African Conference.[25] This not only strengthened Jones's hand as a shipowner, but gave him greater power in dealing with West African merchants, such as John Holt and a multitude of small men working on a commission basis in West Africa. Jones's relationship with merchants had led, and continued to lead, to fierce struggles. These struggles assumed a more persistent character after the formation of the African Association, an association which, with John Holt as a principal member, was a counterbalancing influence to the West African Conference. In general, the merchants, whenever possible, attempted to by-pass the Conference by chartering their own ships. The struggles never lasted very long; Jones was in too powerful a position and the Conference, because of its monopoly, could usually undercut competitors and drive them off the West African route. John Holt and the Association, therefore, usually had to accept the conditions imposed.[26] As time went on, Jones's power increased. In 1895, the same year in which the Conference had been created, he entered into negotiations with King Leopold of the Belgians to provide shipping services to the Congo. By putting a number of his ships under the Belgian flag, he virtually founded the Belgian national shipping line, Compagnie Maritimes Belges. In return, he received large concessions in the carriage of freight between the Congo and Antwerp. In other ways, too, Jones sought to extend his power. He created and owned nearly all the lighterage facilities on the West African Coast and, through these, controlled the handling of cargoes there. He also had a controlling interest in the Bank of British West Africa, an instrument which enabled him to extend credit, not only for trade in the port areas, but also in that of the up-country stores. In other words, he had built up an extensive monopoly position in the rapidly expanding and highly lucrative trade between Liverpool and West Africa. This was a monopoly which confined practically the whole trade to Liverpool, and was an essential element in supplying palm products to Levers' developing soap factories at Port Sunlight, which had been established in 1888.[27]

Liverpool's trading association with the coasts of South America had a long and somewhat erratic history. It grew out of a contraband trade with the West Indies in the eighteenth century. By the nineteenth century, there were numerous voyages made by sailing

ships to Parahiba and other ports, such as, for example, those made
by that interpid master-mariner of the Harrison ships, Richard
Pierre Williamson.[28] These ships usually returned with cargoes of
Brazilian cotton. There was, however, another link. From the end
of the Napoleonic Wars and, later, with the discovery of the South
Shetlands, a fairly extensive whaling and sealing industry was
developed and, in this, Liverpool ships and Liverpool seamen
participated.[29] The South Atlantic, therefore, was an ocean not
entirely outside the scope and influence of the port. On the other
side of the Continent, the western shores of South America, as we
have seen, were brought within range of Liverpool's enterprise by
the early steamships of the Pacific Steam Navigation Co. It was,
however, not until the 1860s that the Atlantic seaboard (and particularly that of Brazil) was brought into regular steamship communication with Liverpool. This was the achievement of the
Booths, the Singlehursts, the Evans and others, who embarked
their capital in what was, for at least a decade, a hazardous and unremunerative venture. The Booth line started in 1865 with two
small steamships, the *Augustine* and the *Jerome*, with a capital of
£40,000. The ships were built in Liverpool to Alfred Holt's specifi-
cations and were not at first successful, either from a technical or
an economic point of view. They barely held their own against the
sailing ship and were worked at a loss. With fiancial help from the
Holts, Rathbones and the Royal Bank of Liverpool (at least until it
closed in 1868) the Booths managed to keep the ships in the
Brazilian trade. Nevertheless, by 1870, new steamship rivals on this
route were making inroads into the trade. This competition came
principally from Singlehurst's Red Cross line and Evans's Maranham Steamship Co. In 1870-1, agreement was reached between the
three companies, allocating sailings and fixing levels of freight
rates. Despite this, there was no great improvement in Booths'
financial position and, for the greater part of the 1870s, the company made only a small return on capital. Towards the end of the
decade, however, prospects became brighter. It was decided to re-
construct the company and expand operations. Accordingly, in
1881, the Booth line was turned into a limited company under the
style of the Booth Steamship Co Ltd, the steamships being managed by Alfred Booth & Co. The newly constituted organisation
had a capital of £550,000.[30] This was the normal form of steamship
company structure; it gave greater flexibility to the managers in the

use of the ships; it provided the expansion of resources within a public company (even though the majority of the shares were held by the Booths and their friends, the Holts); and it created opportune conditions for an enlargement of the fleet. This in turn had to be accompanied by a more efficiently run commercial organisation.

The first few years after 1881, however, were not prosperous. This was due partly to the intensive competition from the French company, Chargeurs Réunis, and partly to the depressed state of trade. After 1886, the trade became better established on four main services (excluding the direct Liverpool–Maranham service): the fast, predominantly passenger route to Para via Lisbon and Oporto for which the Booth line had two ships and the Red Cross line three; the new Continental route via Hamburg, Antwerp, Havre, and Lisbon to the Brazilian ports; the joint monthly service to Ceara and Maranham via Lisbon and Oporto; and finally the subsidised voyages between Manaos and New York. A triangular trade was also started between Brazil, Galveston, and Liverpool, mainly to pick up cargoes of cotton and grain, a service which competed with the Harrison line ships. In general, the prosperity of the Booth shipping company was built up, after 1886, on the homeward cargoes of rubber (a commodity in growing demand from the new bicycle and motor car industries) and on the outward carriage of emigrants from Lisbon and (after 1895) on the carriage of heavy engineering equipment and other capital goods.

This increasing tempo attracted competitors and in 1902 the Hamburg–Amerika line, after having an agreement with the Liverpool companies, broke away and made a determined attempt to capture a greater share of the trade. By this time, however, Booths were in a much stronger position. They had brought their various agencies into one organisation and had amalgamated with Singlehurst's Red Cross line in 1901. As Evans's Maranham Steamship Co had been bought out at the same time, the Booths were able to offer a united front to the Hamburg–Amerika's competition and a fierce rate war followed. The outcome was the acceptance of a new agreement in which Booths received a 70 per cent share of the pool of passenger and freight receipts from Liverpool, and the Hamburg–Amerika line 30 per cent. There was also an agreed list of passenger and freight rates. This allocation worked reasonably well until 1913 when a new agreement was negotiated.[31]

The participation of the Harrison ships in the Brazilian trade was centred on Pernambuco; but this participation was complementary to Harrisons' other Caribbean trades. Their ships sailed to Barbados and thence either northwards to Mexico, where they picked up cargoes of hides, ores and grain, in return for railway equipment and machinery; or southwards to Central America where, via the Isthmus of Panama, cargoes could be shipped to Pacific coast ports. In this trade they were in competition with their Liverpool rivals, the Pacific Steam Navigation Co. It was the extension of this trade to Brazil, in 1876, which gave Harrisons an additional security in the offsetting of trade fluctuations in the area as a whole.[32] If shipments were light in any one region, tonnage could easily be despatched to ports where cargo was more plentiful. Alternatively, holds could be equally well filled with West Indian products.

In the Pernambuco trade, Harrisons encountered increasingly severe competition from both British and German lines. The rivalry had been particularly intense in years of short supply and it eventually became necessary to seek agreement on freight rates and shipping capacity. The four rival British companies, (Lamport & Holt, Royal Mail, Pacific Steam Navigation Co and Harrisons), entered into negotiation with their three German competitors, (Hamburg–Amerika, Norddeutscher Lloyd and Hamburg–Süd–Amerika) and, in 1896, formed a Central Brazilian Conference. Under the terms of this agreement, a classified list of freight rates was put into operation together with a deferred rebate of 10 per cent.[33] In short, this trade, like so many others at this time, emerged from a stage of unregulated growth and had now become subjected (at least in the relationship of shipping space to cargo) to systematic control.

VI

The direct transatlantic trade with the United States was, at certain periods, dominated by the passenger and emigrant traffic. This was (as far as Liverpool was concerned) largely undertaken by the Cunard, White Star, Guion, Oceanic, and National companies. These companies competed for the first-class passenger traffic and built fast liners to accommodate it. In particular, the Guion line, which was created in 1866 from the earlier Black Star line of sailing packets, had an intense rivalry with Cunard until

1894. Thereafter, the Cunard and White Star lines were the principal carriers. All the companies engaged in the carriage of cargo, though this was complementary to passenger services. In periods of trade fluctuation, it was the emigrant trade which maintained profitability, though this traffic was subject to rate-cutting and periodic agreements.

The emigrant traffic, as distinct from the first-class passenger traffic, was a major part of the earning capacity of passenger liner companies serving Liverpool during the latter half of the nineteenth century. There was sound economic sense in the efforts of rival shipping lines to attract emigrants; it was basically a part of the American trade and there were occasions during periods of trade recession when lines (such as the National, for example) could claim that the receipts from the carriage of emigrants had made all the difference between a profit and a loss. Of the estimated 5½ million emigrants departing from Britain between 1860 and 1900, just over 4¾ million went from Liverpool. That Liverpool was able to cope with such a flood of humanity was due to two principal causes. In the first place, the port had the tonnage available and the organisation capable of dealing with agents and government officials, the latter, in particular, being responsible for the administration of a growing volume of government regulation of the trade; and secondly, the railway network serving Liverpool provided adequate feeder services, not only from the industrial areas of Britain, but from the Continent as well. In this, the rail link between Liverpool and Hull was highly important as a short route for Scandinavians and north Germans wishing to cross to the United States.

Despite these obvious advantages, however, the trade was not without financial hazard. Up to 1867, there was a fairly continuous flow of some 20,000 Irish emigrants a year leaving Liverpool; this was often augmented by calls at Queenstown, where many thousands more were taken on board. After 1870, however, English emigrants from the towns formed an increasing proportion of the total.[34] In the 1880s and 1890s, the pattern changed to a growing preponderance of European emigrants. Nevertheless, the traffic did not conform to a continuous flow; between 1860 and 1900, the fluctuations included four troughs and three peaks. As a consequence, there was fierce competition and rate-cutting between steamship companies in the lean years, supplemented by an equally discriminatory structure by railway companies to attract business. The whole trade was subjected to commercial as well as to economic pressures, it was an adjunct of the larger commodity trades and, in its development, the shipping lines of Liverpool, such as Ismay's White Star, Inman's American, McIver's Cunard, the Guion and the National, played a dominant part.

In the Atlantic commodity trades of cotton and grain, the principal Liverpool firms were Harrisons, the Leyland line and the West India & Pacific Steam Ship Co. As we have seen, Harrisons had special rating agreements with American railroad companies for the carriage of grain and cotton to New Orleans, and through-rates from New Orleans on their ships to Liverpool. Both the Leyland and West India companies, however, offered competitive rates and, by the late 1880s, were beginning to cut into the Harrisons' entrenched position. In 1890, therefore, John William Hughes, the new and direct influence in Harrison affairs, concluded a series of agreements with his two rivals, allocating cotton cargoes and fixing freight rates.[35] This arrangement worked satisfactorily for nearly ten years, but in 1899, Sir John Ellerman bought the Leyland line and later purchased the West India & Pacific Steam Ship Co. Thus the working arrangement which Harrisons had with these two companies was placed in jeopardy; but worse was to follow. In 1901, Ellerman sold his West Indian interests to the American railroad magnate, J. Pierpont Morgan. Morgan was greatly interested in building up an American mercantile marine. As a railroad man, he was equally interested in diverting the vast rail freights from cotton and wheat away from New Orleans and the Gulf ports to his own railroad systems serving the Atlantic seaports. Harrisons thus found themselves faced with the prospect of greatly increased competition from American sources and a direct threat to the continued growth of their Gulf trade. For this reason, John William Hughes sought to widen the scope of Harrisons' trading interests.

In 1902, Hughes succeeded in taking Harrisons into the South African Conference and starting a service with Capetown for the carriage of heavy capital goods outwards in return for wool homewards. This also involved a joint service with the Ellerman line and a pooling agreement between Harrisons, Ellermans and the Clan line.[36] Such an agreement was necessary as Harrisons had close working arrangements with Clan ships and, as these ships were much smaller than either those of the Harrisons or the Ellermans, there had to be an equitable distribution of receipts. This move was a wise one. It not only helped in stabilising what otherwise might have been a declining trend in Harrisons' earning capacity, it also identified Liverpool much more closely with South Africa. After 1910, these services were given additional emphasis by the creation of a new trade based on the East African port of Beira and tapping the bulk commodities of cotton and tobacco from that region.[37]

It has not been possible to deal with all of Liverpool's new steam-ship trades which grew up after 1870. Enough had been said, how-ever, to justify the conclusion that Liverpool men with ideas were actively engaged, through the use very largely of their own capital resources, in opening up the whole world to Liverpool. In this process, they worked out for themselves the most effective ways of combating competition and safeguarding their resources. They met the demands of an expanding world trade and, in so doing, their effort was not without its rewards. Capital growth was phenomenal and, if we compare such development for selected companies over the period 1870 to 1914, the inference is obvious:

Employed Capital

	(in £ million)	
	1870	1914
Ocean Steam Ship Co (and after 1902 China Mutual)	0·21	4·90
Charente S.S. Co	0·31	2·58
African S.S. Co British & African Steam N. Co	0·26	1·80
Pacific S.N. Co	0·62	4·20
Booth S.S. Co	0·05	0·90
	1·45	14·38

The above figures are given at current values. If a constant price index is applied capital growth shows a ninefold increase; if also this increase is given the additional support of a fivefold growth in tonnage, a trebling of imports and a quadrupling of exports, by value, one can judge this achievement, largely self-financed, as dynamic and highly profitable.

CHAPTER SEVEN

Port Investment, Administration, and Competition, 1858-1914

I

We have already seen that, by 1858, the investment of some £5¼ million had been expended on the development of the Liverpool Dock Estate. After 1858, however, the flow of investment was directed in three ways: through private investment; through the authorised channel of the Mersey Docks and Harbour Board; and, in a much smaller measure, through the development activities of railway companies. As the new steamship lines introduced Liverpool to a widening range of markets and augmented existing ones, the need for increased accommodation and better dock facilities continued to grow. In turn, this stimulated a two-edged controversy between shipowners and the Dock Board. The passenger liner companies, with an eye on the Atlantic trade, required larger docks, longer quays and wider dock entrances to berth their ships of increasing size and tonnage. On the other hand, the cargo-liner owners, such as Alfred Holt, believed that the steamship had reached an optimum size consistent with the demand for shipping space and the level of costs. The cargo companies, therefore, were not particularly anxious to embark on a vast programme of investment to provide facilities which, as far as they could see into the future, were not likely to be required. In the last resort, these attitudes were seen by merchants and manufacturers as a further attempt on the part of shipowners to secure their vested interests. The Dock Board thus became the focal point of pressures and, as a decision-taker, was often quite unwillingly put into the position of arbiter of the course of Liverpool's future development as a port. This not only affected the flow of resources, but also led to changes in administration, and to the growth of competition from those whose interests demanded a breaking of Liverpool's grip on the import and export trades of the Mersey.

In entering this new phase of Liverpool's growing prosperity, it might be relevant to consider the successive fluctuations in the port's employment of new capital against the background of port investment in the country as a whole. In general, there was a fairly consistent investment demand up to 1866, but something of a decline occurred after that year owing to the aftermath of financial crisis as existing projects were not completed and new ones were not forthcoming. The decline was shortlived. After 1870, under the stimulus of a rapidly growing export trade, national investment began to rise. By 1876, it had reached a peak comparable with that of 1866 and this high level was sustained until 1883, when there was again a period of decline. According to figures produced by A. G. Kenwood, the reflection of extensive alteration to dock systems to accommodate the increase in the size of ships becomes evident.[1] This was distinct from the new and larger docks which were required for these larger ships, particularly in the facility of turn-round and consequent speed-up on voyage. For cargo handling, new and more costly systems were devised involving the use of hydraulic and electrical plant. The subsequent investment period from 1889 to 1910 displayed a fairly wide range of fluctuations. Capital expenditure on British ports reached a peak in 1904, following three distinct stages of growth; it rose initially (in gross terms) from approximately £1·9 million in 1892 to £2·6 million in 1895; it was £4·1 million in 1901; after a short pause, it totalled £4·4 million by 1904. Thereafter annnual investment remained at around this figure until 1907.

In the first ten years after the foundation of the Mersey Docks and Harbour Board, some £1·9 million had been spent on land and works on the Liverpool side of the river as compared with £4·5 million at Birkenhead. This total of £6·4 million represented in gross terms, some 35 per cent of total national expenditure on ports during these years. In the 1870s and 1880s, there was a rapid extension to the sytem, seven new docks being built at Liverpool and one each at Garston and Wallasey. Of the £47 million spent on ports in the twenty years from 1870, the Mersey's share was approximately 22 per cent, and in the following ten years from 1890 (total expenditure £27 million) the Mersey's percentage

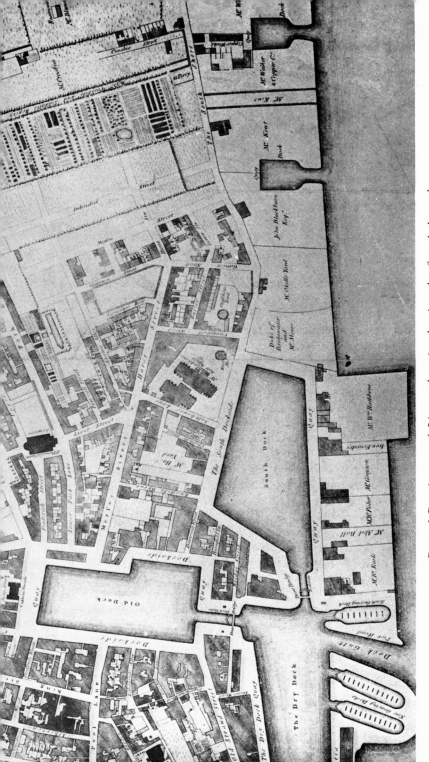

Part of Perry's map of Liverpool, 1769, showing the first docks and industrial sites

William Roscoe, by Sir Martin Archer Shee

remained about the same.[2] Between 1900 and 1909, when total expenditure amounted to some £40 million, the Mersey's contribution was about 20 per cent. In other words, the investment of resources in docks at Liverpool and Birkenhead was maintained at a level consistent not only with the expansion of her own trade, but with the general level of investment in the country as a whole.

As we have seen, the financing of the early docks had been facilitated by borrowing against bonds. This process had led to much criticism.[3] In a report issued in 1870 by the Chamber of Commerce, the suggestion was made that the debt should be funded and perpetual debentures issued. Such debentures, being negotiable on the Stock Exchange, would, it was believed, become a worthwhile security for investors. The whole question concerning the possibility of a new form of security was primarily involved with the payment of high interest charges, and Sir William Forwood was among those who were interested in a funding operation which, at 4 per cent, would save some £52,000 per annum.[4] The controversy went on intermittently throughout the 1880s and into the 1890s. The opponents of a funding system, concentrating their argument on the 4 per cent charge rather than on the principle of funding itself, claimed that it was irrational to have to pay as much as 4 per cent for its money 'when the Corporations of Liverpool and Birmingham could issue their stock at 3½ per cent.[5] This was a telling argument and the board was converted, so much so that as early as 1889 a Bill was promoted to effect the change. The Board drew back, however, when the chairman of the Lords' Committee had insisted that a new form of sinking fund should be adopted, consequent upon the granting of new powers. This was, perhaps, an excellent example of one of an increasing number of instances in which a powerful opposition lobby in Parliament could obstruct the action of the board. On this occasion the imposed condition by the House of Lords that a definite sum of money should be set aside each year, was no amenable substitute for the permissive powers which the board had so long enjoyed and, as a consequence, the whole matter was put into abeyance. In 1896, however, the notice of a motion was given that the board's parliamentary powers to deal with its debt should be enlarged. Finally, an Act of 1899 gave the board power to create redeemable capital stock 'in such amounts and manner and at such prices and times and at such terms and subject to such conditions and to be entitled to such interest as they think fit.[6] The Act did not call for a new sinking fund; the advent of this was to wait for thirty-seven years.

Thus, the board now had power to create stock to raise capital for new works, for conversion of existing securities and for redemption purposes. Unfortunately, the first issue in 1900 was a failure. It was for £5 million at 3 per cent, the terms being setlled after discussion with the Bank of England. The times were not propitious and only £92,000 of this stock was ever issued. As a result of this failure, it was not for another five years that the board went to the market. What was really desirable was that the board should have a more flexible approach to sources of cheap money. In 1905, a new issue was floated for £3½ million at 3½ per cent. It had been the intention to create blocks of this stock for the purpose of offering conversion terms to bondholders, the bonds maturing each quarter—a practice which was continued for some years. On this occasion, however, the stock issue was completely successful, though the response to conversion was disappointing. In the last resort, the dual system of both bonds and stock became an approved and acceptable procedure.

One final point remains to be mentioned. Questions had, from time to time, been raised as to the possibility of making the board's securities into Trustee Stock. This was discussed with Treasury officials, the Liverpool Stock Exchange joining with the board's representatives. The crux of the negotiations turned on the mortgaging of the Dock Estate as security, a procedure not acceptable to the members of the board. 'Our security', said Mr Parker, 'is on the rates and the board did not care to go to Parliament and revise their whole system. You cannot, therefore, comply with this stipulation.'[7] So the matter rested until the passing of the Trustee Investment Act in 1961.

In these various ways resources were made available to the Mersey Docks and Harbour Board, to enable them to extend the Dock Estate on both sides of the river to improve facilities for the steamship and make provision for increased size ships in both the passenger and cargo-liner trades. The vast projects which resulted were not effected without bitter controversy, obstruction and frustration. The outcome, however, was a testimonial to the faith of the men of the time. If they were not always wise in the event, their capacity and imagination in securing the best interests of the port and in particular its future could, more often than not, be given justification.

II

The fairly continuous flow of resources into the construction of docks and harbour works at Liverpool and Birkenhead was accordingly conducted, after 1858, against a background of controversy and demands from vested interests. In one sense, the very nature of the board's constitution made it the forum for critical comment and the instrument of active lobbying by merchants, shipowners, and railway companies. In addition, there was an initial source of rivalry between Liverpool and Birkenhead over the allocation of funds for dock construction. All these opinions, voices and factions were, in some measure, influential in shaping the future development of the Dock Estate; firstly, on the Liverpool side, in the modification of existing docks and in the new building projects to the north and south of Jesse Hartley's line, and secondly, on the Birkenhead side, in the completion of the Morpeth and Egerton system and in the construction of further docks and basins in association with it.

Jesse Hartley and his son had been succeeded by George Fosbery Lyster as dock engineer in 1861. His career in that office was a long one and, before handing over in turn to his son in 1897, he had undertaken a whole series of dock improvements and extensions, mainly at the north end of the estate. After consideration of the mounting pressure building up from steamship owners, he had proposed an extension of docks at the north end. In addition, he recommended a central group of new works east of Sandon dock and a large and reconstructed group at the south end. The outcome of discussions on these proposals resulted in the abandonment of the scheme for a new central system, though approval in principle was given to the north and south extensions. The need for more docks on the Liverpool side of the river was emphasised by the fact that Birkenhead had (at this time) excess capacity whereas Liverpool continually lagged behind need. This was, perhaps, particularly the case in the accommodation required for timber and wheat. Undoubtedly the pressure on space was acute and Lubbock's description of fifty timber ships all following each other up river to try, after being delayed by head winds, to find berths in Brunswick dock, is not an exaggeration.[8] There was an even more insistent pressure from steamship companies. Among those engaging in regular sailings at the beginning of the 1870s (when tonnage passed the six million mark) were Cunard and Inman's transatlantic lines, and Bibby's Mediterranean ships, all berthing in northern docks; the Bramley-Moore was crowded with American packet ships; East Indiamen discharged in Albert and loaded in Salthouse adjoining. Alfred Holt's Far Eastern fleet shortly afterwards adopted the principle of loading in Birkenhead and discharging in Liverpool. In Prince's dock the South American trades discharged on the west side and loaded on the east. 'Georges dock was full of fruit schooners, whilst continental traders used King's dock and Queen's dock'.[9] The Australian wheat clippers, under the auspices of James Baines & Co, Edmund Thompson, H. T. Wilson, and John Galloway, berthing on the Liverpool side, were in process of being persuaded to move to Birkenhead. Thus, Lyster faced formidable problems in connection with the berthing of an increasing volume of tonnage, in providing adequate quays and warehouse space for large ships, in reconciling the particular interests and specific requirements of commodity trades and in keeping a balance between the demands for dock facilities in Liverpool and Birkenhead.

A succession of Acts in the 1860s had maintained the flow of resources into dock improvements and extensions. In 1863, Parliamentary sanction was sought and obtained for £450,000 to construct the north river wall and to build the Waterloo grain warehouses and part, at least, of the Herculaneum dock system. In 1862, Canada half-tide dock, renamed Brocklebank dock, was built east of Canada basin. Another dock, afterwards called Huskisson branch 2, was constructed to the east of Huskisson dock. Another Bill of 1864, seeking to turn Huskisson into a system of docks, had a clause inserted in the Lords requiring that none of the monies authorised to be borrowed was to be expended until the northern entrances at Alfred Dock in Birkenhead were completed.[10] In 1866, powers were obtained to alter and enlarge the Morpeth system at Birkenhead and to convert the low-water basin, previously the river entrance, into a wet-dock. This was later to be known as the Wallasey dock. All these works had been undertaken in the midst of controversy between Birkenhead and Liverpool over the allocation of resources. In retrospect, the heated arguments seem to lack substance for in fact much more capital was expended in Birkenhead than in Liverpool during the first ten years of the Board's administration. A sum of £1,560,000 had been spent at Liverpool on new works, together with a further £340,000 for land. By comparison, at Birkenhead, the original purchase of the dock system had been £1,143,000 plus £2,731,000 on works and £590,000 spent on land making a total expenditure of £4,464,000 as against £1,903,000 at Liverpool.

Lyster's first major enterprise was in the extension of the docks at the north end. In 1873, permission had been given for work to proceed and a sum of £4,100,000 was authorised to finance the projects. Parliament, however, inserted a rather unusual clause limiting the borrowing to a maximum of £500,000 in any one year, a clause which had the effect of delaying rather than expediting the Board's effectiveness in meeting the demands from shipowners for additional berths. Even so, there were some members of the Board, themselves shipowners, who were not happy at the proposed increase in the size of docks at the north end. Among them was Alfred Holt, whose views were based upon a conviction that the steamship had attained an optimum size and that, in consequence, the need for larger docks and entrances was not likely to be a matter of importance in the foreseeable future. One must not forget that Holt's calculations were based on the measurement of his own cargo liners which were, as John Swire proved later, not a reliable guide to the needs of the trade;[11] but there was an overwhelming case for adequate accommodation for the new passenger liners engaged in a growing transatlantic service. Thus, for the first time, the conflicting pressure from steamhip owners played a part in the direction of dock construction.

The new works comprised the building of a sea wall northwards from Canada basin to Rimrose brook, with a return wall the line of which was just short of the Gladstone graving dock.[12] Within this protective cover were built the Langton dock with its branch dock and graving docks, the Alexandra dock with three branches, and the Hornby dock. At the south end, the Toxteth and Harrington systems with additional work on Herculaneum were completed. Langton was opened in 1879, and brought into partial use pending the completion of entrances. The formal opening of the whole system took place in 1881, though the Hornby dock did not come into use until 1884,[13] by which date shipping entering the port had reached 7·8 million tons. One of the more difficult problems which Lyster had to solve was concerned with the siting of dock entrances in relation to width of passage and length of quay. The Liverpool

shore had always been difficult of access because the NNW–SSE
axis was to the beam of prevailing winds and this, with a strong tide
race and heavy surge of water, made navigation into the docks a
hazardous operation, especially when huge ocean-going liners were
involved. The most difficult condition of all (particularly in the days
of the sailing ship) was that in which a stiff north-easterly coincided
with spring tides. Lyster was well acquainted with this problem,
particularly in connection with the outer gate to the 100-foot lock
in Canada basin. This faced north-west and was, under the conditions described, wrongly sited. This gate was a continuous source of
anxiety until after World War II when it was replaced by a
new southern-facing entrance. In Lyster's projects the aim 'was to
allow the entrances to be worked at a depth of twelve feet below Old
Dock Sill' in the hope that ease of access for larger ships could
thereby be effected.[14] A whole series of Acts in the 1890s enabled
further provision to be made in the solution of the problem of access
and easy passage within various systems, as well as for the construction of new docks at the north end and at Birkenhead. Thus, the Act
of 1891 gave power to deepen and lengthen Canada lock to
strengthen and lengthen the west quay of Canada dock and construct
a new branch dock to the east side parallel to Huskisson. In doing
this, the board had taken action contrary to the advice of their chairman, Alfred Holt. He had advocated a reconstruction of the central
system including the more central portion of the southern system.
He still maintained that the size of ship for which Liverpool ought
to cater was approximately 600 feet in length, 70 feet beam with
27 feet draught. This, he thought, would suffice twenty or thirty
years, 'beyond that' he concluded 'we have no need to look at
present'.[15] Holding views which were not generally acceptable to the
board, he was in a weak position and, when this issue was further
aggravated by disagreement on other matters of policy, he decided to
resign from the chairmanship in 1890.[16] In political terms, this
meant that the passenger liner interests had won a victory (though
a minor one as it proved) over the cargo-liner companies.

In June 1892, decisions were taken to widen the Canada-
Huskisson passage and to make a southern entrance to the Sandon
half-tide dock 100 feet instead of 80 feet. This was a wise move,
despite Alfred Holt, because when the two crack Atlantic liners,
the *Lusitania* and the *Mauretania*, were built they had to use the
widened southern entrance. There were still other concessions to

passenger liners. In 1893, provision was made for more adequate berthing at Prince's landing stage, involving the strengthening of the stage and the deepening of the channel so that large liners could come alongside whatever the state of weather or tide, and the building of a railway station there with a connection to the main line. Finally, an Act of 1898 gave effect to a whole series of schemes, long after discussion by the board (some of which have already been mentioned), and virtually completed the improvements of the existing dock systems, improvements which had been discussed and put into effect over a period of twenty years. These included the building of King's docks numbers 1 and 2, on the site of the old King's dock and King's dock tobacco warehouse; the construction of the Queen's graving dock, partly on the site of an existing half-tide entrance and the Queen's branch docks numbers 1 and 2; the deepening of the Brunswick river entrances; the widening of the Sandon half-tide dock and the building of Huskisson branch dock number 1 on the site of the old Sandon graving docks. Perhaps one cannot do better than quote Stuart Mountfield's excellent summary of the dates on which these works came into commission:[17] 1896 and 1903, Canada branches numbers 1 and 2; 1899, Canada graving dock; 1902, Huskisson branch number 1; 1906, Sandon consequential alterations; 1901–2, Sandon half-tide dock and entrances; 1906, King's docks numbers 1 and 2; 1901, Queen's branch number 1; 1905, Queen's branch number 2; 1906, Queen's graving dock; 1905, Brunswick river entrances.

The next important step was to seek the necessary provision for implementing new construction. An Act of 1903 gave power for the acquisition of land to the north of the board's Liverpool estate. This made possible the putting into effect of plans, already agreed, on land in the possession of the board, and the projection of other works on new sites near Seaforth. These schemes were eventually to become the Gladstone system. The board acted with speed and efficiency in face of the increasing pressure from passenger companies for additional berths. By the end of 1903, the chairman was able to give details of extensions to the north of Hornby dock. By 1906, the powers sought were for the building of a half-tide dock with entrances from river; a lock connecting with the Hornby dock; two branch docks and river walls extending to Cambridge Road, Waterloo.[18] At Birkenhead, plans were made for the building of Vittoria dock in the East Float.

As on many previous occasions, the expenditure of capital on new docks raised opposition from diverse interests whose needs, they felt, were being neglected. This time the protests came from the timber trade. As we have seen, this trade used the central and southern area of the docks. As the trade grew, there was at certain seasons an acute shortage of space, and shipowners and merchants alike put forward a strong case for the improvement of facilities and the enlargement of quays at the timber berths. Sir Thomas Harrison Hughes was the chief, though disinterested, spokesman. In 1905, he claimed that, because of lack of development at Liverpool, the timber trade was being driven to Manchester, the Ship Canal claiming to have secured an import of 100,000 tons a year.[19] He regretted that the schemes then being put before Parliament did not give thought to timber.[20] Sir Thomas's voice was in the nature of a cry in the wilderness, the Dock Board being generally convinced of the necessity to build the northern docks. Accordingly in 1908, authorisation was given for work to begin on the Gladstone system, comprising the Gladstone dock, two dock branches, the river entrance locks and the Gladstone-Hornby lock. Although Parliament had sanctioned a double entrance, in fact only one was built. Nevertheless, certain features were introduced on the west side to permit the construction of a second dock. This whole system did not include the graving dock which, later, was to be such an important part of it. In the event, variations were made and a graving dock was included. This dock, in fact, was the first of the new systems to be opened in 1913, the rest of the works not being completed until 1927. The final layout of Gladstone consisted of a vestibule or turning dock and two branch docks with a total water area of $58\frac{1}{4}$ acres and three miles of quays equipped with two single-, one double- and three treble-storey transit sheds. The system was entered by means of a river entrance lock, 1,070 feet long and 130 feet wide, divided into two compartments, having sills '20 feet below Bay Datum or 30 feet below the Old Dock Sill'.[21] This was more than adequate to enable the largest ship (at that time constructed) to find accommodation, and virtually completed the line of Liverpool's Dock estate, stretching from Gladstone in the north to Dingle in the south for a distance of nearly seven miles.[22] In a later chapter, we shall see how modern requirements of new and ultra-large ships engaged in the oil, container, and bulk commodity trades, have not only led to changes in the pattern and use of docks, but have revolutionised concepts of the very nature of ports and port facilities.

Meanwhile, at Birkenhead, the original system, consisting of the Morpeth and Egerton docks and the East and West Floats, had been enlarged by the addition of the Alfred and Wallasey docks, constructed out of the original Low Water Basin in 1866 and 1884 respectively. Together the Birkenhead Docks and Float contained some 148·1 acres but increasing pressure—especially from the food trades—made new works essential. In 1892, the question of purchasing the foreshore stretching towards Cammell Laird's slipway, was raised; and in 1893 an Act sanctioned the purchase. Some two years later, the Board acquired Tranmere Pool. In 1905, powers were implemented to construct a new dock, the Vittoria, in the East Float. In fact, the Board had been in a position to embark on this work at a much earlier date, the provision of the 1905 Act being of a covering nature. Nevertheless, the Vittoria dock greatly added to the facilities at Birkenhead as it increased the quay space for loading purposes and augmented the already considerable service which Birkenhead enjoyed as a loading port.

Just before the outbreak of war in 1914, the tide of opinion began to flow in favour of cargo liners. Their economic importance had been more than emphasised in the long passenger-cargo liner controversy when, in 1907, the White Star line took their express passenger service to Southampton. This was a bitter blow and the view was generally held that, as a matter of future policy, it might be wise to concentrate Liverpool's resources on the development of services for the commodity trades, rather than trust to the uncertainty of passenger trades. Richard Holt, following his uncle Alfred, had long been an exponent of this thesis. Giving evidence before the Royal Commission on Shipping Rings on 10 March 1908, he had said: 'I am interested in the Port of Liverpool and I know that in Liverpool, the general trade of the port is rapidly falling into the hands of regular and Conference liners, at the same time that the whole trade of the port is rapidly expanding.' To an acute observer, the evidence was clear from the activity in the docks. By 1914, the most northerly dock (apart from Gladstone graving) was Hornby; this was now principally used by the timber trade; Alexandra was appropriated, in part, to vessels in the South American trade; some Mediterranean ships also used Alexandra and part of Langton; the Canadian Pacific, Cunard and White Star, mostly passenger, were in Canada, Sandon, and Huskisson; the Dominion and Leyland lines also used Canada and Huskisson for their cargoes; Stotts and Curries were in Wellington and Bramley-Moore; while at the south end, British & Continental were in Queen's; Booths and Larrinagas also in that area, Holts discharging in Queen's north 2, Harrisons using Brunswick and Toxteth, Elder Dempsters in Toxteth and Harrington and, at Birkenhead, the Far Eastern loading trade was firmly established with all the great cargo companies holding berths there.[23] Coasting vessels were in the main accommodated in the central docks. In short, the preponderance of Liverpool's dock space, together with virtually all that in Birkenhead, was occupied by cargo liners. Herein lay Liverpool's strength; perhaps Alfred Holt was wise in judgement after all, for the ships of these companies were carrying approximately 36 per cent of Britain's export trade and 22 to 24 per cent of her imports. This, more than anything else, was the just measure of Merseyside's place in the country's economy in the years before 1914.

III

We must now turn to another matter of importance in a port system; that is, the relationship between shipmen and merchants within the framework of Dock Board administration. It is, obviously, a primary objective of any public institution that the capital resources which it operates and administers, should be so ordered that they are used to capacity and with the greatest possible efficiency. A port is no different from factories or coal mines in this respect. It is therefore appropriate that we should address ourselves to the question as to how the Dock Board administered its estate at Liverpool and Birkenhead in the best interests of its clients. The details of the Dock Board's administrative system are given in Stuart Mountfield's *Western Gateway*. This is an authoritative statement of fact. We propose, however, to emphasise certain important historical developments and relate them to the context of this present volume.

Before 1846, each merchant or consignee was in direct contact with the ship once she had berthed, and sent down to the quay for his own goods. This practice was, to say the least, uneconomic and wasteful of time and energy; it could not stand up to the pressures of a rapidly changing commercial environment. The real point of this was that the merchant, not infrequently suiting his own convenience, delayed the discharge of cargo and thereby the turn-round of the ship and wasted the labour employed. In 1846, therefore, the Dock Committee had taken steps to introduce a system of master porterage, and also made provision for licensing and regulation. The master porter was nominated by the owner or consignee entitled to the largest portion of the cargo, 'the power of appointment passing to the owner of the ship or consignee if no nomination had been made within 48 hours after the ship had reported at Customs.'[24] Usually the consignees arrived, by mutual agreement, at a nomination. These arrangements applied mainly to sailing ships; in the case of steamships, however, there had been, by reason of the high cost of keeping such ships in port, a modification. If the consignees had not agreed on a nomination within one hour of the ship reporting, the steamship owner was given authority to make an appointment.[25] As steamship costs increased rather than diminished during the 1850s and 1860s, the speed of turn-round became a matter of concern and in 1858 a dispute arose between the Board's newly formed Master Porterage Committee and James Bibby. The latter's company had put a clause in their bills of lading under which the consignee waived, in favour of the shipping firm, his right to nominate a master porter. The Committee refused to sanction this proposed arrangement but, as a conciliatory gesture to the shipowner, took action itself in 1861 to tighten up the regulation and discipline of master porters by appointing surveyors to examine and report on stowages. District traffic managers were also given supervisory powers over quays and the work of master porters.[26] Thus, the functions of the three principal categories of person, handling cargoes at the port, were regularised.

The first function involved the master porter who took cargo at a legal point of definition (usually the ship's rail) and performed, for a legally approved scale of charges, the quay operations required for clearance and despatch. The second function devolved upon the master lumper, the person licensed by the Board to discharge the cargo over shipside, the name being derived from an earlier practice by which such port operators were paid a lump sum for the job. Finally, the master stevedore loaded the ship, an operation which was within the competence of the shipowner or his nominee. This was in line with custom, for the Liverpool shipowner had always exercised the right of loading for his freights.[27]

At the beginning of 1862, a newly created Traffic Committee of the Board took over the duties of the Master Porterage Committee. In course of time this Traffic Committee extended its control over the handling, stowage and discharge of cargoes and, in more recent years, by amalgamation with the Warehouse Committee over warehouses as well. Such an organisation was effective in reducing the tensions and clash of interests between importer, exporter, and shipowner in the day-to-day ordering of activity. In matters of overall policy, as we have seen, the major concern of the Dock Board itself, had been with the inauguration of dock building schemes, railway depots and the conciliation of diverse interests among shipowners. Although much had been done to meet the insistent needs of users, Liverpool's share of Britain's total trade, though large, showed a declining trend. There was continuous search for the means of handling larger volumes of traffic, and this was conducted against the background of alternative and competitive sources. As early as 1904, the Board had come to an arrangement with the railway companies concerning the haulage of goods to the dock quays. This arrangement included a system of rebates and was instrumental in creating an efficient organisation under the control of the chief traffic manager. In respect of services rendered by the Board, the railway companies made terminal allowances for operations which they no longer undertook. Such a scheme was mutually satisfactory and, by 1912, the Board was hauling some 350,000 tons annually.[28] This applied only in Liverpool, in Birkenhead the railway companies still continued to control the movement of goods.

In the matter of labour relations the Board played a somewhat negative role. In real terms, the wages of seamen and dockworkers had fallen since the end of the Boer war. Conditions of work in the docks were bad and the casual nature of employment caused bitterness and hostility between gangs in particular dock systems, and between labour employed at the north end and that at the south end. In 1911, matters came to a head. There was a seamen's strike on a national scale, prolongation of which was largely effected by lack of negotiating machinery and by the fact that shipowners, as a whole, refused to recognise the Seamen's Union. In this attitude the shipowners were supported by the Dock Board who declared, as a matter of policy, that while they might listen to grievances from their own employees, they were not prepared to negotiate with those not in their employ.[29] Events deteriorated and the dock-workers began to show sympathy and support for the seamen by refusing to handle 'tainted' ships. Eventually, under the stress of a worsening situation, several shipping companies entered into indivdual negotiations and acceded to the men's request by recog-nising the Union. Far from settling the port's labour unrest, however, these decisions inflamed opinion and, on 28 June, the dockworkers went on strike. The motive behind this action was undoubtedly the belief that what had won the seamen's case could win theirs too. The strike committee was led by Tom Mann and James Sexton and, as in the case of the seamen, negotiations were opened, not with the Dock Board, but with individual shipping companies. As ad hoc settlements were reached the men returned to work, but there was considerable confusion in the absence of an overall settlement. The tugboat men were the next to come out and, before negotiations with them were concluded, the railwaymen had stopped work. The whole transport system of the country had been seized in the grip of strike fever, and nowhere was it more serious than in Liverpool, where the struggle for the recognition of the Unions was being fought as a test case. The port was at a standstill and, as the dispute dragged on into August, tempers became short. Riots broke out and the military were called in; Winston Churchill, the Home Secretary, using his powers for the maintenance of law and order. Thereupon, Mann called a strike of all transport workers and Liverpool was closed to all traffic. Finally, in mid-August, the Government were forced to take action. The Dock Board, after much argument, agreed to take back the men in their employment, while continuing to insist that they would negotiate only with their own men. It was a prolonged battle and the matter of representation was still being argued in 1913 and, although many members of the board and many shipowners con-tinued to be intransigent, the time had come for recognition of the Unions. It is difficult to judge how this fight for recognition would have ended had not war broken out in 1914. There were some signs that opinions were changing. Lord Derby, then Lord Mayor, extended his considerable influence to bring the two sides together, but without much success. In other ways, however, progress had been made, particularly with regard to conditions of employment at the docks. A new and far-reaching plan was proposed for the decasualisation of labour, and reforms of a lasting nature were introduced regulating dock labour as a whole.[30] There were many on both sides who could be given credit for this work, not least among them, Lord Derby, whose gifts were directed towards the realisation of a just and peaceful settlement, James Sexton, whose persistence, very often in the face of unmerited opposition from his fellow dockers, secured the principles underlying a Clearing House system, Charles Booth, whose sympathy for the dockworkers' case ensured his acceptance as a trusted negotiator, and Lawrence Holt, whose patience and administrative skill was generally acknowledged. In his office as secretary of a Joint Committee between shipowners and dockworkers, he did much to effect the establishment of a better administration for the registration of dockworkers and for the clearance of their wages. This is not the place to enter into a detailed exposition of these efforts to bring better conditions to Liverpool's dock system. All that we can do is to suggest that in the attempt to solve the wide range of problems affecting the conditions of dock labour, sincere efforts were made by shipowners, disinterested and influential citizens and dockworkers themselves in bringing enlightenment. In this respect, their efforts may be regarded as marking a turning point in the history of labour relations in the port.

IV

The multiplication of vested interests, whether from the ranks of organised labour, from shipowners, from railway companies or from members of the Dock Board itself, presents an array of forces which were often harmful to the interests of Merseyside's growth as a port. Nevertheless, these were much less serious in their effect on ultimate development than the damaging rivalry of competition from two external sources, both of which were called into being towards the end of the nineteenth century. The first and less important of the two was the establishment of competitive docks by railway companies; the second, a major challenge to Merseyside's shipping and commercial prosperity, was the building of a ship canal linking Manchester with the sea and turning that city into a port of the first order of magnitude.

In one sense, these events grew out of the implacable dock monopoly and monopoly railway charges which had so bedevilled Liverpool's relations with merchants and shipowners alike during the years after 1850. In the rapidly growing export trade in coal, the railway companies turned increasingly to their own ports where the installations, though more modest than those at Liverpool and Birkenhead, were their own creations. These railway ports gave the direct access which Rendel's scheme, for example, had promised but had failed to achieve. Garston, within the Mersey and on the the threshold of Liverpool's dock system, was one such port. It had originally been created by the St Helens Canal and Railway company in an endeavour to secure access to the Mersey for the supplying of coal to the salt fields of Cheshire and for the export of St Helens coal to coastal and overseas markets.[31] The two docks at Widnes, formerly used for this purpose, were quite incapable, owing to the effects of neaping in the lower reaches of the Mersey, of accommodating a vast increase in traffic. The St Helens Railway company had, therefore, extended its line to Garston and built a dock there. This dock was opened on 21 June 1853 and embraced a water area of more than six acres in extent; it was entered from the Mersey through two gates each 50 feet wide. The 30-feet-high coal drops could load 250 tons of coal in 2½ hours, a faster rate than at any other dock on Merseyside. The initial hope was that the loading facilities at Garston, by attracting sea-going vessels on favourably competitive terms, would enable St Helens' coal to rival that from the Wigan coalfield in the export trades from the Mersey.[32] Such hopes, however, were not fulfilled. The dock proved to be difficult of access for large ocean-going ships, and much more capital was needed to deepen the channel before such vessels could berth there in complete safety. Nevertheless, in 1860, the London & North Western Railway took a twenty-one years' lease of the Warrington–Garston section of the St Helens Railway for £12,000 per annum[33] and, in 1870, a new line to Wigan was opened linking the Wigan coalfield with the St Helens–Garston line, so that henceforth Wigan as well as St Helens coal could be exported from the dock.[34] A second dock was opened at Garston in 1875. As a result of improved navigation, the increased capacity of this new system, when later developed by the LNWR, proved to be a considerable rival to Liverpool in the loading of specific commodities. By the end of the century, it was estimated that Garston had diverted more than 50 per cent of Liverpool's coal trade and, at a much earlier date (mainly because of preferential rates offered by railway companies), some ten per cent of Liverpool's grain trade.[35] Thus a competitive dock system, operated by railway companies offering a differential rate structure, could and did affect adversely the domination which Liverpool had so long enjoyed.

The emergence of a small, though powerfully backed, dock system in competition with the might of the Dock Board was no real threat to Liverpool's position as Britain's premier west-coast port. The vital source of effective trouble was centred in Manchester where, for decades, the merchants and manufacturers had struggled to extricate themselves from the grip of Liverpool's dock monopoly. We have seen how they had endeavoured to by-pass Liverpool by creating a railway link with Birkenhead, an effort which was frustrated when the docks on both sides of the Mersey came under a single administration. The new Dock Board, however, did very little to meet the objections of the Manchester men to the payment of excessive rates, and discontent, smouldering in the 1860s and 1870s, finally burst into flame in the early 1880s. In 1883, a Bill to construct a ship canal, linking Manchester with the Mersey was promoted, an action which provoked violent controversy and bitter recrimination among the opposing interests in the two cities.

Fundamentally, the emergence of Manchester as a rival port to Liverpool, was not merely the result of a dock monopoly controlling Machester's trade; it was equally an attempt to break the power of the Liverpool shipowner and, as such, was seen as an insidious attempt to undermine the traditional source of Liverpool's economic strength. From a study of contemporary opinion on this issue, there would appear to be grounds for the justification of this fear.[36] Financial support for the canal came largely from the general body of Manchester cotton merchants and manufacturers. They believed that by securing an outlet from Manchester to the sea, they would achieve a twofold reduction of costs. Direct loading in Manchester would eliminate rail charges from Manchester to Liverpool and Birkenhead; also, by offering alternative (and cheaper) port facilities the competition so engendered would weaken the power of the Conference lines based on Liverpool to control freight rates. In the view of the Liverpool shipowner, the controversy about freight rates assumed unreal significance and was based on misconceptions held by Manchester merchants of prevailing commercial conditions.

(*above*) A famous Liverpool warehouse, the Goree Piazzas, George's Dock; (*below*) Lord Street, with St George's Church in the background

(*above*) Sir Alfred Jones, KCMG; (*below*) Sir Richard Durning Holt 1869–1941

It was arguable that, without Conference agreements, the level of freight rates might have been much higher in times of trade boom and, because of irregularities in the supply of tonnage at such periods, shipping services might, therefore, have been much less efficient. There was no doubt that, even under normal conditions of trade, rebates to merchants were a powerful influence in maintaining loyalty to Conference ships. There was, nevertheless, some force in the contention that German lines, admittedly subsidised, were carrying goods to the Far East, to South America and to West Africa at rates ten to fifteen shillings lower than those from Liverpool.

As a counter to the charge that Conference rates maintained costs at a high level, Liverpool shipowners could always point to the relatively high railway charges. Here was a genuine cause of grievance for both sides. As a practical step towards the removal of such a grievance and as a counter measure to the construction of the Manchester Ship Canal, Alfred Holt had proposed his Lancashire Plateway, a scheme under which goods would be carried direct from the docks to the factory in trucks running on rails and drawn either by horses or by steam engines.[37] This, however, proved to be an abortive idea and, in the end, the views of the Manchester men prevailed and a ship canal was constructed. To the Liverpool shipowner, this scheme, with the original eight docks at Manchester having direct access to the sea and with the prospect of competition from Manchester ships on all the sea routes of the world, presaged nothing but ill-fortune. Surprisingly, the gloomy prophecies were not immediately fulfilled. After waiting for a short time to judge what the effects of the Canal would be on their trade, some Liverpool companies, such as Harrisons, began to send ships to Manchester; but, in general, the main ocean-going companies (Holts, for example) found that they had little to gain from the use of the Canal. Loading at Manchester rather than at Birkenhead or Liverpool would give them no cargo additional to that over which they had so firm a control. This opinion was strengthened by the fact that, within each separate Conference, apportionments of cargo were usually agreed between London, Glasgow, and Liverpool shipping lines. If such agreements were broken, for example, by sending ships to Manchester, the Liverpool owners feared that London- or Glasgow-based companies might retaliate and load there as well. Many Liverpool companies, however, took steps to safeguard their position by instituting an enquiry among their Manchester clients, to ascertain whether or not they held strong preferences for a particular port of loading.[38] The replies were reassuring. The initial enthusiasm for the Canal had waned and it was a matter of indifference whether ships loaded at Manchester, Birkenhead, or Liverpool. The point of controversy with the shipowner was about the level of freight rates rather than with the choice of port.

Nevertheless, the Liverpool shipowners could not afford to be complacent. The Canal Company had powers which it did not hesitate to use and eventually forced the issue with the Conference lines. The chief Indian and China merchants in Manchester were persuaded to sign a formal letter to the Conference, inviting them to send ships to Manchester. This action was seen by the shipping companies as a direct threat to their interests as exporters of piece-goods from Birkenhead; it was also, by implication, an attempt to undermine existing Conference agreements with a view to lowering freight rates.[39] Following negotiations with a committee of Manchester merchants (including a representative of the Canal Company), Liverpool shipowners agreed to send ships to load in Manchester. They did so, only after it became clear that, failing to secure such a concession, Manchester would have been prepared to open its docks to non-Conference vessels.

For a time, therefore, after the opening of the Canal in 1894, Liverpool ships made a limited use of its facilities, but this use, however, was not sufficient to justify the view that Liverpool's docks had been by-passed. This fact was to become more apparent after 1905. Indeed, the Manchester merchant found that he very often incurred financial loss by loading at Manchester rather than at Birkenhead, the reason for this being that it was a costly business to send a large ocean-going ship through the Canal and, consequently, shipping charges increased. On the whole it was less costly to send freight by barge or by railway to Birkenhead. Having thus accepted with ill-grace, the prospect of rivalry with Manchester, the Liverpool shipping interests were not a little agreeably surprised to find that the rivalry was virtually non-existent; but the real source of trouble, namely the railway monopoly, had not been broken and the time had long since passed when that could have been effected. Perhaps Alfred Holt summed up the attitude of many Liverpool men when he declared 'the Board ought years before to have said to traders "we are brothers, the railways are our common foe. Join us against them" '.[40]

V

On the surface, the years from 1860 to 1914 were boom years for Merseyside. Despite periodic fluctuations in trade, vast capital resources had been expended, largely in anticipation of a high rate of growth in the future. Capital had accumulated in the hands of shipping companies to phenomenal levels; new markets and trades had been opened up to the Liverpool steamship; the commercial structure which this development had created and, in turn, revitalised was a pattern of efficiency. Although Liverpool's share of the country's total trade had declined since the 1850s, Merseyside continued to be the United Kingdom's premier exporting port and handled nearly one quarter of total imports. Yet within this prosperity, the seeds of decline had already been sown. This statement is difficult to substantiate because there are many cross and contradictory trends. To a large extent, also, the decline was masked by the steamship prosperity and by the continuous investment in docks. Nevertheless, after 1905, it was becoming apparent even to the casual observer that a slackening in the rate of progress was taking place. It was even more apparent that Manchester was at last beginning to offer competition to Liverpool's hitherto privileged position.

The first really significant indication of decline came from a fall in Dock Board receipts, as follows:

1907	£1,359,000	1911	£1,342,000
1908	£1,319,000	1912	£1,469,000
1909	£1,292,000	1913	£1,579,000
1910	£1,290,000	1914	£1,569,000

These figures bear some correlation with the earnings of shipping companies, and were, up to 1910, consistent with conditions of trade; but thereafter the rate of increase was not in proportion with either the magnitude of the increase in trade or with the increase in the size of shipping companies' earnings.

The declining trend can perhaps be best illustrated from tonnage using the port. For this purpose, we propose to take three projections; the first, based on 1860, taking a ten-year span; the second, based on 1860, with an overlapping eleven-year span and, finally, a trend rate comparison of the same period projected backwards to base year 1716. Annual average percentage rates of growth under the first projection were as follows:

1860–1869	1·5	1890–1899	2·9
1870–1879	2·3	1900–1909	3·4
1880–1889	2·3	1910–1913	3·5

If these figures are arranged somewhat differently, however, a slightly more qualified result is obtained. This second projection uses an eleven-year span with results as follows:

1860–1870	2·0	1890–1900	2·5
1870–1880	2·8	1900–1910	3·0
1880–1890	2·5	1910–1913	3·1

This projection narrows the range of fluctuation and is more nearly consistent with the longer term calculation of annual average rates of growth from base year 1716. Over this latter period of 197 years, annual average rates of growth of tonnage using the port were 4·9 per cent from 1744 to 1850 and 2·6 per cent from 1851 to 1914. The rising percentages in the first two projections from 1860 reflect the increase in the number of trades served by Liverpool steamship companies, and also the general increase in world trade. The second statement is, perhaps a better indication of the rate of growth than the first. It shows a relatively slow rate of growth between 1860 and 1870, the years of transition from sail to steam. It was also a period not yet influenced by the expansion of markets which the steamship made possible. Thereafter, the rate was in correlation with the facts already analysed. A trend rate of 2·8 per cent (base year 1860) would probably be a fair approximation for the period as a whole. On a longer term projection (base year 1716), however, there is a distinct break in trend in 1850 and a slackening in momentum. This reflects a levelling off in the growth of Merseyside's major imports and exports, as well as growing competition from other ports, with a corresponding fall in Merseyside's share of total United Kingdom trade.

The growth rates given above, however, need one further qualification. They are based on gross figures of tonnage using the port. To obtain a trend more closely related with the trade of the port, it is necessary to analyse adjusted figures of tonnage. The Dock Board's accounts differentiate between ships paying tonnage rates (ie those entering and clearing the docks at Liverpool and Birkenhead) and those paying Harbour rates only. The latter rates were charged on ships entering the Mersey but not necessarily berthing at wharf or dockside. By 1890, such tonnage amounted to approximately 12 per cent of all tonnage using the port. With the opening of the Manchester Ship Canal, however, a significant change is noticeable. In 1900, ships paying Harbour rates only had increased to about 18 per cent, and by 1913 to 21 per cent of total tonnage using the port. These latter percentages gave some indication of the impact of the Manchester Ship Canal on shipping entering and leaving the Mersey. In order to obtain a more precise picture of the use of dock facilities at Liverpool and Birkenhead, therefore, it is necessary to take figures based on the payment of tonnage dues. These figures show that, between 1860 and 1914, there was an average annual rate of growth of 2·1 per cent. Although this is less than the rate of growth given above, it is more nearly consistent with the growth of trade and is, therefore, a better indication of port usage.

In general terms, though there was continual growth between 1860 and 1914, the rate was not consistent for all sectors of Merseyside's economy. Whereas port investment and capital of steamship companies increased at high rates, the tonnage using the port had a lower rate of growth after 1850 than before that date. It may well be that the dislocation caused by the war of 1914–18 and the subsequent uncertainty and trade recession in the inter-war years, accelerated what was a declining trend in Liverpool's and Merseyside's prosperity. The means of effective competition had been established, labour unrest had given a brief but frightening glimpse into the future and the shipping companies, despite capital accumulation and the part which they had played in the maintenance of prosperity, were increasingly engaged in struggles with foreign shipping lines. By 1914, the high peak of achievement had been reached and passed; the lean years were about to begin.

CHAPTER EIGHT

War and the Shipping Companies, 1914-39

I

The outbreak of war in 1914 interrupted the long-established trends in the port's trade as well as the political, economic and social pressures activating the life of its inhabitants. The resultant dislocation of accepted practices occasioned by the stress of national emergency, makes the task of comparison and measurement extremely difficult; so that, in effect, the four years from 1914 to 1918 must be regarded not only as an unhappy break in continuity, but as a period of trial in which the efficiency of the port itself was an essential element in national survival.

Merseyside was not altogether unprepared for the disruptive effects of war. A committee had been constituted in 1912 to enquire into the possible steps which might have to be taken to secure the nation's supply of food and raw materials, and it had been generally accepted that the southern and west-coast ports might have to carry additional traffic should the east-coast ports be closed to shipping. In the event, this resolved itself into a problem of accommodation which, in turn, gave rise to many other difficulties. Fundamentally, demands created by war led to a decline in the effectiveness of the Board to promote new schemes. Rising costs and falling revenues, shortage of manpower, pressure on dock and warehouse space were all contributory causes, and the resulting port congestion was severe and persistent.[1] In such circumstances, the administrative machinery had to be subjected to constant revision under the sanction of government intervention.

Worthwhile statistics of the port's wartime activities are not easily discovered. The supplementary information in shipping companies' archives is also meagre due largely to the veil of secrecy which enshrouded shipping movement. Nevertheless, a general assessment can be made. In 1914, some 15,000 ships with a tonnage of 15 million had been berthed, loaded or discharged. The comparable figures for 1915 were 13,555 ships with a tonnage of 15 million; in 1916, 11,337 ships with a tonnage of 12·2 million; in 1917, at the height of the submarine war, 9,832 ships with a tonnage of 11 million; in 1918, only 7,248 ships with a tonnage of just under 10 million.[2] Despite these figures and despite the mounting destruction, the tonnage of cargo was relatively high. Though cargo statistics for this period are not available, it is obvious from the board's statements that, in relative terms, the proportion of income from cargo had increased while that from ships had declined. In this way, the aggregate revenue to the Dock Board remained fairly stable, being £1·56 million in 1914 and £1·66 million in 1918.[3] These figures emphasise the nature of the dilemma facing the Dock Board. Confronted with rapidly rising costs in the shape of increasingly high wage rates, high interest charges and high prices of construction materials, the stable levels of income were not adequate to cover the straining requirements of the port. Only the most urgent and immediate works could be put in hand, while the more fundamental, such as the completion of the Gladstone system of docks, had to be put into abeyance.

An early problem which had to be solved was caused by the rapid depletion of the labour force on the dockside. In the absence of any national scheme of reserved occupations, large numbers of dockworkers had enlisted in the services. By 1916, the situation had become so serious that it was necessary to constitute a Port Labour Committee to deal with the exemption of dock labour essential for transport work in Liverpool. Eventually, a similar control was extended to most of the ancillary trades and this process was greatly facilitated by the use of the Clearing House which, as we have seen, had been established in July 1912. Other precise forms of regulation were imposed by Orders in Council, particularly affecting the clearance of quays and the turn-round of ships. The interests and security of the nation demanded that, in the organisation of labour and in the determination of wage rates, the government rather than individual dock authorities should exercise powers. In June 1916, therefore, a Proclamation brought dockworkers within the framework of the Acts regulating the employment of munitions workers. This led, inevitably, to an increase in wages for both both dock and warehouse men.

In these various ways, therefore, the Dock Board had its former authority superseded. By contrast with these rising costs, the board found itself in a much weakened position in its endeavour to raise revenue. The Crown had always maintained an exemption from rates and dues and, accordingly, payment for services rendered to the government were subjected to Blue Book rates.[4] The discrepancy between these rates and those normally charged under free market conditions was often considerable. After protracted negotiation with the government, the charges were eventually fixed at 75 per cent of normal rates, a figure which was revised and increased from time to time.[5] Nevertheless, the lack of growth in the board's revenue remained a source of anxiety, especially at times when government payments were long overdue. The shortage of funds prevented the most obvious improvements from being made. There was an acute shortage of labour-saving devices and, strange as it may now seem, a totally inadequate supply of cranes. There was virtually no electric power within the whole dock system. Such inadequacies increased the strain on the existing facilities in the port.

In another way the course of the war and the strategy employed in its conduct, created unforeseen difficulties for Merseyside. Following the intensification of submarine warfare in 1917, Joseph Maclay was appointed Shipping Controller with wide powers to make the best possible use of tonnage available.[6] Under his direction, the terrible loss to shipping was checked by the institution of the convoy system; but the effects of this system on the port increased rather than diminished the pressures upon dock space because it resulted in the bunching of ships and cargoes. Furthermore, the entry of the United States into the war in April 1917 led in due course to the disembarkation of considerable forces, some 720,000 in 1918 alone. In order to cover the cost of successive increases in wages, the board had to seek an extension of powers to raise the statutory maximum of charges to 75 per cent above schedule.[7]

The deficiencies in the port's organisation, both materially and otherwise, which the emergency had revealed were not allowed to continue. By 1918, there was a new spirit of enterprise prevailing in the docks; the work on the Gladstone system was restarted with the aid of German prisoners of war; a scheme for electrification was begun, first at the north end and subsequently at the south; railway haulage within the board's estate was increased through the addition of new rails, siding, and locomotives; and finally, a matter of future importance, a lease was arranged with the Union Cold Storage Co for the erection of a cold store at the east end of Alexandra branch dock No 3, a project which eventually added some 50 per cent to the refrigerated capacity of the port.[8] Thus, within the stringent limitations imposed by shortage of resources, measures were taken as a result of the war to improve efficiency. The one serious qualification to this effort was that maintenance was in arrears through shortage of skilled men, a deficiency which had accumulative and long-standing effects after the war had ended.

The shipping companies of Merseyside, no less than the Dock Board were beset by a series of intractable problems during the period of hostilities. Not only had they to face the prospect of heavy capital loss by direct enemy action, but their earning capacity was impaired by the requisitioning of their ships. Set against the national background, these problems can perhaps be given a better perspective. Britain entered the war with 19·2 million tons of shipping representing 39·4 per cent of total world tonnage. By the middle of 1919 the fleet had been reduced to 16·5 million tons, and the share of world tonnage to 32·5 per cent.[9] This, however, is not a true picture, for whereas Britain had lost approximately 3 million tons, foreign fleets had increased by about 7 million tons.[10] For a variety of reasons not relevant in this context, the mercantile marines of the United States, Japan, France, and Italy had all expanded. This change in the balance of power, resulted also in a change in the competitive strength of the major maritime powers in the immediate postwar years. In particular, the United States and Japan, having supplied markets during the war which British ships could no longer serve, were in a strong competitive position to maintain their trade once peace had been restored. For Merseyside, this was a serious threat to the economic future of the port. Liverpool-based companies had lost well over 1·5 million tons of shipping and these losses had to be replaced quickly if advantageous conditions of trade were to be restored; but, in addition, Merseyside had now to face determined competition in her traditional markets in the Pacific, in Central and South America, and in South Africa. The urgent question was how to accumulate resources to re-establish Merseyside's former prestige and economic power in the changed circumstances of a postwar world.

To answer this question, one must look at what had happened to the earnings of Liverpool's shipping lines during the war. In the first place, no broad generalisation can be made. Some companies did extremely well out of the war and were able to add considerably to their reserves, while others were badly hit. Secondly, from the outbreak of war, any British ship was subject to a requisition order. Many such ships were used for naval purposes in the role of armed merchant cruisers, hospital ships, storeships and transports, and government control increased as the war continued. In 1915, all re-frigerated space was requisitioned at Blue Book rates, while the ships themselves were allowed to carry cargo in the non-refrigerated space for their owners. Similarly, at a later date, all grain space was taken over.[11] After 1917, practically 96 per cent of cargo handled was carried at government rates. There was, however, no pattern in the requisition policy. Consequently, very high profits were made by the owners of free ships as distinct from those who had come under requisition. Excess profit duty was a palliative in adjusting the receipts of one company with another, but the unequal effects of war on shipping resources remained as a cause of bitter conten-tion. In general, owners who had whole ships or parts of ships free for cargo, could make large profits because rates were inflated. All Conferences had been subjected to heavy surcharges at a level far beyond that needed to cover increased working costs. This position was maintained (with subsequent increases in rates) until 1917. Thereafter it became much more difficult to secure high returns.[12] A second source of discrepancy between shipping companies was in the unevenness of losses and the inadequacy of insurance payments for such losses. The Liverpool Steam Ship Owners' Association estimated that the replacement costs of ships lost during the war amounted to £280 million, towards which only £140 million was received from war-risk insurance.[13] The difference between what was lost and what was received had to be made up from shipping company reserves.[14] In general, therefore, owners of free ships operating at free market rates profited greatly in the absence of serious loss, whereas those with ships under requisition and working on much lower Blue Book rates, were forced to make sacrifices.

This generally uneven pattern is to be found in the impact of the war on Liverpool-based shipping companies. Heavy losses were sustained, some companies losing more than one quarter of their total tonnage, while none lost less than 15 per cent.[15] As far as passenger-liner companies were concerned, the sinking of the *Lusitania* epitomised the hazards of embarking and operating large, highly capitalised ships in time of war. The cargo-liner companies, on the other hand, suffered much worse loss on some routes rather than on others. The Pacific and Indian routes were relatively more free from attack than the Atlantic and South African routes. Consequently, for ships working outside the restrictions of requisition, the earnings were high, mainly on Indian and Far Eastern voyages. It is not possible to obtain a comprehensive analysis of earnings for the port as a whole, but some figures are available for six Liverpool companies serving the Pacific, Australian, West Indian, South African, South American, and Indian trades. In 1915, net earnings increased fourfold over the levels for 1914; in 1916, sixfold falling to fourfold in 1917 and to about threefold in 1918. In real terms, these increases have to be discounted, but there is no doubt that such earnings, together with refunded excess profits tax after the war, were the basis of considerable expansion in resources. How wisely or otherwise these resources were used in the postwar years was a contributory but nonetheless important factor determining the state of Merseyside's economic well-being during that difficult period. In this context, one can, perhaps, test the validity of S. G. Sturmey's generalisation that 'if shipowners had treated their profits during the war as a windfall to be preserved for fleet replacements, instead of doubling their dividends and using their liquid resources to buy the ships and goodwill of other lines at inflated prices, they would have been at least as well placed at the end of the war as any of their foreign rivals'.[16] Though many Liverpool shipping companies can be criticised in these terms, there were others whose policy was projected into future development. Through their efforts, as we shall see later, it is possible to assert that the spirit of enterprise on Merseyside had not been quenched by war.

II

The immediate need for the Liverpool shipowner after the war was that of re-establishing his competitive strength in the trades which had been served before 1914. To do this, the first objective was to make good losses in tonnage, a difficult task to achieve. Requisitioning was being relaxed gradually; shipbuilding yards were still choked with government orders; ports were congested and rates

were still controlled.[17] As a result, there was a scramble to take over
compsanes with free tonnage, and prices of ships rose to exorbitant
heights involving excessive capital outlay. When controls were lifted
in 1920, freight rates had fallen and thus the return on these high-
priced ships was seriously diminished. This single fact was an
underlying cause of much of the financial strain to be seen in the
balance sheets of many shipping companies during the 1920s. The
alternative policy of laying down new ships was, again, not easy of
achievement. Yards had full order-books and building costs were
high. Nevertheless, by 1922 the situation had begun to ease and
Liverpool shipowners could embark upon planned building programmes. Thereafter, the central problem was one of design and
motive power in the interests of efficiency and competitive operation.
The third impulse in these efforts to return to pre-war conditions,
was through integration of the managerial function by the amalgamation of lines. In this way economies of scale could be effected
and costs could be reduced.

As far as Liverpool was concerned, there was no set pattern of
recovery; each trade had its own particular set of problems and
their solution required a wide and varied range of effort. In the
Far Eastern trade, shipping companies had to keep abreast of all
new technical improvements, to eliminate cut-throat competition
from companies outside Conference agreements and by amalgamations and agreements to command vast capital resources, if they
were to regain their position. To some extent, these processes had
begun as early as 1902 when Holts took over the China Mutual.
Meanwhile, some of the main British competitors in the trade had
either been absorbed or had gone out of existence. In 1906, D.
Jenkins & Co, owners of the Shire line, had sold part of their
interest to Brocklebanks, thus enabling the latter to re-enter the China
trade. They transferred five of their ships to the service. The Royal
Mail acquired the remainder of the Shire resources and in 1911
bought back the Brocklebank share. In the same year, when the
Glen line was absorbed into the Elder Dempster line, a company in
association with the Royal Mail group, ways and means were provided for a joint Shire-Glen service to the Far East. In 1920, the
first of four new motor ships was delivered to the Glen line. These
were fast cargo liners of 9,500 gross tons and were of a high capital
cost; so high in fact that, together with the cost of five other standard government ships, a serious strain was put on their financial

resources.[18] As a result, no new ships were ordered until 1936, the year following the absorption of the Glen line by Alfred Holt & Co. This final grouping within the Holt organisation was reasonably flexible in operation. Apart from certain interlocking directorships, the Mutual and Glen lines retained their individual operating identities.

Confronting this group of shipping interests in the Far Eastern trade was that of the P & O. Although this company's tonnage was centred upon the provision of services to and from India and Australia, it could and did offer serious competition to Holts' Pacific services in general. In 1910, the P & O had embarked upon a policy of purchase and absorption by the acquisition of Lund's Blue Anchor line. This was followed, in 1914, by amalgamation with the British India Steam Navigation Co, a firm which had Australian as well as Indian and Far Eastern connections. During and after the war, a vigorous policy of expansion was pursued by the P & O. By 1939, this formidable group commanded a capital of £14 million with £8,550,000 in debentures, and fleets of steam and motor vessels of 1,950,000 gross tons. By contrast, the Holt group owned some 700,000 tons with a capital of approximately £10 million.

From 1924 to 1926, the net earnings of the companies engaged in the Far Eastern and Pacific trades remained relatively stable. Between 1927 and 1929, these earnings rose some 50 per cent above the level for 1926, but they began to tumble with the onset of the world depression late in 1929. In 1930, there was a fall to 50 per cent and in 1931 to 18 per cent of the 1929 levels. Thereafter, apart from 1935 which was a poor year, earnings increased, though it was not until 1937 that they once again regained the 1929 position. The chief point about these fluctuations is that they bear a closer correlation with the earnings from the foreign trade of Malaya and the Netherlands East Indies than those of China and Japan. In particular, the trade between Singapore and the Islands was badly hit. During the years 1930–1, Malaya's imports fell by 30 per cent and her exports by 50 per cent, while trade with Java, seriously affected by the fall in commodity prices and the abandonment of the gold standard by Britain, fell to unprecedented levels. In fact, shipping earnings from this trade fell by as much as 85 per cent. It became increasingly difficult to compete with the Dutch feeder company, Koninklijke Paketvaart Maatschappij (KPM). By dint of pursuing an active policy designed to give better service to native merchants in the Islands, this Dutch company had succeeded in diverting a share of Singapore's entrepot trade. This was effected by direct links between the rice-exporting countries of South East Asia and the Islands. In the cattle trade also, it had stimulated native enterprise which, in turn, had reacted adversely on the business interests of merchants based in Singapore.[19] The net result of this competition was to increase the importance of Batavia as a rival port to Singapore in the Islands' trades.

Some interesting points arise from a comparison of the earnings of shipping companies serving the Far East and those of British shipping companies as a whole. Because higher freight rates were maintained during the 1920s, the net shipping income was above the pre-war national total of £100 million;[20] the national earnings reached £140 million in 1924 and fell to £65 million in 1933; they recovered to £130 million in 1937, but fell again to £100 million in 1938.[21] This provides a fluctuation of 59: 8: 29 per cent *below* the 1924 level; whereas corresponding fluctuation in the earnings of Far Eastern companies were 3: 76: 107 per cent *above* the 1924 level. What explanation can be given for this relative buoyancy in Far Eastern earnings in times of uncertainty and depression? Apart from the increase in the volume of China cargoes carried after 1931 (China's trade was less affected by depression than that from other sources), the explanation lies partly in the increasing efficiency of the companies themselves and partly in the effectiveness of Conference agreements in maintaining freight rates.

Growing efficiency undoubtedly resulted from the benefits of amalgamation and absorption previously described. The Holt management had much greater flexibility in the accumulation and allocation of resources, in the building up of reserves and in the employment of technical improvements. This was particularly shown in the design and building of new ships. The fleet was re-equipped after 1924 with oil burners and motor vessels. Their managers also developed a more economical type of carrier for both cargo and passengers. After one or two unsuccessful experiments with the Scott-Still combination engine, they fitted diesel engines made by Burmeister & Wain of Copenhagen. Efforts were continuously made to offset rising costs in the shipbuilding industry, but such economies were never made at the expense of new ship construction. Until 1929, at least, Holts could place orders on favourable terms and insist on value for money. On the long haul to China during these years, freights earned amounted to about 5 per cent of the value of the cargo and of this amount less than half of one per cent was required for such items as insurance, dividends, managers' remuneration and provision for further expansion. Thus, reserves were able to be built up and in 1929 Holts ordered new motor ships in anticipation of good trading prospects in the following year. Subsequent events may not have justified this optimism, but their judgement was not in question. When the economic storm broke, those companies with the most efficient ships were able to compete on favourable terms in a shrinking market. Between 1933 and 1939, capital costs were, on the whole, not excessive in relation to the return on capital, while working costs in this trade were reduced by as much as 20 per cent. On the reverse side of the coin, the maintenance of freight rates within strictly operating Conference agreements, led to something approaching a maximisation of receipts. Strenuous attempts were made in the trade with the East Indies to offset the threat of Dutch competition and the decline in the price of, and the demand for, primary commodities. Support was given to Mansfields and the Straits Steam Ship Co to re-establish more favourable trading conditions. In this process, the use of air routes as a subsidiary to sea transport was not overlooked.

Thus, during the years of recovery after the war and during those of uncertainty and depression in the 1920s and 1930s, Holts managed to maintain a position of strength in their Pacific trades. Through technical innovation they increased their efficiency and their competitive position in a highly diversified range of activity. That they were so successful at a time when conditions of trade were adversely affected was due largely to the managerial skill of a most remarkable man, Richard Holt. The impact of his judgement in shipping affairs, was an asset not merely in his own company (Ocean Steam Ship), but, as will be shown later, in that of the prosperity of Merseyside itself.

III

In the Brazilian, Indian, West Indian, Central American, and Gulf trades, the pattern of uncertainty and fluctuations was as severe as that in Merseyside's Far Eastern trade. The incidence of

fluctuation and the impact on the fortunes of the shipping companies engaged in these trades, however, was different in both scope
and magnitude. The problem of keeping ships running to capacity
was aggravated by a serious decline in the cargoes of traditional
products such as cotton, sugar, rubber, wool, and tobacco in the
import trade and of cotton piece-goods and certain classes of
engineering equipment, heavy capital goods and coal in the export
trade. This, in turn, involved the companies in a search for new
markets and new commodities and, as a consequence, the creation
of new voyage patterns.

The Booth line ended the war with a fleet of 18 ships, totalling
72,000 gross tons, approximately half that existing in 1914;
Harrisons, despite serious losses in 1917, had 49 ships, totalling
271,000 gross tons at the end of 1918, a loss of some 25,000 tons on
the 1914 figure. Whereas Harrisons attempted to make good this
depletion by purchasing the fleet of Prentice, Service & Henderson,
Booths preferred to meet their commitments by chartering ships.
In this way, they avoided heavy capital expenditure on ships at inflated prices. One of their staple cargoes in pre-war years had been
Brazilian rubber, the export of which had accounted for 47 per cent
of the world's supply. In the 1920s, having to meet the competition
from Malayan and Netherlands East Indian sources, Brazil's share
of the world's rubber market fell to 5 per cent and, in the following
decade, only occasionally above 2 per cent. This catastrophic fall in
one of the firm's major sources of income considerably reduced the
earning capacity of the Booth ships. In much the same way, the onset of depression affected Harrisons' staple of cotton from the Gulf
ports. Furthermore, as a result of political unrest in India, of action
by the Indian Congress in boycotting British goods and through the
devaluation of the rupee, the export of cotton piece-goods to India,
a chief item in Harrisons' export trade, fell to 20 per cent of the
pre-war volume. In fact, throughout the inter-war years, Harrisons'
Indian trade continued to decline and, by 1939, voyage receipts were
barely covering costs.[22] On the other hand, Brazil's export trade
(apart from rubber) remained relatively prosperous until 1930, the
chief products being cotton, sugar and coffee. Compared with the
pre-war volume of 6.4 million metric tons (average 1911-13) the
increase in Brazilian exports to 7.7 million tons (average 1927-9)
was, under prevailing conditions of trade, a sign of potential
strength. Unfortunately, however, with the coming of worldwide

depression this volume of trade fell by 50 per cent. This, by adding to internal strains, resulted in a depreciation of Brazilian currency, a cause which increased rather than diminished the confusion and stagnation in trade.[23] There was little general improvement until 1936, after which year the 1929 level was again reached. Thus, there were marked changes in the postwar pattern of trade to Brazil. The southern ports were providing more cargoes than those in the north; there were generally smaller cargoes in some traditional products, and falling incomes, coupled with a decrease in capital investment, led to a fall in imports. The situation was only relieved by an increasing trend in the exports of cotton, sugar, and coffee.

How then, did the main Liverpool shipping companies engaged in this trade meet and overcome these adverse conditions? Neither Booths nor Harrisons had equipped their fleets with diesel propulsion, though both companies had undertaken extensive rebuilding programmes in the 1920s and 1930s. Their ships, therefore, had no technical advantage over those of their Continental rivals. Nevertheless, by a series of readjustments, economies were made and profits were maintained, to the extent that, even in the worst years of depression, depreciation was covered by earnings.[24] The Booths reduced the size of their fleet by selling off their old uneconomical ships and concentrated their newer vessels on the carriage of cargo from the more profitable ports. In this way, the tonnage of the fleet was adjusted to the space required for cargo on offer and costs were kept stable. Charters were used for the meeting of seasonal demands. The pattern of voyages was changed; the reduction of passenger ships to two was sufficient to maintain services between Liverpool and Manaos, but the other passenger services were discontinued. Economies were also made by reducing the number of Brazilian agencies by acquiring cheaper berthing space and by the reorganisation of stevedoring and porterage facilities.[25] In general terms, the Booths expended £1 million on new ships between 1927 and 1939; these ships carried an average of 135,000 tons of cargo annually between 1932 and 1938 and their earning capacity, though less than in pre-war years (apart from 1934-6 and 1938) was always adequate to provide for new tonnage. By 1939, the Booth fleet consisted of nine ships totalling 46,500 tons and the firm had an employed capital of something over £2·5 million.[26]

The losses which Harrisons sustained in their Indian and Gulf trades were more than offset by increases in other trades. Sir

Thomas Harrison Hughes, now the active director of policy, concentrated the firm's resources in giving the most efficient services on potentially the most profitable routes. The Leyland line was purchased, not for the value of its tonnage, but for the access which the acquisition gave to new routes. A determined attempt was made to increase trade with South Africa. Following a period of intense competition with the Thomas line of tramp steamships in the 1920s and with the rival Conference line, the Union Castle, Harrisons put four oil-fired turbine ships, which had been bought from the Prince line, on to the South African service. These ships showed an immediate profit.[27] New ships were also built for the West Indian cargo and passenger trades and these earned substantial profits. In the Indian trade, cotton was abandoned in favour of a new staple— gunny bags. Above all, Hughes made wise decisions, not only in the allocation of resources but also in the use of income from reserve investments. The existence of large reserves was regarded by him, partly as a fighting fund to be used as a weapon against any possible takeover and partly as a source of strength in time of depression.[28] As a result of these policies, Harrisons emerged from the uncertainties of the 1920s and the stagnation of the early 1930s with a faster income growth rate than any other British firm of comparable size.[29] In 1939, the Harrison fleet totalled 280,400 gross tons and the company had an employed capital of £7.9 million.[30]

IV

The vicissitudes of Merseyside's shipping connection with West Africa were coincidental with the aims, objectives and personalities of two men, Lord Kylsant and Sir Richard Holt (of the Blue Funnel line). After Alfred Jone's death in 1909, there was evidence of strain in the West African Conference and, on the outbreak of war in 1914, Woermann ceased to be a member. The existing agreements came to an end. It was therefore in a different set of circumstances that the West African Conference was re-established in 1924. By this year, the two most powerful interests outside the Conference were John Holt and Lever Bros, and these interests were in a potentially stronger position to affect decisions than in the period before 1914.

In the first place, Holts had acquired a small fleet of their own under the title of John Holt and Co (Liverpool) Ltd. With these ships the company was able to operate a regular fortnightly service between Liverpool and West African ports. Though Lever had acquired the Bromport line in 1916 with a fleet of eight ships, there was no direct engagement in shipping operation by this firm until 1929. This was largely due to the fact that after re-establishment of the West African Conference in 1924, the competition from the Conference vessels was intense and unbreakable.[31] In order to create a larger and more powerfully competitive organisation, therefore, Lever Bros founded the United Africa Company in 1929, by amalgamating the old Niger Company and the African & Eastern Trade Corporation. This was a serious attempt to challenge the Conference lines. Furthermore, as new ships were added to the UAC's fleet, there was concentration on the construction of vessels for the carriage of palm oil in bulk. From 1934 to 1938, no fewer than fourteen new ships were built to meet the special needs of the trade. Thus, both Holts and Levers were much less dependent on Conference ships than they had been before the war, and after 1929, though Elder Dempsters carried up to 50 per cent of John Holt's cargoes, they virtually ceased to carry for the UAC.

It will be remembered that Owen Philipps had taken over Alfred Jones's shipping interests. These interests were subsequently taken into the Royal Mail Group, an organisation which Philipps, under his title as Lord Kylsant, controlled. His dream as a shipowner had been to build up a centrally organised British mercantile marine, equal in competitive strength with that which Pierpont Morgan had hoped to create for the United States. A fair amount of Liverpool tonnage was involved in this scheme, including Elder Dempsters, Lamport & Holt, the White Star line, the Pacific Steam Navigation Co, Coast Lines, the Moss line and other smaller shipping companies. It was, therefore, a serious matter of concern to the economic status of the port as a whole when Kylsant became enmeshed in financial difficulties. These difficulties were in turn exacerbated by worsening trading conditions throughout the world. As a result, Kylsant's shipping empire disintegrated and Elder Dempster, together with the other Liverpool companies, were brought down in the general ruin.[32] The Kylsant disclosures were much too complex to be discussed in this present volume; but the attempts, which were made by Liverpool shipowners to salvage some financial order from the wreckage, needs to be mentioned.

Elder Dempsters' resources were reorganised under the title Elder Dempster Lines Ltd, and Richard Holt, senior partner of the Blue Funnel line, was placed very largely in an advisory capacity, in the position of chairman and manager of the new company. It says much for his skill as a shipowner that he was able, with the active help of Sir Alan Tod, to secure financial assistance and so work the ships that by 1939 Elder Dempsters were on the road to recovery. It is an even greater testimony to his judgement that, following such a severe financial crash, the company could have been restarted in business and given new life and hope. In 1939, the company had ships with a tonnage of 213,000 gross tons and an employed capital of approximately £3 million.[33] Liverpool's connections with West Africa were maintained despite unprecedented difficulty in both trading conditions and financial management. The company endeavoured to uphold the technical efficiency of the fleet by the addition of diesel-driven ships, a fact which undoubtedly gave a competitive advantage in the years after 1934. For Merseyside as a whole, the Kylsant crash meant a loss of effective resources at a time when many traditional trades were in process of decline. That more serious and irreparable damage was not done was largely due to the skill and wisdom of Liverpool's own shipping men. In the struggle, something of the old inspirational force and enterprise had shown itself. The great cargo liner companies based on the port had, by a process of attrition, emerged from the lean years with a stronger competitive instinct and a more realistic desire to maintain their hold over the major sea routes of the world.

V

The passenger liner companies, no less than the cargo-liner companies, emerged from war with depleted fleets and lost operational sea routes. On the north Atlantic, both Cunard and White Star sought to reinforce their services from Liverpol. The former continued sailings to the St Lawrence (started in 1910 with the acquisition of the Thompson line) and using ships of the size of the *Laconia* on the Liverpool–Boston–New York route; while the latter built new motor ships of the *Britannic* and *Georgic* class. It was the intensity of competition from German, French, and Italian lines in their endeavour to capture the cream of the transatlantic passenger traffic, which led the two long-established British rivals, Cunard and White Star, to consider a redisposition of their resources. Only by such means could passenger traffic be regained and fill the ships sailing from Liverpool and Southampton.[34]

The identity of interests, however, was not easily accomplished. Since 1900, White Star had been subjected to competitive pressures other than those from Cunard. The share capital of the company had been taken over by the Morgan combine in 1902, though the ships were not transferred to the American flag. One of the results of this merger had been that the White Star had taken over the Dominion line's Liverpool–Boston service; but after the war the American group had sought to disengage itself from European commitments. Accordingly, in 1927, White Star share capital once again changed hands, this time, passing into Kylsant's Royal Mail group.[35] It was a chequered history of enterprise in which success and failure had their direct influence on the economic well-being of Merseyside. Apart from the disruptive effects of the disintegration of Kylsant's colossus upon the financial structure of White Star, the inroads of foreign competition seriously impaired the efforts of the managers to increase revenue. In a similar context, White Star's chief British rival, Cunard, was encountering mounting difficulties. Accordingly, in an attempt to achieve economies of scale and sharpen their competitive strength, Cunard and White Star were merged in 1934.[36] The merger was a precondition of government help for the completion of the *Queen Mary*, the building of which had been suspended during the worst year of the depression. The amalgamation, in this form, lasted until 1949 when the name White Star was dropped and Cunard took over the whole of the Atlantic services. Thus ended a competitive struggle in the north Atlantic passenger trade which had lasted upwards of a hundred years.

Most of the other Liverpool passenger trades were variously affected after 1919, either by the harmful incursions of foreign competition or from the stultifying consequences of a scarcity of resources. The Pacific Steam Navigation's services to South America had already been subjected to severe competition from Compagnia Sud-Americana de Vapores; but the greater blow fell in 1922 when the Chilean government promulgated a decree restricting the carriage of coastwise cargoes to national vessels. The Pacific Steam Navigation Company had embarked upon a large-scale building programme to cater for both cargo and passenger services to Pacific west-coast ports, the large liner, the *Reina del Pacifico*, being among the ships included in the list. The effect of the Chilean government's decree was to compel the Pacific Steam Navigation to withdraw all services (both cargo and passenger) from Chilean ports;[37] a move of considerable consequence for Pacific Steam Navigation's organisation as a whole. Whereas formerly a large proportion of tonnage had been routed via the Straits of Magellan, the company was henceforth to sail its ships via the Bahamas, Bermuda, and the Panama Canal. Trading conditions, however, were not easy. Apart from the discriminatory effects of preferential legislation, both the Royal Mail and Pacific Steam Navigation companies were adversely affected in their passenger receipts by the cheaper services on offer from foreign companies and, in cargo services, from a powerful British rival, Vesty's Blue Star line. As in the case of other Liverpool companies, such as Lamport & Holt and Elder Dempsters, the potential competitive strength of the Pacific Steam Navigation Company was sapped by the financial dislocation following the Royal Mail crash, and it was not until 1937, when the company entered the Furness group, that better prospects were anticipated and eventually realised. On other long-established sea routes served by Liverpool, there were somewhat attenuated passenger services after 1920. The Canadian traffic was mainly in the hands of the Canadian Pacific Company, its connections with Liverpool having begun in 1891.[38] Though there was severe but intermittent competition from Cunard during years of depression, the Canadian Pacific was carrying the majority of passengers to Canadian ports by the end of the 1930s. The Blue Funnel joint service with Shaw Savill to Australia and Elder Dempster's service to Lagos and other West African ports were maintained but not appreciably extended. On the South American run, Booth's sailed two passenger liners to Manaos. In contrast with these, the Harrisons' highly-advertised and reasonably remunerative passenger services to the West Indies were something of an innovation during the inter-war years.[39]

It has not been possible to embark upon the vicissitudes of all of Liverpool's shipping companies during the inter-war years. Enough has been said to emphasise three main conclusions. In the first place, there had been a considerable regrouping of Liverpool's shipping resources. This had been a consequence of the need to achieve competitive strength in conditions of severe fluctuations in trade and by the chaos following the Royal Mail crash. It will not have been lost upon the reader that this latter event touched the prosperity of many a Liverpool-based firm. In fact, the crash involved seven major Liverpool companies with a total of 1.5 million gross tons of shipping and employed capitals approximating £20 million. Few ports could have survived a disaster of this magnitude and it argues much for Liverpool's strength that, at the depth of a world-wide depression in trade, survival and recovery could have taken place. A second conclusion must be sought in the character and skill of Merseyside's own shipping men. The adaptability to changing circumstances and the organisational capacity of such men as Sir Richard Holt, Sir Alan Tod, Sir Thomas Harrison Hughes, Sir Percy Bates and a host of others saved shipping companies from financial disaster. They may be open to criticism on the grounds that they did not introduce technical improvements to their ships at a fast enough rate, but they did much to sustain employment by keeping the majority of their ships afloat and very often ran them at a near loss. Through their activities, Merseyside continued to be a lifeline for the supply of food and raw materials.

Finally, through the dislocation caused by war and by the subsequent years of uncertainty and trade depression, one cannot escape the obvious fact that the usage of Merseyside's port systems, as evinced by the demand for her cargo and passenger services, fell very considerably. The trend rate, as compared with previous periods, for shipping using the port fell to 0·03 per cent per annum. In the worst years of depression from 1931–3, there were minus deviations of some magnitude from this trend. Yet, after 1934, most shipping companies began to recover; by 1937, a boom year in comparative terms, profits were again substantial. The real substance of this recovery, however, can only be judged if it is set against the background of events in the rest of Merseyside's economic development. It is our purpose, therefore, to put the record of Liverpool's shipping activities into broader perspective and, in the following chapter, attempt some measurement of its significance to the welfare of Merseyside as a whole.

CHAPTER NINE

The Port and Fluctuations in Trade, 1919-39

I

The measurement of Merseyside's position as a port is a complex matter involving detailed statistical analysis. It is not possible in this chapter to give the details, though these have been worked out and form the body of material on which conclusions have been based. Our objective is twofold. First, an attempt will be made to consider the relative position of the port during the inter-war years within the framework of fluctuations in the trade of the United Kingdom as a whole. From this, one can be given a better perspective of the influences for good or ill on the shipping of the port which were discussed in the previous chapter. Secondly, we propose to analyse the effects of changing patterns of trade on the well-being of Merseyside, not only from the point of view of allocation of resources, but also within the context of social and political conscience; for it was during these years that the gulf between wealth and poverty became more noticeable and the bonds linking civic pride with past achievement were sundered by bitterness and disillusion about future prospects.

It will be remembered that in the years before 1914 Merseyside's share of total United Kingdom trade had amounted to 31 per cent, being made up by 36 per cent of total exports and approximately 25 per cent of imports.[1] By 1938, this overall position had altered. As a percentage of total value, Merseyside's share had fallen to 20·8 as against London's 38·1, Hull's 6·0, Manchester's 4·4, Glasgow's 4·2, Southampton's 4·3, and Bristol's 2·3.[2] In short, London and Merseyside were still by far the kingdom's largest ports, but whereas London had maintained its position, Liverpool had lost heavily to London and other ports. The explanation of this substantial change in Liverpool's relative position must be sought in the decline in the basic industries which she served, and in the fact that handling costs, as between Liverpool and London, had become more competitive. As a result, more manufacturers in the Midlands began to use London as a port of supply and distribution.

Turning to an examination of Merseyside's share of the United Kingdom's trade, by commodity, we have the following statement for 1938:

IMPORTS

Liverpool's and Birkenhead's percentage of UK trade (by value)

Dairy products	5·9
Grain and flour	19·1
Meat	15·8
Fruit	23·4
Oilseeds	25·0
Timber	12·5
Wool	24·6
Woollens and worsteds	1·2
Petroleum	6·2
Cotton and linters	67·5
Rubber	28·9
Tobacco	30·2
Sugar	35·0
Tin	89·1

EXPORTS

Liverpool's and Birkenhead's percentage of UK trade (by value)

Cotton yarns and piece-goods	52·2
Woollens and worsteds	33·0
Iron and steel manufactures	29·0
Non-ferrous metals and manufactures	40·5
Machinery	37·9
Vehicles (including ships, locomotives and aircraft)	26·4

[It will be observed that the relative position of both imports and exports had undergone considerable change in the twenty-five years from 1913. In general terms, the level of imports, which had risen to 36 per cent of the United Kingdom total in 1918, fell to 22 per cent by 1922. Thereafter, the exceptional importance of Liverpool and Merseyside in the import trade of the United Kingdom no longer obtained. Even when figures are adjusted for the exclusion of Eire after 1923, the fact is obvious that London had become the major port of entry; Merseyside taking second place with about half London's total.]

[The trend in Merseyside's imports dropped steadily from 1925 to 1931, after which it started to rise again until a peak was reached in 1936–7. Fitting a linear trend to the percentage share of Merseyside, the indications are that the port was losing trade to the other ports of the United Kingdom at the rate of 0·2 per cent of the trade of the United Kingdom each year (ie about 1 per cent of her own share in that trade each year). The general conclusion is that Merseyside was losing trade to other importing ports during this period, but that superimposed upon the trend was a strong cyclical influence tending to make her share lower in the years of depression.[3] The comparison of Merseyside with London, whose linear trend showed an increase of 0·4 per cent of the trade of the United Kingdom, was wholly unfavourable. In fact, London's position was the reverse of that on Merseyside. There was a strong upward trend, combined with a cyclical influence, tending to making London's share higher in years of depression. The fact that the peak in London was reached three years later than the trough on Merseyside is significant. The discrepancy can be attributed to the difference in the relative importance of the trend and cyclical influences.[4] In London the trend was sufficiently strong to mask these influences, whereas on Merseyside it was not such a dominating factor.

In particular commodities, the import trade showed a surprising range of fluctuation. Raw cotton, on which so much of Liverpool's prosperity had been founded, continued to hold a premier place until 1926. By 1931, however, Liverpool's share had dropped to 67·7 per cent and never rose above 70 per cent during the 1930s. Liverpool's loss had been Manchester's gain, particularly in the import of Indian and Egyptian cottons.[5] On the other hand, wool was a commodity which went against the general trend, Merseyside's share rising at the expense of London. The total gain in terms of relative shares was about 10 per cent over the period as a whole.[6] In rubber there was widespread fluctuation, though in actual volume the import remained steady. This was due to the fact that Merseyside did not share in the general increase in the demand for supplies of Far Eastern rubber. Before 1914, Merseyside had imported approximately half of Britain's annual supply, but during the 1920s this share fell to less than 10 per cent, rising once again to approximately 30 per cent in the 1930s.[7] There was in general an increasing trend in the import of oilseeds and vegetable oils in response to the demand from the crushing plants and soap-making factories at Port Sunlight.[8] In Liverpool's oldest and, therefore, basically traditional commodities of tobacco and sugar, there were degrees of fluctuation. Merseyside's share of the tobacco trade varied between 24·3 per cent in 1931 and 45·6 per cent in 1934. Sugar, however, was an import commodity in which Liverpool maintained her position. Before 1914, about 20 per cent of the country's supply of sugar came through Liverpool. By 1920, this share had increased to 32·4 per cent. Although there was some falling off in the next few years, the relative importance of Liverpool in this commodity remained considerably higher than in the pre-war years; the extent of the fluctuation varied between 26·1 per cent in 1925 and 36·0 per cent in 1936.[9] The importance of wheat in Merseyside's import trade was diminished. Before 1914, she had been the chief port, but by 1921 London had overtaken Liverpool. Only in 1923 and 1929 did Liverpool's imports of wheat exceed those of London; in other years her share of the trade fell from 26 per cent to 17·4 per cent. Both Hull and Manchester were strong competitors to Liverpool in this commodity.[10] Finally, Liverpool's predominance as a centre for the import of tin was maintained throughout the whole of the period from 1924 to 1938, amounting to some 90 per cent of United Kingdom imports. The only years in which supplies fell below this percentage were 1930-2 and 1938.[11]

From the above analysis, it is clear that Merseyside (chiefly represented by Liverpool as the unloading port) suffered a declining trend in her import trades. While some individual commodities, such as wool and sugar, increased in both volume and value, other traditional products such as cotton and tobacco declined. On the whole, Liverpool did rather worse in times of depression than other rival ports but, generally speaking, made a fairly rapid recovery in time of increasing trade. These fluctuations correlate closely with the earnings of Liverpool shipping companies and suggest a growing sensitivity to the fluctuations in effective demand from all sections of the consuming public. In other words, Liverpool's import trade, because of economic considerations, had to maintain itself if it were to retain its former magnitude, by competitive rates and services. In those commodities where costs could be kept low or in those where Liverpool had an obvious geographical advantage, the trades increased; but in others in which supply costs were lower in other ports, Liverpool lost her former importance. Trade went elsewhere and, in some instances, never returned.

[In Merseyside's export trade, there was, as might have been expected, an equally sensitive reaction to economic conditions. This was so with particular commodities. There was, in addition, a broad change in the pattern of markets served. From the then record height of £480 million in 1920, her exports fell to £234 million in 1922 and to £103 million in 1932. Despite this decline, Merseyside remained the country's premier exporting port, except in 1938, when London took the lead.[12] In that year, London's share by value of United Kingdom exports (including re-exports) was 32.3 per cent while that of Liverpool was 26.1. The extent of the decline between 1920 and 1932 was exaggerated by falling price levels, the actual volumes were not so adversely affected. From 1932, there was a slight improvement, but even in 1937, the next peak year before World War II, the total only reached £155 million. In general terms, Merseyside retained her share of just under one third of United Kingdom exports, a position equal to that in 1914; and this was achieved against a background of falling levels of trade throughout the world.]

In some export commodities the fall in demand was such that it produced an adverse reaction on the import trade. For example, the unprecedented fall in the export of cotton piece-goods led to depression in the cotton textile industry and consequently to a fall in demand for raw cotton. A change with a magnitude of this dimension created widespread dislocation in the port's commercial organisation, in this case, to a structure which had been geared to an expanding, rather than to a contracting market. As a result, cotton firms went out of business; links with traditional markets were lost and uncertainty about future prospects of trade in the port, increased. The extent of the change can, perhaps, be best illustrated from the changes in the composition of the export trade

[itself. From 1922 to 1924, 55 per cent of Liverpool's export trade consisted of cotton yarn, piece-goods and other textiles; 24 per cent was metals, cutlery, road vehicles, machinery, and hardware and only 3 per cent chemicals. The chief markets were then the USA, Canada, West Indies, West Africa, and the Far East. By 1934 to 1938, the position had changed radically; the composition being 36 per cent cotton yarns, piece-goods, and other textiles, 37 per cent metals, cutlery, machinery, and hardware and 6 per cent chemicals. As we shall see in a subsequent chapter, this process of change begun in the inter-war years was long-term, and irrevocably altered the composition of the export trade. By 1950, cotton yarns, piece-goods and other textiles had fallen to 28 per cent, whereas metals, etc, had risen to 45 per cent. At this latter date, the markets for Liverpool's exports, in order of priority, were the Far East taking 22 per cent, South and Central America and the West Indies 16·4 per cent, Australia, New Zealand and Fiji 11·8 per cent, Europe 10·5 per cent, West and South Africa 6·9 per cent, the USA, Canada and Newfoundland 5·8 per cent. This pattern is but further confirmation of the rise and fall of particular trades as expressed in the terms of the earning capacity of shipping lines. Those companies engaged in the China, South African, and West Indian trades made greater net voyage profits than those in the American and Indian trades.]

[What can be most usefully learned from this analysis? The most obvious fact was that the pressing difficulties besetting the port's trade during the inter-war years, required a completely new outlook for their solution. As a result of certain accidental causes, the trade of the port began to be more broadly based, both as to commodities handled and to markets served and supplied. By exporting a greater percentage of 'newer' products, which, in their manufacture, contained a smaller proportion of high-cost imported raw material, the port, to some extent, began to safeguard her future position against the effects of prospective depression. After 1945, as we shall see, the process of introducing counter-cyclical factors into the port's economy was carried many stages further. To this extent, the experience gained from 1920 to 1939 caused such changes to be made that links with some 200 years of past history were broken, traditional modes of thought and commercial organisation were discarded, and a more realistic attitude towards future growth and development was adopted.]

II

We must now turn to the effects of change upon the overall activity of the port as seen through the eyes of administration, namely through the records of the Mersey Docks and Harbour Board. In the first place, the Board was under some pressure from the government after 1929, to institute a public works policy in an endeavour to combat rising unemployment. Accordingly, new works were proposed including five bascule bridges as a replacement for swing bridges at Birkenhead and at Stanley dock; extension of the West Float (Bidston dock); replacement of pumps at Langton graving docks; and improvements to Clarence dock. Of these, the five bridges, the Clarence dock scheme and the Bidston dock were all accepted for the provision of grants.[13] The total cost was over £2 million.[14] In the second place, the Board itself attempted to increase traffic to the port. Following a somewhat optimistic appraisal of future prospects in 1929, port charges were reduced. These reductions were made possible from the countervailing benefits received under the De-Rating Acts of 1929. In these various ways, the port's administrative authority was used as a means of checking adverse trends in activity.

As far as the Board was concerned, however, the indicators of uncertainty and depression were found, not so much in fluctuations in tonnage or in the rise and fall of particular commodity trades, as in the ratios of costs to revenue. Apart from 1927, when the Board's total revenue increased to £2·9 million, and in the years of depression when it fell to £2·3 million, there was a remarkable stability at around £2·6 million as the annual return for nearly the whole of the inter-war period. In face of increasing costs, therefore, the need for economy was of some urgency. Accordingly, a twofold policy was adopted to achieve this end; the first, involved the cutting of costs on new works, maintenance and repair; the second, on reducing interest charges payable on the Board's debt.

In 1931, Richard Holt, after a period of absence, had resumed his chairmanship of the Board. As a staunch Liberal, he was active in his pursuit of economies; as a shipowner, he insisted that it was a duty to reduce the charges on goods rather than on ships.[15] This, it was thought, would attract cargoes to Liverpool and give her competitive strength over other ports. Another decision taken was that to reduce the length of Bidston dock to 1,000 feet instead of the projected 1,600 feet.[16] Further steps were also taken to clarify the position with regard to Bromborough dock, a dock which had been constructed for Lever Bros under powers obtained shortly after the end of the war. The objective of the first Lord Leverhulme had been to by-pass the Board's dock monopoly by building his own system. As Bromborough was within the port of Liverpool, however, the payment of town dues was required and a small rate on cargoes not shipped by Lever Bros on their own behalf. Negotiations for the settlement of these claims were concluded in 1932.[17] The net effect of all these proposals would, it was believed, save resources and directly increase revenue. By far the biggest saving, however, came from the various attempts to reduce interest charges. In 1932, the government reduced the rate on War Loan to $3\frac{1}{2}$ per cent. There was, therefore, an incentive to take advantage of this lower rate, particularly as large amounts of bonds were falling due in 1933-4. Accordingly, a new issue of $3\frac{1}{2}$ per cent stock (1935-65) which had originally been created before 1914, was offered at $96\frac{1}{2}$ as a conversion to holders of bonds. A new class of stock was created in 1934; this was for £500,000 of stock at $3\frac{1}{2}$ per cent (1975-85). As the downward trend in interest rates continued, an offer was made to the holders of £9,800,000 of $3\frac{1}{2}$ per cent stock (1935-65) then outstanding to convert into a $3\frac{1}{4}$ per cent stock (1970-80).[18]

We have already touched upon the controversy regarding the provision of a Sinking Fund for the extinction of the Board's debt. The matter was raised again in 1928 and a greater degree of precision was given to the establishment of such a fund when, in 1936, it was related to capital expenditure on a calculated basis over a period of 90 years at 3 per cent. The setting up of such a fund enabled the then existing fund to be used to cover the old debt taken over by the Board in 1858, and was undoubtedly a wise move.

Finally, in the generally improving conditions of trade in 1937, consideration was given to the modernisation of the Dock Estate. The first proposal was designed to help the coasting trade by facilitating the turn-round of ships. This resulted in a new entrance lock, 45 feet long and 65 feet 6 inches wide at the west side of Waterloo dock, enabling vessels drawing up to 17 feet to enter and leave berths at any state of the tide. The second scheme was, in due time, to become the Langton-Canada improvement scheme. This not only led to the reconstruction of the Langton entrances but to the remodelling of the estate in that area. Such latter improvements, however, were not effected until after the second world war. Nevertheless, the range of effort implied a determination to overcome the effects of adverse fluctuations in the port's economic well-being. The monetary value of trade through a port is not necessarily the only index by which to judge periods of relative prosperity or decline. So it was with Liverpool during the 1920s and 1930s. Tonnages of cargoes, both before and after the years of depression, showed a far less disproportionate reduction than their values, and it was upon tonnages handled rather than upon values that employment was maintained in the docks. We must, therefore, turn to an examination of tonnages in order to obtain a clearer perspective of the effects of fluctuation on the general levels of employment and unemployment on Merseyside during these years.

In terms of crude statistics, Merseyside dealt with 17,115 ships totalling 16.52 million net registered tons in 1920.[19] There were shortfalls in 1921 and 1922, but in 1923 the respective totals were 20,074 ships totalling 18.0 million tons. The two following years showed a continuous rise and, though there was a slight decline in 1926, the figures in 1929 had reached 20,583 ships and 20.5 million tons.[20] By 1930, there was a record peak of 20,771 ships totalling 21.31 million tons. Thereafter there was a decline, falling to 17,074 ships with 18.75 million tons in 1933; it was not until 1937 that the 1930 peak was reached and passed.[21] The net effect of this analysis shows that, from the point of view of the Dock Board, the measure of the depression was a drop of 12.2 per cent from the peak of 1930. There was in addition a somewhat different time scale for the deepening of the depression on dockside compared with that experienced by shipowners. The latter had, during 1931 and 1932, been struggling with falls of far greater magnitude in their earning capacity.

The above figures of port usage are given as indicators of the Dock Board's revenue earning capacity in that they include all shipping paying both tonnage rates and harbour dues. As already stated, however, much of the shipping paying harbour dues only, did not berth in Liverpool or Birkenhead, but passed through via the Ship Canal to Manchester. We have already seen that in 1914 such tonnage amounted to 21 per cent af all vessels entering the Mersey. During the inter-war years, this percentage rose from 18.8 per cent in 1920 to 24.1 per cent (average 1930-3) and to 28.4 per cent by 1937. To obtain a closer definition of port usage and fluctuations in trade, it is therefore necessary to use figures of shipping paying tonnage rates. These tonnages were as follows:

Million tons

1914	15·1	1932	14·5
1920	13·4	1933	14·2
1924	14·4	1937	16·1
1930	16·2	1938	16·5
1931	15·1	1939	16·6

Taking 1914 as base year, the increase of tonnage over the twenty-five year period to 1939 was small, and there were many years within this period when there were sizeable deviations below trend. If these figures are compared with net earnings of Liverpool shipping companies there is a fair degree of correlation, particularly in the years of recovery after 1934. As a broad generalisation, the dock system tended to recover from depression at a slightly faster rate than did shipping companies, apart from one or two notable exceptions. If the magnitude of the loss of Liverpool's import trade to London be offset against the strength of the export trade (in relative terms), the inference might well be justified that there was a disproportionate fall in the earnings of shipping companies engaged in the carriage of primary products.

A further measure of activity during these difficult and confused years in the history of the port may be made by comparing trends of the two principal sets of tonnage figures. It will be remembered that, from 1860 to 1914, an annual average rate of growth of 2·8 per cent was calculated on all tonnage entering the Mersey; but that for shipping berthing and using the services of the Dock Board, the annual rate was 2·1 per cent. The corresponding percentages for the period 1920 to 1939 were 0·7 and 0·03. This argues virtually a nil rate of growth in the years between the two world wars. Such a statement, however, is too broad and needs much qualification. As we have already seen, Liverpool had increased her share of some trades, while in others she sustained heavy losses. Thus, in the years of uncertainty and depression, the Dock Board was faced with a static revenue and rising costs with a very low rate of growth in dock usage and with serious losses of trade to other ports. These unfavourable factors were aggravated by world-wide depression in trade. To meet such difficulties, an active policy of reorganisation in the Board's finances was made and, as a result, economies were achieved, particularly in the scale of interest charges on the Board's debt. New works were put in hand (some, admittedly in the nature of public works to maintain employment), and these not only enlarged the port's capacity, but also added to the efficiency of the whole system. The watershed had been crossed, albeit somewhat painfully, but henceforth, Merseyside's relative position as a port was to be prescribed far less by traditional attitudes from the past and much more by a realistic appraisal of new needs and future prospects.

III

Having discussed the varied factors affecting the trade and administration of the port, we turn finally to the industrial structure of Merseyside, in order to assess the effects of these years on employment and on the well-being of the individual. In this respect, the great weakness lay in the fact that since there was no compensatory growth of local industry nor an influx of new industry, the normal outlets for employment were shrinking. The result was a large pool of surplus labour even in the more prosperous of the inter-war years. During the 1930s, the rate of unemployment on Merseyside never fell below 18 per cent of the insured population. Arising from such unpropitious conditions, one might infer considerable labour unrest. The collapse of the postwar boom, after 1921, and the uncertain trading prospects which followed had led to an ebbing of strike activity and rising labour militancy. Efforts by Labour leaders were concentrated in an attack on unemployment. This, in the main took the form of daily protest marches of the unemployed through Liverpool. The impact of the General Strike of 1926 upon this situation is, therefore, perhaps worthy of analysis.

By this latter year, a good deal of the sectionalism in Trade Unionism had been overcome and this had resulted in a consolidation of union strength within the city. A major step to consolidation had been the creation, in 1921, of the Transport and General Workers' Union, an organisation which replaced the numerous unions which had formerly catered for dockworkers and road transport men. In the same year, the local Labour party and the Trades Council amalgamated. This action had virtually nullified the effectiveness of the opposition provided by the breakaway movement of dockers and seamen, in 1917, to form a rival Trades Council. As a result, there was a growing tendency for sympathetic action and this, coupled with a waning of religious differences (a main stumbling block to concerted labour activity in Liverpool), gave labour a much more important voice in Merseyside affairs.[22] This was so, despite the undoubted fact that the government of the city, under the direction of Sir Archibald Salvidge, was dominated throughout the period by an anti-labour majority. In the event, Merseyside was one of the few areas in the country prepared for strike action in 1926. Machinery for the co-ordination of activity by the various unions was quickly put into operation. It appeared that the long tradition of militancy and the troubled years of labour dispute were about to be brought to a climax. The inescapable truth is, however, that the Strike on Merseyside was by no means general.[23] Furthermore, there is evidence to show that the unions themselves had increasing difficulty in maintaining the strike.[24] The tramway men were soon back at work. Many whose families could not subsist on strike pay enrolled as safety volunteers in their own industries; some transport workers even took jobs as tugboat men.[25] By the time the strike was called off, there had been a considerable drift back to work. Thus, in itself, the General Strike had not achieved very much to enhance the power of organised labour. The resultant effects upon the trade and industry of the port were, however, more deep-seated and lasting. To understand the reason for this, one must consider the relationship between the service occupations of the port and those in manufacturing industry. The most obvious characteristic of Merseyside's occupational structure was that services accounted for a greater proportion than manufacturing. There were, nevertheless, precise numerical relationships in the fluctuations of employment between the two. One interesting point (brought out by Wilfred Smith) was that, since 1924, the actual numbers of insured employed workers registered at Merseyside labour exchanges grew at a faster rate than for those in the country as a whole. Accordingly, it is possible to make a rather more comprehensive analysis of change on Merseyside than in the rest of Britain.[26]

The second characteristic was that there was a large percentage of employment in transport as distinct from other services. This was a phenomenon common to Merseyside throughout the inter-war period, though there was a declining trend in such employment during the 1930s.[27] In general, while it is true that the industrial structure of Merseyside was maintained in its fundamental features, it was less sharply differentiated by 1939 than it had been in the early 1920s. The evidence for the above statement can be summarised as follows:

Share of employment on Merseyside of Insured persons

Industry	(per cent) 1924	1931	1939	Gt. Britain 1939
Food, drink, tobacco	10·1	9·7	8·4	4·3
Textiles, clothing	4·0	4·0	3·9	11·1
Metals, engineering	12·7	8·9	13·6	18·8
Other manufacturing industry	12·8	12·6	13·8	11·8
Transport	21·6	18·2	15·1	6·1
Distributive trades	17·7	25·2	19·1	14·8

As a further summary, it can be stated that, during the period from 1924 to 1939, the share of employment in manufacturing industry on Merseyside fell from 40·2 to 39·7 per cent, whereas in Britain as a whole the fall was from 61·7 to 52·8 per cent. The corresponding figures for the service trades on Merseyside showed a rise from 59·8 to 60·3 per cent as against a rise from 38·3 to 47·5 per cent for Great Britain as a whole.[28] If these percentages are translated into actual totals of persons employed, there was a rise from 116,000 in 1924 to 138,000 in 1937 of persons engaged in manufacturing; for the service trades, from 174,000 to 207,000. As the population of Merseyside remained constant at 1·4 million between 1924 and 1939, the relevance of an over-dependence on service trades for employment assumes a weakness in the economy. Ever since the relative decline in industrial activity at the end of the eighteenth century, Liverpool had been pouring resources into the service side of the port. This had rendered her vulnerable, both in trade and in employment, to sudden changes in demand, whether for industrial products from overseas or from Britain's changing capacity for raw materials. For this reason, it was decided, as part of an active policy by the City Council, to widen the base of Liverpool's employment structure. After World War II, there was a promotion of trading estates on the perimeter of the city and, later still, the inducement to large employers of labour such as the motorcar industry, to build factories on Merseyside. This, as we shall see later, helped in changing the whole pattern of employment in the area and strengthened the economy by avoiding a repetition of what had happened in the 1930s. Even so, the basic source of weakness was difficult to eradicate. Despite new industry with injections of new capital, Merseyside's percentage of unemployment remained, until comparatively recently, at approximately double that of the national average.

Compared with the dynamism of late nineteenth and early twentieth centuries in the motivation of Merseyside's economic development, the period from 1920 to 1939 presents a gloomy prospect of general stagnation in trade, capital growth and employment. This, however, is too facile a picture. The effects of trade fluctuation and depression, though severe, were perhaps less so on Merseyside than in other parts of the country. Although the port lost trade to London and elsewhere, there was a relatively fast rate of recovery after 1933. The shipping companies weathered the storm of depression and the Royal Mail crash with remarkable tenacity. The dock system was enlarged by 18 per cent of total area, and the finances of the Board were put upon a more realistic basis. All this was done despite a long-term drop in the trend of growth. One can only ascribe such activity as springing from a spirit of faith and optimism rather than from one of calculation.

IV

The various attempts which were made to improve housing, communications and other amenites in Liverpool and Birkenhead during these years, involved the use of both corporate and private resources. Relatively large sums were expended and the resultant cash flows acted as a counter-cyclical influence, particularly in the field of employment. Without such resources, the depression would undoubtedly have run a much deeper course on Merseyside and its effects would have been more serious and lasting.

The physical extent of Liverpool had grown continuously since 1900. The building line had reached out beyond Sefton Park, the Dingle, Rice Lane, and Old Swan. In 1902, the boundary had been taken beyond Garston, and Fazakerley was added in 1905; later came Allerton, Childwall and Much and Little Woolton. Amidst a chorus of public protest, Queen's Drive, a fine example of one of the first ring roads, was being driven through fields as yet untouched by bricks and mortar; but the prospect of a green countryside skirting the outward circular perimeter of the new road was not of long duration. The tramway tracks extended their tentacles outwards from Pier Head and, with them, services to a rapidly growing area of new streets. By contrast, the older parts of Liverpool and Birkenhead were cleared in an endeavour to remove the worst of the squalid legacy of eighteenth- and nineteenth-century construc-tion. Numerous blocks of flats had been built throughout Liverpool under the provisions of the Sanitation Amendment Act of 1864 and the Housing of the Working Classes Act of 1890. Yet it was not until after 1919 that Liverpool's housing programme can be said to have made an effective start. One by one vast suburbs of council-owned property appeared, stretching from the gates of Knowsley Hall in an arc through Roby to Allerton, Speke, and Dingle. Beyond Queen's Drive was the Norris Green estate (brought within the city boundary in 1927), covering 680 acres, containing 7,700 houses together with shops, schools, churches and cinemas; the whole being built in a pleasant neo-Georgian style of architecture. The counterpart of this housing development by the Corporation on the outskirts of the city was in the clearance of much high density and insanitary housing between London Road, Brownlow Hill and Myrtle Street, and also in the area behind Islington. The new blocks of flats which replaced the old early nineteenth-century courts were, at the time of construction, a model of enlightened redevelopment. The total amount expended on these housing projects (as represented by the amounts borrowed) was £24·60 million.[29]

On the Cheshire side of the river, building development had taken place comparable with that on the Liverpool side. Birkenhead had grown outwards from the original early nineteenth-century plan to

engulf Tranmere, Oxton, Prenton, and Claughton. It had also
stretched along the shore to become contiguous with Port Sunlight
to the east and Wallasey and New Brighton at the mouth of the
estuary. By the 1920s the boundaries had reached Upton in mid-
Wirral and claims were being made to land for further expansion
reaching out almost to Clatterbridge on the one hand and to
Greasby and Frankby on the other. The delineation of present-day
Merseyside, therefore, was almost completed and was contained
within a triangle with its apex just short of Warrington in the east,
just beyond Blundellsands to the north and to a point running
midway through Wirral to the south. This is not an official description of Merseyside, but it will suffice for our purposes. If the new
Redcliffe Maud proposals become effective, this whole area will, for
the purposes of local government, be organised as a metropolitan
region, though the area, as defined above, will contain a very much
larger part of Cheshire within its jurisdiction.

The second field involving the employment of resources during
the inter-war years was that of improvement in communications.
The growing demand for a better access between Liverpool and
Birkenhead as well as for a shorter route to the south led to the
building of the Mersey Tunnel. This considerable feat of engineering was begun in December 1925. The works began with the driving
of two pilot headings, one from each side of the river, and these
met midway under the Mersey in April 1928. The headings were
then enlarged into the full-sized tunnel. The sandstone rock which
was excavated formed the hard core of reclaimed land on which, at
a later date, the Dingle oil jetty and the Otterspool promenade were
built. A cast-iron lining to the tunnel was fitted and between the
excavation and the lining a concrete grouting was pumped in under
high pressure which, in effect, welded the tunnel casing to the river
bed-rock. The main tunnel, which was opened in 1934, with dock
branches on either side of the river, was 2·87 miles in length and
cost upwards of £7·5 million, towards which the government contributed £2·5 million. The balance of expenditure was met from loans,
the interest on which was covered partly by tolls and partly from
rates levied in Liverpool and Birkenhead.[30] As a promotor of
primary and secondary sources of employment, this enterprise must
be judged, not merely from the flow of resources in Merseyside
itself, but also from the demand for such items as 82,000 tons of
cast iron and 270,000 tons of concrete used in its construction.

Another forward-looking development during these years was also in the linking of Merseyside by air with the rest of the British Isles. The city purchased some 2,000 acres from Speke Hall estate and allowed the site to be used as an aerodrome. In 1933, however, an airport, owned by the Corporation, was opened, the terminal building being completed in 1939. Three miles of perimeter track were added in 1940, three runways in 1942, and two brick hangars, six Bellman hangars and numerous workshops were completed shortly afterwards. The control tower, containing all the latest communication devices, was an additional feature of Liverpool's skyline.

In fact the skyline of Merseyside as a whole began to assume a different shape. The monolithic tower of the Tunnel pumping-station was superseded by the rising mass of Sir Giles Scott's tower on the Anglican Cathedral. This dominating structure, the Cathedral, had been building since 1904 and was a monument to private, as distinct from corporate, generosity. In the 1920s the Vestey family had given £227,000 (later increased) to provide the central tower and a peal of thirteen bells.[31] Though not finally completed until the 1950s, this tower was, perhaps, symbolic of Liverpool's struggle against adverse conditions in a period of uncertainty and depression.

From what has been analysed in the preceding pages, the conclusions must be that the port was under severe strain for this period of twenty years. In both her import and export trades there were fluctuations of serious magnitude; the service industries were badly disorganised and widespread unemployment was a consequence. In terms of tonnage using the port, the average annual rate of growth fell to a low level. Yet, despite this, the period was not wholly one of stagnation. Both in Liverpool and in Birkenhead, effective measures were taken to improve housing conditions, to extend communications and to create new capital works in the dock system. By all these promotional efforts, it is estimated that some £40 million was injected into the economy of Merseyside from 1920 to 1939.[32] If the long lines of unemployed dock workers in Liverpool, Birkenhead, and Garston did not readily appreciate the prospect of rising towers in the sky, their future, because of the measures taken, was less sombre than might have been forecast at the time. The rate of recovery of Merseyside from depression was one sign of hope. Another was that Liverpool's economic structure was in process of re-organisation. As a result, by the end of

World War II, the whole economy of the area was more broadly based and less likely to be disrupted by the unbalancing effects of a trade cycle. The scourge of unemployment, coupled with bad housing conditions, had been greatly alleviated. It had yet to be proved that Merseyside could regain her dominant position in sustaining the country during a second world war and of resuming, through her own dynamism, an upward trend in her rate of economic growth.

CHAPTER TEN

War, Reconstruction, and Growth, 1940-70

I

The full story of the impact of World War II on Merseyside has yet to be told. It is only possible here to attempt some measurement of its effects upon shipping and port installations. These effects were, by any standard, extremely serious, not only to Merseyside as a whole, but to the nation at large. The reason for this was that London ceased to be operative for lengthy periods, and, as a consequence, Merseyside became the most vital source of supply and despatch. The devastation caused by the increasing ferocity of attack from the air had to be overcome by an increasingly effective and efficient organisation in which all sections of the community were co-ordinated. This involved co-operation with the armed forces, with civil defence and medical organisations, with trade unions, with shipowners and merchant bodies. As a consequence, there was a variation of authority in certain important areas of control; by the Dock Board in matters of finance and rate-fixing; by the trade unions in the organisation of labour; and by shipowners in the free use of their ships.

The intensity of bombardment from the air increased after July 1940 and culminated in a series of destructive raids in May 1941. Thereafter, the port remained comparatively free from attack. Not only had the dock and warehouse system sustained vast loss in these attacks, but a large part of the central area, including Lord Street and the inner wards stretching from Scotland Road to Ranelagh Street, had been virtually demolished. In addition, large numbers of streets along the line of the docks from Bootle in the north to Garston in the south had suffered severe damage. The greatest devastation of all had been caused by the blowing up of an ammunition ship in Huskisson branch dock number 2. Apart from the tremendous loss of life and property sustained during this period, the net result on the effectiveness of the port had been the elimination of berthing and storage space; enemy action had closed the port for 1,310 hours; 91 ships, excluding naval vessels, had been sunk or seriously damaged within the dock system; and by the end of May 1941, out of 144 berths, only 96 were still in operation.[1] To salvage the sunken ships, to clear the channels and waterways to repair damaged quays and to find adequate storage space was a formidable task. For the most part, however, Jesse Hartley's walls withstood aerial high explosive, and the port was kept open. During the whole conflict it handled 70 million tons of cargo and maintained vital coastwise traffic to the extent of 2·5 million tons annually.[2] No fewer than 1,285 convoys arrived in the port, the largest consisting of 60 ships.[3] This was some measure of Merseyside's corporate effort in helping to win the war; but the effort was made at high cost in lives, property, and capital resources.

In the day-to-day financial management of the port's affairs, the exigencies of war brought considerable anxiety. In the first place, there was an erratic fluctuation (as might have been expected) in the volume of tonnage entering and clearing the port. In 1940, there was a fall of approximately 2·3 million tons on that of the previous year; in 1942, there was a corresponding drop of 6 million tons and, in the following year, nearly 5·7 million tons.[4] This was caused by the effectiveness of submarine warfare and by the loss of facilities consequent upon air attack. There was a slight recovery in 1943 and a rise of nearly 4 million tons in 1944; by 1945, Merseyside was again handling the same amount of tonnage as in 1939.[5] The unpredictable nature of these figures had a correspondingly unprecdictable effect on year-to-year revenue, even when allowance is made for changes in rates. In 1939, the board had received a total of £2·58 million; in 1940, the amount had risen to £2·64 million; but in 1941, there was a fall to £2·37 million. Despite falling tonnages, the revenue increased in 1942 to £3·57 million and £4·06 million in 1943.[6] Thereafter, the rise to £4·88 million in 1944 and £4·24 million in 1945, was more nearly consistent with tonnage figures.

Although the Port Emergency Committee, which had been created at the outbreak of the war, had been given authority to deal with movement of ships and other relevant functions, they could not override statutes or by-laws without reference to the Minister of War Transport. In order to meet increasing costs, permission had been obtained, in 1940, to raise dues; and further increases were sought in 1941. The effects of the May attacks, however, made all forecasts null and void, and a flat 100 per cent increase was envisaged; this, after considerable argument was reduced to 60 per cent,[7] a level which proved to be sufficient throughout the remaining years of the war. Thus, the figures for the board's revenue were maintained, despite falling tonnages in 1942 and 1943. Secondly, on the capital side of the board's accounts, the situation was serious, partly because of destruction of physical assets and partly because of difficulties in forecasting and in estimating values. Permission had to be obtained from the Capital Issues Committee for the renewal and replacement of bonds, and ministerial approval had to be given to the suspension of the Sinking Fund for the year 1941.[8] Nevertheless, despite control from Whitehall, the board managed, by 1945, to obtain a statutory increase in their borrowing powers and sanction to proceed with the new northern entrance to the Langton system. In the third place, the measure of control over the port's administration during the war was most noticeable in the field of employment and labour relations. The most obvious sign of this was to be found in changes affecting the master porterage system. As a means of speeding up the turn-round of ships, a decision was taken, in 1941, that all registered dock workers should be employed by the Ministry of War Transport. As Stuart Mountfield has pointed out, this meant the adoption of specific control points serving definite areas of the docks. It also led to the establishment of zones with employers allocated to each zone.[9] Thus, by the end of the war, the port was largely under the direction and control of central authority; the estate had been extensively damaged and resources for postwar reconstruction were neither accurately defined nor in sight of settlement.

The first postwar year, 1946, was no good augury for the future. By July of this year, the deficit on revnue account stood at £774,000. This had been caused by a fall in tonnage after the end of the war, resulting in a loss of £1·25 million in income compared with the previous year, while expenditure had remained constant.[10] The whole position was further aggravated by a dock strike at the end of 1945 and to delay in receiving ministerial approval for an increase in dues, from 25 per cent to 75 per cent over the 1933 schedule.[11] Before any major step could be taken, however, it was necessary to settle claims for war damage. It was not until 1948 that agreement was attained on the magnitude of the sum involved.[12] Final payment of £10,976,000 was made in June 1949. The active phase of reconstruction did not, therefore, begin until the 1950s and, throughout the decade, the port operated against a background of mounting difficulty and unforeseen dislocation. A large number of berths were out of commission and repair work was slow owing to shortage of labour; this accommodation problem coincided with an upswing in the export trade, a circumstance which required ships to hold their berths for much longer periods than did the process of importing. The lack of space was made more acute by a series of disastrous fires; the first in 1949, gutting cargo stored on the upper floors of sheds in Gladstone south 2 dock, the second, in August 1950, virtually destroying the shedding in Canada south 3; and the third gutting and sinking the *Empress of Canada* on the north side of Gladstone branch dock No 1 in January 1953.[13]

The reconstruction of the docks was, therefore, partly as a result of tardy government action, partly because of trade pressures and partly owing to destruction by fire; a slow, frustrating and painful process. That so much was achieved is remarkable when one considers the nature of the obstacles which had to be overcome. Before a start could be made on the new Langton entrances, a great deal of preliminary work had to be put in hand for the clearance of war damage to the Gladstone-Hornby lock, to complete the Waterloo entrance and to overhaul the gates at Sandon. The Langton-Canada scheme, involving the replanning of the estate in that area, was begun in 1949. It comprised the new Langton river entrance, the widening of the Canada-Brocklebank passage and the remodelling of the old Canada entrance and the Canada basin.[14] These improvements, which were not completed until 1962, gave a safe and protected passage for ships from the river to this part of the dock system. Though this project was the major one of construction in postwar years, there were other smaller works carried out at Birkenhead. The Vittoria dock was extended at the western end. The main purpose of this was to provide better berthing facilities for larger ships engaged in the Far Eastern trade. The north side of Bidston dock was also converted to an iron-ore berth and new sheds were erected to cater for the export traffic to the East and to Africa.[15]

There was, therefore, a slow recovery after the destruction and dislocation of war. In general, the pace of such recovery had to be determined by the new needs of an expanding world; in particular, it was governed by a range of difficult and obstructive problems, all of which had to be overcome, as they eventually were. At the same time, Merseyside's position as a port was subject to a constantly changing pattern of priorities. The task of measurement in such context therefore becomes excessively difficult. Accordingly, all that will be attempted is to put a few important facts into relationship in the hope that, by inference, the conclusions will not be inconsistent or too inaccurate.

II

If, in physical terms, the port had recovered from the destruction of war and the postwar dislocations of trade, the full measure of the conflict had yet to be assessed. Some 21.7 million tons had entered the Mersey in 1939. Apart from 1945, which was a good year, it was not until 1952 that shipping activity once again equalled that of 1939. The intervening years, including those of war, were subject to depressive influences, and it was not really until the period after 1953 that the strong upward trend in the rate of growth was resumed.

In 1949, Merseyside's share of the total trade of the country was 28.5 per cent compared with London's 31.5.[16] Thus, between them, the two major ports accounted for 60 per cent, their nearest rivals being Hull, Manchester, and Glasgow. In the export trade, Merseyside had once again regained first place from London, the respective shares being 32.9 and 30.8 per cent; while in the import trade, Merseyside's share had remained reasonably constant at 24.8 per cent compared with London's 30 per cent.[17] During the course of the 1950s, however, there was a constantly shifting pattern in the composition of trade and in the markets served. At the beginning of the decade, Merseyside imported, by value, one fifth of all grain and flour consumed in the country, one fifth of imported meat supplies, nearly one fifth of all fruit and vegetables, two fifths of all oilseeds and vegetable oils, 15 per cent of timber, nearly two fifths of raw wool and about three fifths of a shrinking total supply of raw cotton.[18] The share of the major export commodities was two thirds of all cotton piece-goods, approximately two fifths of woollens and worsteds, one third of the exports of iron and steel, nearly 30 per cent of non-ferrous metals, 38 per cent of machinery and 27 per cent of vehicles of all descriptions.[19] This rather boring catalogue is of relevance only in so far as it provides a basis for a discussion of future change in comparative terms. For example, Liverpool's imports of raw cotton were one-third less in 1955 than they had been in 1950, but in wool Liverpool managed to increase her share at the expense of London. The position with regard to grain had not materially altered since the 1930s, the two ports, Liverpool and London, handling about 40 per cent of total supplies.[20] In some of the more traditional trades such as sugar, Merseyside retained her place in relative terms; in timber and oilseeds, on the other hand, she maintained a fluctuating rivalry with London and Hull.[21] By 1955, for instance, the relative shares of imported timber between Liverpool, London and Hull approximated 36, 14, and 10 per cent respectively.[22] In oilseeds, however, a great change in the relative positions took place, Hull losing her predominant share to Liverpool with London also gaining at her expense.[23] In a whole range of other commodities in which the changing pattern of consumer demand has called into existence in the twentieth century, very large increases occurred, thus helping to fill the gaps caused by a decline in some of the older and longer-established import trades.[24] In such a category one must place fuel oil and petroleum, commodities which assumed an increasing importance to Merseyside's trade following the building of the oil port and refinery at Stanlow on the Cheshire bank of the Mersey estuary. As we have seen, Merseyside regained her position as the principal exporting port during certain years after 1945; but by the mid-1950s, London had once again re-established her supremacy, exporting some 33 per cent by value, of all United Kingdom exports and re-exports, whereas Liverpool's percentage fell to 27.[25]

 Turning now to the composition of Merseyside's export trade, the structure at the beginning of the 1950s was that cotton-piece-goods accounted for 28 per cent, by value, of her total, and metals, vehicles and machinery had risen to 45 per cent. Up to 1955, the chief markets for such exports in order of priority (based on the port's trade with each market as a percentage of Liverpool's total export trade), were the Far East, 22 per cent; South and Central America and the West Indies, 16·4; Australia, New Zealand and Fiji, 11·8; Europe, 10·5; West Africa, 9·6; the USA, Canada and Newfoundland, 5·8. By the end of the decade still further changes had taken place in both the composition of the trade and in markets supplied. Cotton yarns and piece-goods, once so important, now accounted for only 8 per cent of the total value, machinery of all kinds, road vehicles, cutlery, hardware and metal manufactures had risen to 53 per cent.[26] There was also large expansion to 15 per cent in chemicals, salt, coal, soap, and vegetable oil. A broad geographical division of markets for such products showed that Africa and the Americas took roughly one-half, India and the Far East one-quarter, Australia and New Zealand 14 per cent and Europe 11 per cent.[27]

From this brief survey, it is clear that Liverpool's business community had learnt the lessons of the inter-war years. The damaging effects of a long and painful process of transition from an individualistic type of economy to a controlled one, was not made without correspondingly painful re-adjustments. By 1960, it was at least hopeful that, within the existing pattern of world trade, Liverpool could retain an essential element of flexibility which, if rightly used, might both strengthen and maintain Merseyside's role as a major port. A main source of strength in this respect had occurred through the alteration of Merseyside's occupational ratio between manufacturing and service industries.

Under the Distribution of Industry Act of 1945, the government did not seek to impose rigid control over industrial location; but rather to take such steps as were necessary to prevent the recurrence of heavily localised unemployment.[28] It was not intended to encourage the development of certain selected areas so that their population should eventually undergo a substantial increase. The essential points in this policy were concerned with the offering of inducements to manufacturers to site their factories in specified areas. As wartime restrictions were still in operation, the inducements took the form of building priorities and the provision of financial facilities. Though Merseyside was not scheduled as a Development Area until some considerable time later, the side effects of this policy were elements in the subsequent changes in the balance of employment. One of the reasons why Merseyside was excluded at that time was that a disproportionately large share of the new government factories, built during the war, had been located there. It happened, however, that the Liverpool Corporation held a unique position among local authorities in the powers which it possessed for the attraction of new enterprises. These powers were conferred by Act of Parliament and enabled it to acquire land adjacent to the East Lancashire road for the purpose of promoting industrial development. In the assistance of this process, they were also empowered to make long-term advances to industrialists who wished to establish themselves there. Thus, the possession of these powers put Liverpool in much the same position as that of a Development Area.[29]

Although by 1951, the percentage change in numbers employed, as between manufacturing and service industries, had not altered very much since 1939, the long-term effects were to be considerable. At the beginning of the 1950s, 39·1 per cent of the insured population was engaged in manufacturing as against 60·9 in services; this compared with 47·6 and 52·4 per cent for the United Kingdom as a whole. Transport was twice as important in the industrial structure of Merseyside as in that of the country at large. Today, the balance has shifted towards manufacturing, particularly as a result of the establishment of large-scale motor-car units by Ford, Vauxhall, and Standard, and the oil refineries at Stanlow, and Cadbury's large chocolate-biscuit factory at Moreton. These, however, are but additional to the more intensive development of electrical and engineering factories on the industrial and trading estates at Aintree, Speke, Fazackerley, and Kirkby.

Much of this new development was separate from the older, lighter type of industry on the trading estates. The Edgehill, Old Swan, Fazackerley group included a wide range such as biscuits, sweets, jams, metal manufacturers, tin boxes, toys, and telephones; textiles (such as rayon), rubber, soap, and polishes.[30] The Speke and Kirkby estates, on the other hand, were newly built and capable of expansion into heavier and more highly capitalised industries. They included cars, rubber goods, metal safes and non-ferrous metals, vehicle assembly and machinery, industrial chemicals, fine chemicals and medical preparations, paints and varnishes and drums.[31] In this way, a strenuous attempt had been made, since the war, to help an area with a high birth rate and a large labour force. Before it is possible to discuss whether or not such an aspiration was capable of realisation, however, it is necessary to link these physical changes in trade with the diminished economic function of Liverpool's merchant body and with the alterations in status of her shipowners. In postwar years, a revolution, almost unnoticed by commentators and shipping historians, had taken place in the various spheres of economic sanction. For Liverpool, the changes were profound and none the less essential if the port were to meet the challenge of competition from other ports, the threat of militant labour unrest and the potential development of container traffic, with any degree of confidence.

III

Defoe's description of the Liverpool trader as the 'universal merchant', was applicable not only because such a person dealt in a wide variety of products and served scattered markets, but also because he possessed width and scope in his economic functions. He worked on open indent, buying in the cheapest and selling in the dearest markets; he financed trade, he hired and sailed ships and insured his own ventures. Such individualistic activity persisted throughout the eighteenth and nineteenth centuries, though by the beginning of the present century, the merchanting function was being more narrowly defined, very largely because specialist groups, such as bankers, shipowners and insurance firms, had encroached upon his ancient prerogatives.[32] The limitation of function was taken many stages further after the end of World War II. As a result, the merchant *qua* merchant, once so powerful in the political and economic life of the city, was reduced in status.

What effect did such a change have upon the commercial mechanism of the port? By the 1950s, the merchant, and especially the export merchant, had a narrower range of specialisms. These very largely depended on his skill in choosing, blending and using his knowledge in order to provide a cheap and efficient distribution channel. It was a change which, while retaining the merchant within the commercial framework, nevertheless left him with a reduced economic status. He no longer controlled the channel through which trade passed; manufacturers at home and importers abroad so developed that they were able to to take the initiative in creating trade. Agents, bankers and other specialists were employed to provide supplementary action.[33] Such groups worked on a large enough scale internationally to establish and maintain contact.

To some extent, the nature of the product determined the range and facility of its distribution. In the sale of unbranded goods, for example, Liverpool merchants were still able to exercise merchanting skills; these skills were particularly effective in those goods available at different prices and at different qualities from numerous sources of supply. There was, therefore, considerable scope during the 1950s for the older-type merchant to deal in cheap textiles, dried fish, unbranded soap, nuts, bolts, and rivets, commodities in which the merchant could find the cheapest source of supply from a wide range of manufacturers and fulfil the requirements of his customers. Profit margins were low and, accordingly, there was little inducement for manufacturers to set up competitive selling organisations abroad. On the other hand, in the sale of unbranded goods which were standardised and available only from a limited number of manufacturers, there was much less scope for the individual merchant. The buying of cement or sulphate of copper required no skill in choosing sources of supply. Importers and manufacturers could, and did, make contact with each other directly or through commission agents.[34] Another group of products not well adapted to merchant trade included art and fashion goods, such as women's clothes and any sort of speciality in which personal taste was involved. By the mid-1950s, foreign importers of these goods were preferring to contact British manufacturers directly. Similarly, in highly specialised equipment, such as machinery, electric cables, transformers and other industrial products, the scope for the merchant had become restricted. He generally lacked the requisite knowledge for the provision of a technical service. In such trade, therefore, direct contact had become the practice between manufacturer and customer. Technical liaison having been established, the merchant might, on a limited number of occasions, be brought in to finance the transaction.[35] For the most part, however, this type of product (which was assuming a larger share of Liverpool's export trade) was no longer suitable for merchant transaction.

Another considerable percentage of Merseyside's export trade consisted of branded products. In this group, also, there was a marked movement away from selling by independent merchants. Products such as bicycles, motor-cars, chocolates, biscuits, speciality toys, and toilet preparations came more and more to be sold through commission agents, through manufacturers' own selling departments abroad, or directly to the importer or his buying agent in Britain. The very act of branding implied that the manufacturer intended to use intensive selling methods and his efforts might well have been nullified if his products were sold by a general merchant dealing in vast numbers of competing lines. The weapon of resale price maintenance, which accompanied branding, virtually turned the merchant who dealt in such products into a commission agent. Finally, in the sale of highly specialised mechanical equipment, the service required the provision of spare parts, a service which the manufacturer, rather than the merchant could perform.[36] By the 1950s, the greatest scope for the merchant lay in the handling of small lots of a large number of goods and in exploring and opening up new markets. Irregularity of demand and small orders for one product presented no problem to him. He was able to combine many small orders into one big one so that a steady flow of trade passed through his hands.

Translated into terms of markets served, these remaining functions of the merchant were able to be maintained in those areas of the world which were relatively underdeveloped. In such markets, communications were usually poor and importers could not be relied on to maintain contacts. Furthermore, as orders were small, such importers needed credit to enable them to sell goods before they could pay for them. The Liverpool merchant exporter, by advancing credit and bearing risks, operated effectively in these areas. The best example of a merchant market at this time was West Africa. Before independence was granted to Nigeria and Ghana, the vast hinterland was relatively underdeveloped in a commercial sense; banking and communications were insufficient for the needs of trade and native importers had little capital and needed much credit. Native buying habits were not conducive to the direct selling methods of large-scale manufacturers. The need was for a large amount of cheap consumer goods and the area was, therefore, ideally suitable for small type merchanting activity. This conclusion held good, even though a larger share of the trade had passed into the hands of big companies such as the United Africa Company and John Holt. As we have seen, these companies operated their own ships and banking facilities and had branch houses and stores throughout the whole market. Nevertheless, these trading companies gradually succumbed to the pressure of manufacturers' trademarks. Long before the mid-1950s, they had been forced into exclusive selling arrangements with manufacturers of proprietory goods, though such arrangements rarely operated on a fixed-price basis.[37]

By contrast, the USA, which, in the eighteenth and nineteenth centuries, had been such a fruitful field for Liverpool merchants, had seriously declined in importance (ie as a merchant market). One factor in this decline had been the falling off in the supply of raw cotton and, consequently, the export trade complementary to that commodity. The closing of the Liverpool Cotton Exchange was a further factor in the situation. The size of the US market, the closely integrated commercial organisation, together with the highly industrialised structure of the country and protective tariffs, all combined to operate against the merchant. If he had any dealings with it at all, it was in the role of agent rather than merchant. In Central and South America, Liverpool men had also lost a great deal of ground. The old trade supremacy in such countries as Mexico, Brazil, and Argentina disappeared before the numerous inhibitions similar to those in the American market, namely, high tariffs, intense local competition and the confining of demand to a narrow range of high-class speciality products. Added to these difficulties, however, were the impositions of currency restrictions, trade restrictions, active competition from US traders and the growing tendency towards direct buying.[38]

Thus, by the end of the 1950s, the Liverpool export merchant no longer dominated trade as he did in the past. The initiative in trading, so long his exclusive function, was now perforce shared by the manufacturer or the importer, depending upon the type of commodity, the size and organisation of the market and the size of the manufacturer. At the same time, the auxiliary functions were being performed by the merchant, importer or manufacturer, or by specialist firms and agents. Greatly reduced in status though he may have been, he still was able to play some part in international trade, especially in the services which he could still offer. This was particularly the case in his dealings with small, hazardous and under-developed markets and in linking together small manufacturers and importers.

IV

The impact of change on the channels of Merseyside's trade did not influence the trend of trade as a whole, apart, that is, from adding to its strength and size in certain markets. It did, however, affect the old relationship between shipowner and merchant and shipowner and dock authority. In general, a high-value low-volume trade, such as, for example, the exports of a manufacturing nation, does not require an excessively large tonnage of ships. What Merseyside needed was a larger trade in quantum terms. To some extent, despite the drop in raw cotton, large volumes were maintained in the import trade; but in exports, owing to the increasing percentage of metal, engineering and high speciality cargoes, volumes tended to diminish. In these circumstances, the nominator of the vessel played an increasingly important part in the direction of trade. If the exporter (as we have seen, increasingly the manufacturer) nominates the vessels, it can only be the volume of exports which determines the demand for shipping. Conversely, the same applies if the importer is the nominator. How did such considerations affect the Liverpool shipowner in the 1950s? The possession of the right to nominate the carrying vessel did not always mean that a Liverpool (or even a British) ship would be chosen. In times of boom or depression this uncertainty applied with added force. The true safeguard lay in the power of the Liverpool shipowner to offer a really competitive service and to bring the products of the seller to the warehouse of the buyer as quickly and as efficiently as possible.

The shipowners themselves had already taken action to strengthen their effectiveness in meeting the changing circumstances of trade. This had very largely taken the form of combination in which managements were kept intact, though capital resources and tonnages were used as competitive instruments.[39] This process had gone on apace during the 1930s; but by the end of the 1950s shipping power was vested in the following groups: P & O, 2,399,000 gross tons; Furness Withy, 1,420,000; Holts (Blue Funnel), 971,000; Cunard, 947,000; British & Commonwealth, 872,000; Ellerman, 631,000; Vestey, 466,000; T & J. Harrison, 268,000; Canadian Pacific, 121,000, and Palm line, 111,000. Today, the various Liverpool shipping companies whose histories have been traced in this volume are members of one or other of these groups. The Houlder, Alexander, Johnston-Warren, Royal Mail and Pacific Steam Navigation companies are within the Furness group. The Blue Funnel group, as we have seen, was the most powerful Merseyside group in its own right, containing the Blue Funnel, Glen, Elder Dempster and China Mutual lines. The Cunard group includes the Port line and T. & J. Brocklebank, while the Clan line and Houston line are in the British & Commonwealth group. The Ellerman group contained the Ellerman and Papayanni lines, Hall line, Ellerman's & Wilson line and, finally, the Booth line and Lamport and Holts are contained within the Vestey group. In such context, the multi-farious activities of the past private enterprise have been drawn to-gether in a few precisely identifiable capital structures.[40] The power of such groups with their vast reserves is still potent in the direc-tion of Merseyside's economic position as it is also in the wider sphere of competition with equally identifiable groups of shipping companies in other maritime countries throughout the world.

There is, however, another interpretation of this picture. If the shipowners have consolidated their position, the militant forces within (and, for that matter, without) the ranks of organised labour have also grown in strength. A presage of future activity occurred in 1955 when twenty-nine years of peace in the shipping industry were brought to an end by a seamen's strike. This lasted from May to June and was confined to two ports, London and Liverpool. Though only 1,700 seamen were involved, it was officially estimated that 25,000 working days were lost. In July to September 1960, another more serious strike took place. In this particular case, there were two phases, together lasting for nine weeks, some 5,000 sea-men being involved in the first phase and 4,000 in the second.[41] This time, some 123,000 working days were lost. Finally, the most disastrous strike of all in the summer of 1966, virtually brought all the ports of the country to a standstill. The grievances which occasioned these actions were evidence not only of discontent with wages and hours of work; they were as much concerned with union representation on board ship and with the terms of the Merchant Shipping Acts which controlled such matters as discipline at sea.[42]

Parallel to this unrest was the equally serious action taken by dockworkers. As we have already stated, the board's financial difficulties in 1945 were increased by a dock strike. Growing dis-content concerning wages, hours of work and payment for dirty cargoes, finally culminated in 1955 in a struggle between the Trans-port and General Workers Union and the Association of Stevedores and Dockers, the Blue Union. The resultant strike, very serious, though not complete, ran from 23 May to 2 July. This involved great loss to the port and a fall in revenue to the Dock Board of some £250,000. During the last ten years, the incidence of strike activity has increased. The present uncertain situation in labour relations, therefore, presents itself, in general terms, as a struggle between the organised groups of shipowners and port employers on the one hand and the equally powerful organisation of the unions on the other. Negotiations between the two groups, however, are made more difficult and complicated by the unofficial activities of militant groups and rivalry among the unions themselves. Such internecine strife, however valid grievances might be, can only bring decline to the prosperity of the port as it is presently constituted.

We must now return to the 1950s in order to examine the impact of these events on the progress of Merseyside's shipping trades. On the whole, they were prosperous years, despite increasing competition from foreign companies in nearly all of the major trades, despite strikes and despite rising costs. The demand for shipping increased as a result of the outbreak of the Korean war, primarily because of stockpiling of raw materials and of increases in consumer demand for food products. In terms of total shipping entering the Mersey, there was a rate of growth comparable with that in the years before 1914. There was a rise from 21·1 million tons in 1950, to 29·3 milion in 1960; the only year in which there had been a fall being 1957 when there had been a decrease of half a million tons on that of the previous year. Even in 1955, the year of the strikes by seamen and dockworkers, the figure remained the same as that in 1954.[43] Actual volumes of cargoes were also increasing at a faster rate than at any time since 1914. The explanation for this was that wartime controls had been lifted, and trade was once again beginning to flow in free and unrestricted channels. The average annual rates of growth for aggregate tonnage entering the Mersey during the 1950s can be represented in two ways. In the first place, there was a rapid growth until 1955 at 5·4 per cent per annum with a distinct break in trend in that year. Secondly, from 1955 to 1960 there was a slowing down in the annual rate of growth to 2·3 per cent per annum. Just over a quarter of this tonnage, however, passed through Liverpool to dock either in Manchester or at points in the estuary where tonnage dues were not chargeable. A more precise definition of tonnage unloading cargo in the Dock estate is therefore necessary if one requires a trend more closely identified with the port's growth.

If the rates of growth, based on aggregate tonnage using the Mersey, are adjusted by calculations based on tonnages berthing and clearing the port (ie paying tonnage dues), it becomes clear that the very low rate of growth of 0·03 per cent per annum, during the inter-war years, persisted until 1953.[44] Thereafter, despite shortfalls in 1955 and 1962, there was a considerable rate of growth until 1966 of 3·5 per cent per annum. The effect of the seamen's strike in 1966 is clearly discernible and, in the following years, 1967 and 1968, there were falls of 3·5 and 2·9 million tons respectively from the 1965 levels. There was, therefore, a break in the upward trend in 1966, a break from which the port does not yet appear to have recovered.

These latter trend rates, though different from those calculated from figures of aggregate tonnages entering the Mersey, are not entirely inconsistent. The main discrepancy in the post-1953 trend rate implies some acceleration beyond that evident in the alternative data. One possible explanation may lie in the increasing tanker tonnage discharging at Tranmere for the Stanlow oil refineries. Roughly one-sixth of all tonnage entering Liverpool's dock system is now tanker tonnage. Some 11,000,000 tons of petroleum and bunker oil are unloaded annually at Dingle and Tranmere, and it is likely that this figure will be greatly augmented during the 1970s. As a source of revenue to the Dock authority, tanker tonnage is undoubtedly valuable, but it is not labour-productive and, therefore, much less a determinant of growth than cargo-liner tonnage in the general well-being of the port as a whole. A very real danger threatening Liverpool's status and relative position might occur if tanker tonnages should outstrip those of the cargo and bulk commodity trades. On the whole, however, the upward trend in the rate of growth of shipping using the port, between 1953 and 1966, is in accord with an upward trend in the rate of earnings by shipping companies. It also reflects an increase in activity in the economy of Merseyside as a whole.

In general, the 1950s were relatively good years for Liverpool shipping companies. This was true for the larger companies whose capital resources enabled them to maintain the efficiency of their fleets, despite a virtual doubling of shipbuilding costs; it was also true with regard to changing patterns of trade in which they were able to achieve flexibility in the use and allocation of their considerable resources. The generalisation, however, was not so true for the smaller companies whose funds were not adequate to provide cover against an increase in competition from foreign shipping lines and a general rise in operational costs. The extent of this comparison can, perhaps, be best illustrated by reference to specific trades in which Merseyside had long-established connections. In the Far Eastern trade, as we have seen, the two powerful groups, P & O and Holts, controlled most of the British trade; the Dutch shipping companies offered severe competition in the Island trades but this was, to some extent, mitigated after the establishment of Indonesian independence. Though the two British groups were in control of the major share of the carriage of cargo to and from the United Kingdom, they held no exclusive position. There was competition from tramp steamers and from other cargo lines. For example, the Ben line increased its services after 1950, sending at least one ship a month to Singapore and Japan and one ship every month to Indonesia.[45] The Ellerman group, which had some connections in this trade since the establishment of the Ellerman & Bucknall Steamship Co but which, nevertheless, had never been a very serious competitor, sent one ship a month homewards from Indonesia.[46] However loosely-knit the structure of these company groupings may have been, their effectiveness was never in question. Within the framework of Conference agreements, they provided adequate safeguards for the maintenance of earning capacity. By the efficient use of large fleets of ships, equipped with the latest technical devices and powered by diesels, they were able to keep working costs at a minimum and sustain voyage profits. The relative position was one of strength and this strength was but little impaired even when China became a prohibied area to British ships. Though Holts, for example, were forced to write off capital assets in Shanghai and other Chinese ports, their loss of revenue from the closure of ports along the coast was offset by changes in the pattern of voyages. Henceforth, the loading line extended from the northern tip of Japan to Hong Kong, the Philippines and southwards through the territories of Borneo, Malaya and the islands of Indonesia to the Australian coasts.[47] Despite this radical change in the traditional pattern of voyages, regular calls continued to be made at well over thirty loading ports in the Far East. In addition, fleets of small feeder ships served the Holt main line ships in exactly the same way as they had performed like services in the days of Alfred Holt, the founder of the firm.

In much the same way, Harrisons were faced with the loss of traditional markets in India and Brazil. The fall in earning capacity caused by withdrawal from these markets was further accentuated by a falling off in the demand for one of their staple cargoes, cotton from the Gulf ports. In short, Harrisons, like Holts, had to meet change by a considerable redeployment of resources. In this case, the gaps were filled by a more intensive working of the trades with South Africa, the West Indies, Mexico and Central America, Venezuela and, until the advent of Fidel Castro, Cuba.[48] With new diesel-powered ships and with freight rates maintained in the various conferences, Harrisons were successful in coping with serious changes in the traditional patterns of trade and in promoting keenly competitive services in newer markets. In this process, there was considerable change in the composition of their cargoes. Rubber and cotton gave way to sugar and flour, the latter being carried in bulk in competition with other companies' fleets of bulk carriers. On the South African run, however, wool gave way to a broader range of miscellaneous commodities.

In the West African trade, once wartime restrictions were lifted, Elder Dempsters operated their fleet under relatively prosperous conditions. The two main British competitors, John Holt & Co and the United Africa Co, had, during the war, sailed their ships together with those of Elder Dempster as common carriers on the open berth. This system was continued after the war in the interests of fair allocation of the limited cargo space available. Consequently, when trade with the Coast began to increase in response to consumer demand for vegetable oils, it was decided to put the wartime relationship on a more permanent basis.[49] At the same time, it was thought desirable that merchants ought to be given the right to deal with independent shipping companies. Accordingly, in 1950, the John Holt Line Ltd was established to control the ships of the John Holt enterprise; the Palm line, at the same time, being formed to take over the fleet of the United Africa Co.[50] Both these new lines were admitted to the West Africa Conference. So it was, that after some thirty years of rivalry, all the British interests engaged in trade with West Africa were brought under one umbrella.

Following these re-organisations, came the sale of some of the Holt ships, and the Holt Line Ltd was transformed into the Guinea Gulf Line Ltd in 1954. This new line found some difficulty in competing (even within the framework of the Conference) with the more powerfully capitalised companies such as Elder Dempsters.

In 1957, a change of policy occurred when the Red Rose Navigation Co, a wholly-owned subsidiary, was registered in Bermuda.[51] The first and only ship of this concern, the *Rose of Lancaster*, was placed on charter to the Guinea Gulf Line, a temporary expedient towards the solution of mounting difficulties. To some extent, these difficulties were increased when the various African territories became independent. Traffic which had, in the immediate postwar period, been concentrated on the United Kingdom and Continental routes, now became more widely dispersed; outward cargoes fell as native industry was encouraged and as non-European sources of supply developed. At the same time, the small, but persistently promoted, lines of Ghana and Nigeria took an increasing share of declining export cargoes. This was, perhaps, inevitable as most of the exports of cocoa and vegetable oils and seeds were controlled by state marketing boards. These factors might have been successfully overcome had it not been for other adverse financial considerations, considerations which seriously weakened Guinea Gulf's competitive position in a greater measure than those already described.

There had been a large increase in operational costs at a time when freight rates could not be raised. Elder Dempsters' resources were sufficient to cover a temporary difficulty of this kind, but Holts' were not. Consequently, the Holt fleet was reduced to four ships. Many of the costs were fixed and did not vary with the number of ships. As a result, profit margins fell and the company was forced to re-examine their whole position as shipowners.[52] In 1962, a management agreement was made with Messrs T. & J. Brocklebank. This solved one difficulty, but others remained. The four ships were fitted with oil-fired turbines, a mode of propulsion which, as we have seen, was eminently successful in operating Harrisons' ships during the 1930s; but in the 1960s, the cost structure of shipping companies had changed. Such ships could no longer compete with diesel-powered cargo-liners. The decision was, therefore, taken to sell the ships. After an abortive sale to the Nigerian National Shipping line, Elder Dempsters became interested and, on 1 March 1965, John Holts' shipping interests were bought by Liner Holdings Ltd.[53] Thus ended an interesting chapter in Liverpool's shipping history in which the functions of a purely merchanting firm had retained the subsidiary function of shipowner; this function had to be abandoned at a time when there was a down-turn in trade.

In retrospect, the years from 1939 to 1969 witnessed three distinct factors affecting Merseyside's position as a port. In the first place, the rate of recovery in the postwar years was painfully slow. It was not until after 1952 that noticeable progress was made in the clearance of irksome wartime controls and, in physical terms, in bringing order out of the chaos and destruction in the dock system. Thereafter, progress was rapid and dock usage began to increase at a rate comparable with that of certain periods before 1914. On a long-term projection, however, (ie base year 1860), there would appear to be a break in trend in 1955 for aggregate tonnage entering the Mersey, though a comparable break did not occur in shipping loading and discharging within the Dock Board's system until 1966. Secondly, the earnings of shipping companies continued to be maintained at remunerative levels until the middle of the 1960s. Markets were enlarged, exports increased, especially in technically high-grade products. Capital structures had been re-organised within a few powerful groups and, in general, greater efficiency in the working of fleets had been achieved. Against this background had to be set the growing strength of trade union activity and, in particular, the militancy of non-official action by both seamen and dockworkers. Finally, the face of Merseyside itself had been lifted, not only by a better provision for industrial employment, but by the rebuilding of the central area largely destroyed by enemy action and by the provision of new housing estates on the outskirts. In this context, it is relevant to mention that the Overhead Railway, which had carried dockworkers and sightseers along the line of docks from Seaforth to Dingle since the 1890s, was dismantled, thereby giving a more spacious aspect to the buildings at Pier Head and a more imposing entrance to Britain's 'western gateway'.

The general impression obtained from a study of Liverpool's postwar history is one of considerable development, despite frustration and radical changes in the patterns of trade. According to the way in which one interprets figures of port usage, there might be two watersheds in this development; but whether the year 1955 or 1966 will be the more significant date in which trends changed, must be left to the judgement of future historians. We can only put the achievement of these past thirty years against that of the preceding two and a half centuries. One must readily admit that, from the procedures adopted, only a general impression can be obtained. Nevertheless, the conclusions which emerge are not greatly at variance with the body of qualitative evidence analysed in this volume. The lessons of nearly three hundred years of history may, it is hoped, be of some help in shaping future progress on Merseyside. Such an aspiration directs the theme and analysis in our final chapter.

CHAPTER ELEVEN

Past, Present, and Future

I

The first record of Liverpool is that of King John's so-called charter of 1207. References thereafter are sparse, though not altogether uninformative. It is not until the middle of the sixteenth century that a composite body of records gives us a reasonably continuous picture of the town and the life of its inhabitants.[1] One can surmise that for a period of 350 years after King John, the small community of less than 1,000 souls lived and worked on the shores of a turbulent river under the shadow of a protective castle, virtually cut off, on the landward side, by creeks, mosses and bogs, from easy access to the hinterland. Yet, despite the conclusions of many observers at the end of the seventeenth century that Liverpool had not grown much beyond the confines of a fishing village,[2] there is evidence of a burst of commercial and trading activity in Elizabeth's reign. Liverpool ships were beginning to develop a varied trade with Ireland and were reaching out to the Mediterranean, to French, Spanish, and Baltic ports. It is also true that much of this activity, for reasons already given, declined in the seventeenth century. The inhabitants were, therefore, thrown back on agriculture to sustain themselves in livelihood. The upsurge of activity which occurred after 1670, was not therefore, connected with a previously continuous rate of growth, but was primarily caused by new and, very largely, external forces.

During the first half of the eighteenth century, however, the growth of the port was determined as much by the increase in Liverpool's own industrial potentiality as by a rapid development of overseas trade. The interaction of the two prime factors created secondary movements for the improvement of communications, for the establishment of banking and insurance facilities, for the building of docks and for the generation of a commercial policy in Liverpool's own interest. As a result, the port became an attractive source of enterprise where young men with initiative and ability could found their family fortunes. This process tended to accentuate commercial rather than industrial growth. By the beginning of the nineteenth century, Manchester and the Midlands were beginning to outpace Liverpool's industrial capacity, so that henceforth her effort was confined primarily to those industries required for the building, maintenance, and servicing of ships. In the nineteenth century, as we have seen, the flow of resources was directed into service rather than into manufacturing industries. After 1920, a more static situation was achieved and, following the end of World War II, the wheel once again began to turn full circle so that, today, the importance of manufacture to the economic well-being of Merseyside, has assumed a more distinctive and important place.

In this process of constant change the power and influence of the Corporation played its part. In strictly economic terms, it became responsible, in the eighteenth century, for the promotion and ad-ministration of funds, under successive acts of Parliament, for docks and other systems of communication within the area of its jurisdic-tion; it maintained liquidity as in 1793 when it issued its own notes; and, through the Liverpool Office in London, it exerted pressure, particularly in commercial matters on the central government. For a time after 1860, the power of the Dock Board in the direction of economic affairs, together with that of the railway companies, rivalled the influences exerted by the Corporation; but in the present century, the dominating role of city government has re-asserted itself. This power is very largely twofold, first, in the con-trol and allocation of land for industrial purposes and, secondly, in the exercise of financial sanction. It was used as a motivating force in the 1920s and 1930s and has increased in scope and magnitude. The indications are that, in any subsequent re-organisation of local government, the authority, however widely constituted, will increase rather than diminish.

The end product of this sustained effort in the accumulation of resources and in the exploitation of economic gain in the far corners of the earth, is that over a period of three hundred years Merseyside has grown outwards from a small cluster of houses on Mersey's shore to a vast conurbation embracing both sides of the estuary. The capital stock is, by historical evolution, designed to serve not only the shipping, banking, industrial and social needs of the area alone, but also the needs of the nation as a whole. To these ends the population, which has now grown to something over two million, is conditioned partly by history and partly by economic necessity. The final questions which an enquiry of this kind must attempt to answer are three in number. How can we measure Merseyside's progress over the past three hundred years? Can Merseyside's historic role as a universal provider of food and raw materials and as a supplier of capital and consumer goods be maintained? Finally, what are the factors likely to affect the port's economic position in the future?

II

It is not easy to measure human endeavour. All that can be attempted here is to match specific rates of growth, in concrete terms, in the hope that important points in trends may be considered and tentative conclusions be drawn. Let it be stated at the outset that, owing to the destruction of official records, sequences of figures for the main items in Liverpool's import and export lists are not available for the eighteenth century as a whole. The figures used in this volume have been collected by a painful process of reconstruction from Port Books, cargo lists published in newspapers, merchants' handbills and, after 1820, published import returns. For purposes of simplification, all commodity figures used have been those of volume rather than value. The measurement of growth in population refers only to Liverpool with subsequential changes in boundaries, the population of the Wirral shore of Merseyside being minimal until the middle years of the nineteenth century.

With these qualifications in mind, we can begin by examining the upsurge of Liverpool's import trade in the eighteenth century. Sugar and tobacco imported into Liverpool exhibit fairly constant growth from 1710 to 1913. The growth for sugar is 2·9 per cent per annum, while that for tobacco is 1·6 per cent. The fluctuations around these trends are minor, indicating that the two traditional staples of Liverpool's early trade in commodities followed a consistent pattern in response to increasing demand. The impact of the newer plantation commodities after 1750 is most marked; raw cotton grew at the rate of 7·1 per cent per annum, between 1770 and 1850 though there was a dramatic slowing down to 1 per cent per annum during the years 1850 to 1912. This change was due to a number of reasons, not least the equating of supply more nearly with demand and the levelling-off process through the building-up of stocks and the operation of the Liverpool Cotton Market; secondly, to the shortages caused by the cotton famine in the 1860s and, later, to the carriage of cotton direct to Manchester via the Ship Canal. Since cotton was such an important item in the port's import trade before 1850, the slackening in the rate of growth after that date may help to offer a partial explanation of a similar falling-off in the rate of growth of shipping tonnage using the port *after* 1850. The effect of the more highly diversified list of commodities can be judged from the following annual rates of growth after 1785; cocoa (1785–1810), 13.5 per cent; coffee (1785–1810), 5.2 per cent; rum (1785–1850), 2.3 per cent, with no break in intermediate years; in grain and allied products there is also rapid growth from 1810 to 1850; flour (with a low base year) rose at an annual rate of 12.6 per cent, while American wheat imports rose at the rate of 5.8 per cent. Thereafter, from the years from 1852 to 1913, the evidence of expansion in the grain trade is displayed in rates of growth as follows: wheat, 3.9 per cent, barley, 2.4, oats, 1.2. For all grain combined, the rate of growth, after 1852, was 3.4 per cent per annum. These percentages merely serve as emphasis to an already established fact, namely that as the relative importance of some major commodities declined, others, equally important, took their place. This may be a truism but it is, nevertheless, one which goes far to explaining the real nature of Liverpool's growth over a period of two centuries.

In the export trade, the two basic commodities in Liverpool's rise were coal and salt, but in the latter half of the eighteenth century there was a more highly diversified export list consisting of an increasing quantity of small items of manufacture. These are impossible to measure in the absence of any figures of volume. It is, therefore, not until the nineteenth century that a real indicator of Liverpool's export trade can be found to supply a reasonable source of measurement. This is provided by cotton piece-goods which accounted for more than 40 per cent of Liverpool's total exports after 1840. These exports showed a continuous rate of growth of 2.6 per cent per annum between 1852 and 1913. It was in the years after 1920 that the serious decline in Liverpool's trade with India took place and, as a consequence, her share of the export of cotton piece-goods began to diminish. This caused a fundamental change in the pattern of Liverpool's outward cargoes and led, as we have seen, to a concentration on other manufactured goods, such as metal products, machinery, road vehicles and chemicals.

If we turn next to figures of shipping tonnage entering the Mersey, some interesting points of correlation begin to appear. Between 1716 and 1914, there were three distinct periods of growth. *periods* The first, from 1716 to 1744, when there was a low rate of growth of 0·7 per cent per annum; the second, from 1744 to 1851, was a period of rapid growth estimated at an annual rate of 4·9 per cent and the third period, from 1851 to 1914, with a growth rate of 2·6 per cent. This indicates a distinct break in the trend in 1851, a break which is identifiable with similar breaks in the rates of growth of cotton imports and, incidentally, with that of population which showed an annual increase of 2·9 per cent between 1705 and 1831 and 1·8 per cent from 1831 to 1921.[3] It will be recalled that the previous figures of tonnage entering the Mersey from 1860 onwards gave a rate of growth of 2·8 per cent per annum.[4] There is little to choose between this figure and the 2·6 per cent per annum calculated for the longer period from 1716. The inference is that up to the middle of the eighteenth century, the facilities which Liverpool could offer as a port, though increasing, were confined chiefly to the needs of her own industrial development. After 1750, however, the insistent pressure of demand from her hinterland, coupled with a broadening scope of trade in West African, West Indian, and South American products, raised levels of growth to an unprecedented height. Superimposed upon this diversification of trading interests was the added pressure of commercial relationship with the United States, at first in the supply of cotton and tobacco and later in that of grain. Furthermore, after 1813, trade with India was opened up to Liverpool ships and, after 1833, China and the Far East came within the acquisitive orbit of Liverpool's merchants and shipowners. Between 1750 and 1850, Liverpool was presented with the opportunity of trading with the whole world and, by a continuously improving system of road, canal and railway communication, of supplying all parts of the United Kingdom market. The establishment of Liverpool's maritime supremacy in the years from 1820 to 1860 was further evidence of the way in which opportunity was grasped and turned to account. After 1850, despite the coming of the steamship and the regularity and speeding-up of services to a wider range of markets, the pace of growth slackened. This was caused partly by growing competition from other ports, from growing competition from foreign shipping lines on all the major sea routes of the world and, above all, from a declining trend in Britain's own rate of industrial growth after 1880. Even so, there was still considerable scope (at least until 1914) for the employment of resources within a system that was becoming rather more established and conservative in operation; witness the growth of new trades and new shipping companies after 1870. Up to the outbreak of World War I, Liverpool's relative strength remained virtually unimpaired, even though the dynamism which had created that strength had long since passed its peak

By contrast, the years from 1920 to 1939 saw a considerable decline and a slackening of momentum in the activity of the port. As already stated, the trend rate for shipping entering the Mersey during this period was 0.7 per cent per annum. In the postwar period from 1945, however, there was a short revival. The projection from the rate of growth during the inter-war years shows that after 1949 there was a rapid increase to 1954–5 at a rate of 5.4 per cent per annum. This was caused by the growing volume of trade during the recovery period which ended in 1955. There followed a growth rate of 2.0 per cent from 1955 to 1963. The 1967 and 1968 figures show a distinct drop, very probably a consequence of mounting labour difficulties. If, however, one chooses to discount these latter figures, then the break in trend in 1955 seems obvious,[5] though, from 1955 to 1966, the growth is slightly lower at 1.7 per cent per annum. Alternatively, if one chose to represent the whole of the 1960s as a period of zero growth following two periods of rapid change (the first, to 1955, at 5.4 per cent per annum, the second, 1955–60 at 2.3 per cent), the trend would break in 1960. This interpretation, however, is probably less acceptable than that which indicates rapid growth, interrupted by excessive problems induced by labour unrest, managerial upheavals and growing competition from foreign ports and foreign shipping companies.

On the other hand, a rather more reliable indicator of the port's activity may be found in the figures of shipping using dock facilities (ie paying tonnage rates) as distinct from that entering the Mersey. From 1860 onwards, there was a steady rate of growth of 2.1 per cent per annum. This lasted until 1914. The next forty years, a period in which Liverpool's strength was sapped by the destruction of two world wars and by trade depression, witnessed general stagnation with a rate of growth of only 0·03 per cent per annum. After 1952–3, however, there was a good recovery at a rate of 3·5 per cent per annum, a trend which lasted until 1966. The reasons for a break in trend in this latter year have already been given. The decline since that date has been persistent, amounting to some 15 per cent below trend with further depressive tendencies.

Finally, we turn to the growth of investment in dock works and harbour facilities. These figures include expenditure not only on the building of docks, but also on the construction of warehouses. After 1840, the cost of a major part of warehouse and shed construction was included within the aggregate cost; before 1840, the amount expended by private warehouse companies has been assessed from general historical sources. One other explanation is necessary and will become apparent from the following figures. In order to obtain a more reliable comparison, all figures have been expressed in terms of 1968 prices. This operation, in itself, is subject to degrees of error arising from the conversion factor used—a matter of considerable relevance for figures before 1800.[6] Nevertheless, despite the lack of statistical precision, the figures give a general picture over a period of two hundred years.

	Actual Investment	At 1968 prices	Annual average rate of growth
	£ million	£ million	per cent
1709–1830	2·5	29·4	0·24
1830–1860	3·1	31·1	1·0
1860–1870	6·4	58·5	5·32
1870–1890	10·4	88·3	4·21
1890–1900	5·5	49·6	4·51
1900–1909	8·0	68·6	6·86

Before 1860, the figures refer only to expenditure on the Liverpool side of the river, after that date they include those for construction at Birkenhead and incorporate liabilities incurred there before 1858. There is some ambiguity arising from the time periods involved, all such periods having an overlap in one year (ie 1830, 1860, 1870 etc).

If these overlaps were eliminated, however, the overall result would not be significantly altered.

The first and most obvious conclusion to be drawn is that investment grew faster than pressure of demand for dock space. Between 1860 and 1909, tonnage using the port virtually trebled, whereas investment (at current prices) increased nearly sixfold. Converted into 1968 prices there was a fourfold increase. This was more nearly in line with the increase in the volume of cargoes, but this should not be taken to imply that, pound for pound, there was a corresponding increase in the areas of accommodation. It is, rather, a reflection of rising costs of construction, of the more capital intensive requirements of a steamship, as opposed to a sailing-ship port, and of the needs of passenger-liner owners as distinct from cargo-liner and tramp-steamer operators. The second striking fact is that Jesse Hartley's works, both as to area provided and for solidity of construction, were much cheaper per unit than subsequent systems. Again, such a statement needs qualification. While some of Jesse Hartley's docks were designed for steamships, the majority were for sailing ships. These ships required less elaborate (and, therefore, cheaper) dock installations and berthing facilities than did steamships. In short, though the pace of investment increased to something in advance of anticipated needs, the effectiveness of such investment was contained by rapid change in technological terms. Even so, in the 56 years between 1858 and 1914, the Mersey Docks and Harbour Board had raised some £31.5 million in an endeavour to meet the needs and give a surety to future expansion.

In whatever way one may care to measure the achievement and enterprise on Merseyside over the past two hundred and fifty years, the record is one of astonishing growth, growth very often in times of adversity and despite unpropitious physical difficulties. Perhaps the most dynamic growth was during the century from 1750 to 1850 in terms of port usage; but one cannot fail to ascribe to the period 1870 to 1914 the golden age of material prosperity. The steamship transformed both the commercial and economic horizons. The spirit and the momentum which it created have not been sustained since the end of the first world war, though there were periods in time of war and in the equally dark days of depression when a sense of urgency prevailed; but, since 1966, conditions have changed in a more distinct and drastic way. The future of the port, once so securely an article of faith, is now less sure and less capable of

discernment than at any time in its long history. In 1965, Liverpool's
share of total United Kingdom trade was 18·3 per cent;[7] her share
of total imports had fallen to 16·2 per cent and her share of exports
(including re-exports) to 20·7 per cent. Thus, under conditions of an
expanding world trade, Liverpool's share has fallen in recent years.
The implication must be that she was losing trade to other ports,
both British and European, which had a lower cost structure and
more efficient systems of cargo handling.

III

The disturbing nature of the magnitude of the problems, outlined
above, is likely to be accentuated by other considerations of a lasting
character. One cannot escape the conclusion that, in the field of
labour relations, Merseyside has presented a bad image to the world.
On the one hand, the employers see strike action as a frustrating
challenge to their competitive strength, while dockworkers regard
such activity as legitimate in the interest of livelihood and in the
maintenance of standards of living. The damaging effects of militant
and, very often, unofficial strike action has had a reaction on the
policy of shipping companies and upon that of the Dock Board.
The problem of uncertainty in labour relations has been further
exacerbated in recent years by changes in the cost structure of the
port. Whereas, in the past, a shipping company could usually cover
rising costs by an increase in receipts, the past six years have shown
that this is no longer the case. In general terms, costs (mainly labour)
have risen sixfold while shipping earnings have risen twofold.
There has thus been a tendency for ships which have for generations
used the port of Liverpool to seek out cheaper ports. In this context,
continental ports, such as Rotterdam and Antwerp, have profited
greatly at Liverpool's expense. The first inevitable conclusion is that,
if Merseyside is to maintain a rate of growth in the future comparable with that in past times of prosperity, the existence of a large
dock labour force is no longer a viable factor in the make-up of the
port. The answer must lie in intensive mechanisation of the dock
system. In the second place and as a corollary, the coming of container traffic must be given adequate port facilities in which a highly
skilled man can operate large volumes of cargo by electrically
controlled and automatic systems; this also presupposes that much

cargo movement could be controlled by computer-programming and that ships of an optimal size be used for specific sea routes.[8] Already some of these ideas are in process of realisation through the building of a new container port north of Gladstone.

Good intentions, however, may not always work out profitably in practice. The great Ocean group, the outgrowth from Alfred Holt's Blue Funnel line, capitalised at over £140 million, with more than 100 ships, is one of four partners in Overseas Containers Ltd. This consortium, which operates container services to Australia, now plans to mount a bigger container service to the Far East. In a few years it is anticipated that more than half of Ocean's business will find its way into containers. 'I would think,' stated Sir John Nicholson, the chairman of Ocean's, 'that during the next decade, containers look like being the most economic vehicle for the vast majority of manufactured goods. However, it is a precision operation which depends on the ability to rely on precise port operations not yet found in the less developed parts of the world. I do not think that it will extend in a hurry to Africa or, for the same reason, to parts of Asia.'[9] Nevertheless, despite initial difficulties, the implications are plain for all to see. Most of Britain's cargo-liner trades will be eventually carried by one or other of the two container consortia, Overseas Containers and Associated Container Transportation. As already stated, Blue Funnel and other associated companies are members of the former consortium, while Harrisons are members of the latter.

Under agreements controlling the operations of these consortia, all trade, when in containers, passes from the control of individual companies to the container companies. As a corollary to this, the emphasis has tended to shift away from shipping and dock services (though these are still needed) to skilled operations in road and other land transport. Thus, the new consortia are staffed by men trained in land as well as in sea transport. It is the land movement of containers which is the critical part of the operation for it is precisely at this point that the whole system might break down. Running the ships is comparatively simple for an experienced organisation; it is (again according to Sir John Nicholson) the misuse of containers and land transport which costs money and makes the difference between profit and loss on the overall operation. To overcome initial difficulties for their Australian trade, Blue Funnel and associates have built six ships accommodating about 1,400 containers each. This, however, is but an interim stage in a prospectively extensive business.

The final question to pose is how does Merseyside compare with other ports in being able to offer facilities for this new type of traffic? The answer should depend primarily on three factors: the relative cost advantage or disadvantage of Liverpool's geographical position; the effectiveness of Merseyside's system of communications with the rest of the country; and finally, the effectiveness of local government authority to institute, regulate and control services within the area. At the moment, the signs are not auspicious. Apart from the underlying consideration of Liverpool's present cost structure, it seems likely that, if container ships have to cover continental Europe as well as the United Kingdom simultaneously, they will not call at Liverpool. This is because of the geographical disadvantages of doing so when ships are running on tight schedules. In such circumstances, therefore, Liverpool would be used only when the distribution of cargoes makes Liverpool a convenient port. In basic terms, Merseyside is better situated, geographically, than any other port for container trade with North America. In the development of internal communications something has already begun with the building of a second Mersey Tunnel, linking Merseyside with the principal motorways; but the problem of a well-planned system throughout the area as a whole still lacks drive and a constructively prepared scheme. To a large extent, this problem is bound up with spheres of local authority as well as with that of finance. Whether or not the Redcliffe Maud proposals for a more unified system of government within a metropolitan area will be accepted is a matter of future concern. The need certainly exists for an overriding authority on such an important issue as communications and transport. The past history of Liverpool shows quite clearly that her life depended on efficient networks of roads, canals and railways. The Corporation and the citizens of Liverpool were always conscious of the need for promotional effort in this particular sphere of economic development. It is inconceivable that they should now disregard either the wisdom, judgement and experience of her progenitors or the lessons which can usefully be learnt from history.

There is, however, one big difference between the Liverpool of the 1960s and that of the 1860s. In the eighteenth and early nineteenth centuries, the merchants, shipowners, manufacturers and dock workers were more closely identified with the port than they are today. The capital stock of their various enterprises was as much a Liverpool entity as the men who managed it and the employees who worked for it. The Claytons, Williamsons, Gladstones, Athertons, Bensons, Gregsons, and Roscoes, no less than the Holts, Rathbones, Booths, and Harrisons took an active part in the government of the town as well as in the sponsoring of social and cultural activity. It will be remembered that Paul Mantoux asserted that Liverpool's commercial expansion was, in the eighteenth century running parallel to the rest of the country. Her merchants and shipowners, bankers and insurance brokers, had wielded a powerful influence on the direction of a national economic policy. Liverpool has lost this supremacy. Independence in cotton and insurance has gone; many of her shipping lines are part of groups with their headquarters in London. The upsurge of new industries in the area, such as the motor industry, is a vital factor in the port's development; but, almost in every case, the industrial companies are offshoots of larger companies based elsewhere. The men in charge are not of Merseyside and, consequently, have no inbred interest in its welfare. For the most part, they can only form transient links and, therefore, it is not easy for them to provide a forum in which local pressures can develop.

What can be done to arrest these centrifugal tendencies? As these final words are being written, the news has been made public that the Far Eastern container trade is to leave Liverpool for Southampton. There is a strong opinion that other trades (such as that with South Africa) will follow. Do we face the prospect of the docks of Jesse Hartley and his successors being filled in? Can Britain allow her second largest port to go into a state of decline? Can the presently proposed nationalisation of our ports provide the answer to Merseyside's difficulties? Rhetorical questions, perhaps, but the future of Merseyside as a port is beset with incalculable problems. That it will continue to serve the country in particular bulk trades is certain; that it will be a container port of sorts is admitted; but will it ever again be a promoter of national economic growth as it was in the years of King Cotton?

IV

In view of Liverpool's past history, it would be a grave mistake to end this survey on a pessimistic note. Much time, thought, and energy have already been given to the future of Liverpool's role in the country's economy. The motivation for this undoubtedly derives from a committee set up by the Minister of Transport and headed by Lord Rochdale. As a result of its investigation the National Ports' Council was established with the object of creating central organisation for the collection and dissemination of knowledge covering every aspect of port working and development. Unfortunately the full implementation of the committee's recommendations have not taken place, whereby a National Port Authority would have been set up with non-operational responsibility directed towards the safeguarding of both local and national interests in port reorganisation. The need for such authority is obvious, though political decision may eventually dictate the structure as to form.

Let us, however, assume that such a national authority will be created. How could Liverpool profit from its coverage during the next decade? The premise must be set by the size of Britain's overseas trade and the types of transport likely to be demanded. Within the bounds of such authority, tanker traffic may be ignored for, though it will obviously be of great importance to the economy as a whole, one may assume that the oil companies will provide accurate statements of their needs, and that ports will continue to meet these needs without any serious obstruction to dry cargo requirements. According to recent estimates made by the National Ports Council, there may well be a rise of between 70 and 80 per cent in dry cargo handling by 1980.[10] It is much more difficult to ascertain how this increase in cargo will be carried. Air transport is a natural and possible source, since in recent years carriage of cargo by air has risen from 3 per cent to 12 per cent of total value of imports and exports. Much of this increase, however, is accounted for by the very high value (and low volume) of the traffic so despatched. It is unlikely, despite the growing capacity of the jet plane, that air transport could make serious inroads on the anticipated rapid rise in bulk cargo handling. Nevertheless, aircraft companies could take over some types of cargo from the normal and accepted channels of shipping companies. To meet such eventuality, ports must work more quickly and efficiently than in the past.

Turning next to the role of the ocean-going ship, it is becoming obvious that container ships will not be suitable for all types of trade. There may be some demand for so-called 'lash ships'[11] carrying barges loaded in various ways. The bulk carrier for primary commodities, developed so successfully in the 1950s, might well increase in size and require a whole new range of handling facilities. Such changes and improvements, presently under active consideration, are primarily designed to cut shipping costs, but their acceptance and use must, of necessity, require extensive alteration to port layout and general structure. We propose, therefore as a final exercise to apply the foregoing ideas to Liverpool herself in an endeavour to see how this port might profit from new ideas springing from present adversity. Let it be emphasised that the following scheme (which is basic, though capable of alteration in detail) is at source the result of forward-thinking by Liverpool's own shipowners and business men. To be adopted, it requires not only the goodwill, but also the capability of all sections in the port's service industries, of trade unionists, of administrative staffs, of shipowners and of transport workers as a whole. In essence, it represents something of the complexity which the evolution of the port of Liverpool will present to its planners, whoever they may be.

It has become obvious, through the course of this volume, that the privileged position which Liverpool and her river once held, now no longer obtains. Neither her hinterland nor her shipping and trade associations can pursue her traditional role as Britain's premier cargo-liner port. The outcome must be that Liverpool will have to find a new role based largely on specialised services, which will maintain the best of old business and attract new. How can this be done?

In the first place, the new container port north of Gladstone (at Seaforth) should be established by the late 1970s as a modern harbour, handling as much general cargo as now passes through the whole port. It will contain highly specialised berths for meat, grain, and timber, together with container facilities to compete, on more than favourable terms, with any other port in the country. In the second place, as the ports of our southern coasts become more congested (as they are likely to do, should Britain enter the Common Market) a west-coast terminal at Liverpool, served by liner trains with roll-on roll-off facilities, might be a nationally desirable development. What, then, of Jesse Hartley's monuments on the east side of the Mersey and the extensive systems of docks at Birkenhead on the west? The essential point to grasp is that, as a result of operations at Seaforth, Liverpool will have, for the first time in a hundred years, dock space to spare. Such space will not only enable transport to be marshalled intelligently, but will provide facilities for efficient cargo-handling. By 1975, it should be possible to take whole docks out of commission, demolish old sheds and fill in between piers to provide areas of land faced on three sides by modern sheds. In such circumstances, whole parts of the existing dock estate could be reallocated to specific trades and for specific functions. For example, it is suggested that the area from Prince's dock to the south side of Bramley Moore would be suitable for a new Irish sea terminal, including container-loading depots, self-adjusting ramps and marshalling yards. This terminal could not only make Liverpool the central port for trade between Ireland and the United Kingdom, but also for much of the Irish trade with Scandinavian, German, and Belgian ports. Finally, as standards of living increase, there will be growing demands for such things as berths in King's and Harrington docks, but further development is impeded by the limitations of the south dock systems. By redesigning the docks between the proposed new Irish terminal and Huskisson as a fruit-importing complex (including a wholesale market, air conditioned warehouses, banking and telex facilities) Liverpool would be able to offer amenities to attract all the fruit and vegetables likely to be consumed between the Severn and the Clyde. Huskisson dock could then become a general cargo-loading terminal for the ships that had discharged at the fruit complex. Further to the north, Gladstone, Langton, Canada, Brocklebank and Alexandra docks, backed by the Birkenhead system, would be able to cope with residual conventional trades.[12] It is conceivable that if the predictions of the National Ports Council are well based, the volume of such residual traffic handled by Liverpool in 1980 will be only slightly less than the total conventional cargo passing through the port today.

During the next ten years, it is reasonably certain that there will be industrial development along the banks of the Mersey and the Manchester Ship Canal. Many of the industries, so sited, will be able to make use of lash services for the carriage of their products.

These services could be adequately located south of the Tranmere oil jetties while, at the same time, a barge-parking pool could be established in the south-end docks. Barge terminals of this kind could also be under cover, the barges being docked at right angles to the quay and served by gantries running from the shed area over the water.[13] Such facilities are already in operation at some continental ports, such as Hamburg.

Is this projected reorganisation of Liverpool's port services nothing more than fantasy, the pipe dream of a few forward-looking Liverpool businessmen? Certainly not. Some part of the proposal is already in process of construction and the resultant development is a logical extension of the new works. The realisation of the whole, however, depends primarily on two factors: first, upon the capability of men to solve Liverpool's problems within the framework of national need and, secondly, upon the goodwill and determination of Merseyside's citizens themselves to grasp at these possibilities, apply and work them, and thus prevent such ideas and their fulfilment from passing to other ports.

If there is anything in the foregoing pages worthy of notice, it is the fact that Liverpool's capacity for recovery, in times of adversity, has been that of the capacity of men and women to act in defence of their river and their port. It is a spirit which may take a variety of forms, from defiance in the face of aerial bombardment to the vociferous rivalry between the supporters of the two first division football teams. The hope must be that the native intelligence of Merseyside's own citizens will be adequate for the promotion of her continuing prosperity, for the preservation of a dynamic self-interest and for the application of that self-interest in the wider perspective of Britain and the world as a whole.

Notes

The following abbreviations are used:

Blue Funnel	Hyde, F. E. *Blue Funnel: A History Alfred Holt & Co of Liverpool 1865–1914* (1965).
Mountfield	Mountfield, Stuart. *Western Gateway: A History of the Mersey Docks and Harbour Board* (1965).
Shipping Enterprise	Hyde, F. E. *Shipping Enterprise and Management: Harrisons of Liverpool* (1967).
THSLC	*Transactions of the Historic Society of Lancashire and Cheshire.*

NOTES TO CHAPTER 1

1. J. A. Picton, *Memorials of Liverpool* (1873), vol 2, 2–3. Picton examines the documentary evidence for the origins of Liverpool castle.
2. J. A. Twemlow, *Liverpool Town Books, 1550–1862* (1918), vol 1, 280 (hereafter cited LTB). A list of Liverpool ships dated 12 November 1565 included *Thaygle* (40 tons), *George* (36), *Saviour* (30) and *Bartholemewe* (16). Ten barques and two boats together totalled 223 tons, and employed 75 seamen.
3. Estimates based on freemen's and other rolls; see T. N. Morton, *Extracts from the First Minute Book of the Corporation of Liverpool.*

4. LTB, vol 1, 107, 247, *et passim*.
5. W. Fergusson Irvine, *Liverpool in the Reign of Charles II* (1889), 89, 91.
6. LTB, vol 1, 129, 398.
7. LTB, vol 2, 45.
8. *ibid*.
9. Municipal records, 19 December 1611 and 25 October 1619; quoted by J. Picton, *Selections from the Municipal Archives and Records* (1883), 179. Atkinson produced salt at 1s a bushell, whereas Breton salt sold at an average of 2s 4d a bushell.
10. LTB, vol 1, 179; vol 2, 149, 172.
11. LTB, vol 2, 786.
12. LTB, *passim*.
13. Irvine, *Liverpool. . .* , 99–100.
14. Picton Library, Moore Papers, 920 MOO 315.
15. Apart from records in H. Peet, *Liverpool Vestry Books* (2 vols, 1912–15), see H. A. Ormerod, *The Liverpool Free School, 1515–1803* (1951), 22.
16. D. Defoe, *A Tour thro' the whole Island of Great Britain* (1724–1727), (ed) G. D. H. Cole (1927), vol 2, 665.
17. H. Peet, *Liverpool in the Reign of Queen Anne* (1908), 130.
18. Irvine, *Liverpool . . .* , 104.

NOTES TO CHAPTER 2

1. For a short account of the Collins chart, see J. B. Harley, 'Ogilby and Collins: Cheshire by Road and Sea', *Cheshire Round*, 1 no 7 (1967), 210–25.
2. See particularly the Chart of the Harbour of Liverpool by P. Burdett, published in W. Enfield, *An Essay towards the History of Liverpool* (1774); and a cartographic survey of the country surrounding Liverpool published in T. Troughton, *The History of Liverpool* (1810).
3. C. Morris (ed), *The Journeys of Celia Fiennes* (1947), 180.
4. Public Record Office, Liverpool Ports Books 1704–11, E 190/1365/18, E 190/1370/11, E 190/1380/6. The author is indebted to Mrs Brenda Poole for permission to quote figures from her unpublished thesis 'Liverpool's Trade in the Reign of Queen Anne' (Liverpool MA, 1960).

5. This map, somewhat stylised, shows that Liverpool had expanded since 1710 by the addition of some 25 streets.
6. 8 Anne, c 12 (1709).
7. LTB, *passim*; *Reasons humbly offered to the Honourable House of Commons against laying a Duty on ships towards building a Dock at Liverpool, which they cannot make use of* (1709).
8. C. Northcote Parkinson, *The Rise of the Port of Liverpool* (1952), 80.
9. Estimated from relevant Minutes in Liverpool Town Books and from title deeds of land transferred in Derby MSS and Okill Papers, Picton Library.
10. *ibid*.
11. W. H. Chaloner, 'Charles Roe of Macclesfield (1715–81): an Eighteenth Century Industrialist', *Transactions of the Lancashire and Cheshire Antiquarian Society*, vol 63 (1952–3), 55. The copper works opened in 1768.
12. Estimates compiled from Dock Acts and privately owned title deeds in Municipal Records, Derby MSS and Okill Papers.
13. For the calculation of this estimate see below, note 22.
14. Abstracts of title deeds, 1725–60.
15. Irvine, *Liverpool . . .*, 99–100.
16. Leyland and Bullin Papers, Memorandum of assets, 1812; see also Picton, *Memorials*, vol 2, 159.
17. Lancashire Record Office, will of Moses Benson, dated 15 May 1806, probate granted 27 June 1806.
18. Abstract of deeds on land known as Higher Weaver, Lower Weaver and Black Half Acre, 1797 to date, used by kind permission of Mr T. Whitley Moran.
19. *Diary of Nicholas Blundell of Crosby*, (ed) Rev T. E. Gibson (1895), 154; see also J. R. Harris, 'The Employment of Steam Power in the Eighteenth Century', *History*, vol 7 (1967), 133–48; and T. C. Barker and J. R. Harris, *A Merseyside Town in the Industrial Revolution: St Helens 1750–1900* (1954), 55–6.
20. T. Baines, *History of the Commerce and Town of Liverpool* (1852), 418, quoting a secondary source.
21. *ibid*.
22. This figure represents initial expenditure on ships built over the period 1740–50. It is not, therefore, a figure of current value. It is calculated on an average of 2,300 tons per annum at building costs given in Fisher and Grayson's Ships' Books, of

average £8 per ton, plus £6 per ton for prime fitting out. Thus, expenditure on ships built amounted to £322,000. To this must be added some £25,000 for ships in the process of building, making a total of £347,000. These costs compare with those quoted by R. Davis, *The Rise of the English Shipping Industry* (1962), 374, though fitting costs seem to have been lower in Liverpool than in London. See also R. Stewart-Brown, *Liverpool Ships in the Eighteenth Century* (1932), 7–15.

23. L. S. Pressnell, *Country Banking in the Industrial Revolution* (1906), relevant references to Liverpool.
24. F. E. Hyde, B. B. Parkinson and S. Marriner, 'The Port of Liverpool and the Crisis of 1793', *Economica*, new series, 18 (1951), 363–78.
25. G. Wills, *English Pottery and Porcelain* (1969), 292–304.
26. The author is greatly indebted to Mr Alan Smith, Keeper of Ceramics and Applied Art, Liverpool Museum, for information about the Herculaneum Pottery works. His book, *An Illustrated Guide to Liverpool Herculaneum Pottery* (1970), is an authoritative work on the subject.
27. F. A. Bailey and T. C. Barker, 'The Seventeenth Century Origins of Watchmaking in South-West Lancashire', *Liverpool and Merseyside: essays in the Economic and Social History of the Port and its Hinterland*, (ed) J. R. Harris (1969), 1–15.
28. Picton, *Memorials*, vol 2, 179.
29. H. A. Ormerod, *Liverpool Free School*, 15–28; for the wills of William Clayton and Richard Houghton, see H. Peet, *Liverpool in the Reign of Queen Anne*, 139, 144.
30. P. Mantoux, *The Industrial Revolution in the Eighteenth Century* (1928), 110.

NOTES TO CHAPTER 3

1. Lancashire Record Office, Probate records; information kindly supplied by Mr R. Sharpe France.
2. Public Record Office, Liverpool Port Books, 1700–15, quoted in Mrs Brenda Poole's thesis, 'Liverpool's Trade in the Reign of Queen Anne', Appendix I, Tables 1(a) and 1(b).
3. *ibid.*
4. Picton Library, Newspaper Files. An analysis of ships' cargoes

entering Liverpool for quinquennial years from 1785 to 1835 Main sources used were: for 1785–1810, Corrie's Merchant Handbills, *Liverpool General Advertiser, Billinge's Liverpool Advertiser, Liverpool Chronicle and Commercial Advertiser, Liverpool Courier and Commercial Advertiser*; after 1815, *Gore's General Advertiser.*

5. Municipal Records, 13 October 1648; the tobacco was brought in by Jenkinson in the *Friendship* and sold to Mr Shepard.

6. C. N. Parkinson, 54, quoting from Blundell's Diary.

7. Holt and Gregson MSS, vol 10, 253.

8. Municipal Records, 19 December 1611 and 25 October 1619; quoted by J. Picton, *Selections from the Municipal Archives*, 179.

9. Blackburne petitioned the Common Council in June 1696 to be permitted to establish a refinery (LTB, 3 & 29 June 1696). Thomas Johnson was associated with the Dungeon Salt works, near Hale, afterwards taken over by John Ashton (see T. C. Barker, 'Lancashire Coal, Cheshire Salt and the Rise of Liverpool', *THSLC*, vol 103 (1951), 93, note 7.

10. T. S. Willan, *The Navigation of the River Weaver in the Eighteenth Century*, Chetham Society, 3rd series (1951), 39–40.

11. W. Enfield, *An Essay towards the History of Liverpool*, 87–8.

12. From an estimate made in 1773 it was calculated that 15 cwt of coal was needed to produce 20 cwt of white salt. Based on this ratio, the demand for coal from Cheshire salt boilers must have increased from approximately 4,000 to 12,000 tons between 1732 and 1750; see A. F. Calvert, *Salt in Cheshire* (1915), 284, 942.

13. This included improvements to the navigation of the Weaver; Willan, *passim.*

14. T. C. Barker, 'The Sankey Navigation', *THSLC*, vol 100 (1948), 126.

15. *ibid.*

16. *ibid*; from a letter transcribed by F. A. Bailey from the vicar of Prescot to the provost of King's College, Cambridge, 7 April 1759, in which it was stated that the price of coal had been raised and continued 'for four or five years past'.

17. The Common Council ordered two surveyors to make a survey of the Sankey Brook (then called Dallam Brook). One of the surveyors was Henry Berry, who was afterwards responsible for constructing the canal, and who was the Liverpool Dock Engineer, 1752–89.

18. Among the petitioners were James Crosbie (mayor), Charles Goore, Richard Trafford, John Ashton and John Blackburne Jnr.
19. T. C. Barker, 'Lancashire Coal . . .'.
20. *Parliamentary Report on the Sankey Navigation* (1771).
21. The proposed site of this dock is marked on the Perry map of 1769.
22. W. Enfield, 80–8.
23. Troughton, *History of Liverpool*, 264.
24. Willan, 219–20.
25. Anonymous, *Remarks on the Salt Trade of the counties of Chester and Lancaster* (1804), 11–12.
26. Willan, 224–8.
27. The Davies-Davenport Papers and other voyage accounts confirm this. The Davies-Davenport Papers, now housed at Keele, were originally used by kind permission of Mr Raymond Richards of Gawsworth, Cheshire.
28. Records of the *Liverpool Merchant*, which sailed to Barbados in 1700 carrying 220 negroes.
29. Davies-Davenport Papers; Letter Book, William Davenport to captain of the *King of Prussia* (May 1771).
30. F. E. Hyde, B. B. Parkinson and S. Marriner, 'The Nature and Profitability of the Liverpool Slave Trade', *Economic History Review*, 2nd series, vol V (1953), 368–77; also B. B. Parkinson, 'A Slaver's Accounts', *Accountancy Research*, vol 2 (1951), 144–50.
31. R. Pares, *A West Indian Fortune* (1950), 280–92.
32. Analysis of voyages made, from the Davies-Davenport records and other ships' voyage accounts in the Picton Library and other privately owned sources.
33. For a full discussion, see Hyde, Parkinson and Marriner, 'The Nature and Profitability of the Liverpool Slave Trade'.
34. J. E. Merritt, 'The Triangular Trade', *Business History*, vol 3 no 1 (1960), 1–7.
35. Lancashire Record Office, Probate Records. From information supplied by Mr R. Sharpe France.
36. Holt and Gregson MSS, vol 10, 444.
37. Picton Library, Newspaper Files, *passim*.
38. F. Armytage, *The Free Port System in the British West Indies: a study of commercial policy, 1766–1822* (1953), *passim*.

39. These differentiations of market have been calculated from cargo lists and other relevant information in Liverpool newspaper sources.

40. Hyde, Parkinson and Marriner, 'The Port of Liverpool and the Crisis of 1793', 363–78.

41. J. Wheeler, *Manchester, its Political, Commercial and Social History* (1836).

42. T. S. Ashton, *Economic Fluctuations in England, 1700–1800* (1959), 171.

43. B. H. Tolley, 'The Liverpool Campaign against the Orders in Council and the War of 1812', *Liverpool and Merseyside*, 131. In terms of tonnage there was a fall from 734,000 tons in 1810 to 446,000 tons in 1812.

44. *ibid*.

45. R. Stewart-Brown, *Liverpool Ships in the Eighteenth Century*, 5.

46. *ibid*, 32.

47. F. Neal, 'Liverpool Shipping in the early Nineteenth Century', *Liverpool and Merseyside*, 170.

48. *ibid*, 166.

49. T. C. Barker, 'Lancashire Coal and Cheshire Salt', 98.

50. C. Walford, *A Review of the Causes which have led to the Commercial Greatness of Liverpool* (1883), *passim*.

51. T. C. Barker, *Pilkington Brothers and the Glass Industry* (1960), 130ff; also T. C. Barker and J. R. Harris, *A Merseyside Town in the Industrial Revolution, passim*.

52. T. Baines, *History of the Commerce and Town of Liverpool*, 768; also D. W. F. Hardie, *A History of the Chemical Industry in Widnes* (1950).

53. Minute Books of the West India Association, 1799–1807.

54. References from *Gazeta de Buenos Aires*, 1813–14, 1817 and 1819, kindly supplied by Mr A. G. E. Jones.

55. W. O. Henderson, 'The American Chamber of Commerce in Liverpool', *THSLC*, vol 85 (1935), 1–61.

56. G. S. Veitch, *The Struggle for the Liverpool and Manchester Railway* (1930), 21–3; fr additional information on the Liverpool financial interest in the line, see H. Pollins, 'The Finances of the Liverpool and Manchester Railway', *Economic History Review*, 2nd series, vol V (1952), 90–7; also R. E. Carlson, *The Liverpool and Manchester Railway Project, 1821–31* (1969), 64ff.

NOTES TO CHAPTER 4

1. H. A. Ormerod, *The Liverpool Royal Institution* (1953), 9.
2. *Catalogue of the Library of William Roscoe* (1816).
3. R. Brooke, *Liverpool during the last quarter of the Eighteenth Century*, 71–4.
4. *ibid*.
5. R. Anderson, *White Star* (1964), 41.
6. Compiled from T. Baines, 773ff.
7. This was an outgrowth from earlier commercial developments as described in R. Davis, *A Commercial Revolution* (1967), 22.
8. F. E. Hyde, *Shipping Enterprise and Management: Harrisons of Liverpool* (1967), 9–10.
9. Cammell Laird & Co, *Builders of Great Ships* (1959), 9.
10. *ibid*, 12.
11. For the story of Alfred Holt's experiments on the steamship, see F. E. Hyde, *Blue Funnel: a History of Alfred Holt & Company of Liverpool, 1865–1914* (1956), 9–19.
12. *Shipping Enterprise*, 22.
13. A. C. Wardle, *Steam conquers the Pacific* (1940), 106ff.
14. For a description of these technical problems, see H. J. Dyos and D. H. Aldcroft, *British Transport* (1969), 243ff.
15. *ibid*, 239.
16. D. Lobley (ed), *The Cunarders* (published for the Company, 1969), 27. The American end is admirably covered by R. G. Albion, *The Rise of New York Port, 1815–60* (Scribner's, 1939, reprinted by Archon, Hambden, Connecticut, 1961), especially chapter 15.
17. *ibid*, 31.
18. *ibid*.
19. From information kindly supplied by Mr Philip Cottrell of the Department of Economic History, University of Liverpool.
20. *Blue Funnel*, 32ff.
21. *Shipping Enterprise*, 23ff.
22. From information kindly supplied by Dr P. N. Davies of the Department of Economic History, University of Liverpool. The material from his two theses—'Sir Alfred Jones and the Development of West African Trade' (Liverpool MA, 1964) and 'British Shipping and the Growth of the West African

Economy, 1910–50' (Liverpool PhD, 1967)—has been incorporated and will shortly be published as a history of Elder Dempsters.

23. *Shipping Enterprise*, 47, 52ff.
24. S. Marriner, *Rathbones of Liverpool, 1845–73* (1961), 18.
25. *Blue Funnel*, 29, 30.
26. Marriner, *Rathbones*, 90–4.
27. For information about the Swires, see S. Marriner and F. E. Hyde, *The Senior: John Samuel Swire, 1825–98* (1967), 10ff.
28. *Blue Funnel*, 33ff.
29. *ibid*, 35–6.
30. Marriner and Hyde, *The Senior*, chapters 4 and 5.
31. P. N. Davies, 'Sir Alfred Jones and the Development of West African Trade', for Liverpool's connection with West Africa.
32. *Merchant Adventure* (printed for John Holt & Co, undated), 22; also *The Diary of John Holt and the Voyage of the Maria*, (ed) Cecil R. Holt (1948), 136ff.
33. D. Williams, 'Liverpool Merchants and the Cotton Trade, 1820–50', *Liverpool & Merseyside*, 182–211.
34. *Shipping Enterprise*, 23–4.
35. *ibid*, 33–4.
36. *Report of the Liverpool Steam Ship Owners' Association* (1880).
37. G. Chandler, *Liverpool Shipping* (1960), 120.
38. Anderson, *White Star*, 42ff.
39. F. E. Hyde, *Mr Gladstone at the Board of Trade* (1934), 202ff.
40. W. O. Henderson, 'The Liverpool Office in London', *Economica*, 42 (1933), 473–9.
41. Enfield, *An Essay towards the History of Liverpool*, 24–5.
42. *A General and Descriptive History of Liverpool* (1797), 68–70; quoted by R. Lawton, 'Genesis of Population', *Merseyside: a Scientific Survey*, (ed) W. Smith (1953), 120.
43. R. Lawton, *ibid*, 122.

NOTES TO CHAPTER 5

1. T. Baines, *History of the Commerce and Town of Liverpool*, 349.
2. Minutes of Council, 11 January 1737.

3. R. Brooke, *Liverpool during the last quarter of the Eighteenth Century*, 99.
4. 2 Geo III, c 86, preamble and clauses; Brooke, 99–100.
5. *ibid.*
6. *ibid.*
7. Preamble to the Act 25 Geo III, c 15.
8. S. A. Harris and T. C. Barker, 'Henry Berry (1719–1812): an inventory of his professional papers', vol 112, 57–63.
9. Picton, *Memorials of Liverpool*, vol 1, 642.
10. 6 Geo IV, c 186; see also Stuart Mountfield, *Western Gateway* (1965), 2–3. For details of the important step towards a more autonomous Port Authority, see S. Mountfield, 'Liverpool Docks and the Municipal Commissioners' Inquiry of 1833 for Liverpool', *THSLC*, vol 115 (1963), 163–74.
11. 9 Geo IV, c 55; 11 Geo IV, c 14; 4 Vic, c 30; 7 & 8 Vic, c 30.
12. Picton, *Memorials*, vol I, 654.
13. Roderick Stephenson, 'The Development of the Liverpool Dock System', *Transactions of the Liverpool Nautical Research Society*, vol 8 (1953–4, 1954–5), 61–75.
14. The Report of Thomas Telford, Robert Stevenson and Alexander Nimmo (16 May 1828), recommended two extensive sea ports on the rivers Dee and Mersey adjacent to Liverpool, with a floating harbour or ship canal to connect them.
15. 7 & 8 Vic, c 79; for further information, see T. Webster, *The Port and Docks of Birkenhead* (1848), and *Minutes of Evidence and of Proceedings on the Liverpool and Birkenhead Dock Bills in the Sessions of 1848–52 and 1855–6* (2 vols, 1857), *passim*.
16. Birkenhead Town Hall Archives; letter from J. M. Rendel to Birkenhead Dock Commissioners, 14 August 1848, quoted in P. J. Emery, 'Wallasey Pool—the birth pangs of a Port' (unpublished thesis, University of Liverpool MA, 1959).
17. Webster, *Minutes of Evidence*, 24 May 1852.
18. Birkenhead Town Hall Archives; Robert Stephenson to J. M. Rendel, 24 July 1848, confirms his opinion that the docks were well-designed, substantially built and executed, and with every regard to economy. J. Murray, an engineer called upon by the Liverpool Dock Trustees to give an estimate, put the cost at £462,298.
19. *ibid.*

20. *Liverpool Mercury*, 7 June 1853.
21. P. J. Emery, 'Wallasey Pool', 93.
22. *ibid*.
23. Mountfield, 1–15.
24. Picton, *Memorials*, vol 2, 54, 55.
25. J. R. Kellet, *The Impact of Railways on Victorian Cities* (1969), 179.
26. Gladstone MSS; Memo on railways by W. E. Gladstone, 30 June 1847.
27. Hatfield MSS; Agent's report to the Marquis of Salisbury, 1850.
28. Gladstone MSS; W. E. Gladstone to the Earl of Derby, 14 February 1850. Cf Seymour Broadbridge, *Studies in Railway Expansion and the Capital Market in England, 1825–73* (1970), 123, 131.
29. Quoted in Kellet, 190.
30. See W. H. Chaloner, *The Social and Economic Development of Crewe* (1950), 19ff.
31. Kellet, 191.
32. *ibid*, 191.
33. *ibid*.
34. Smith, *Merseyside: a Scientific Survey*, 189.

NOTES TO CHAPTER 6

1. D. A. Farnie, *East and West of Suez* (1969).
2. *ibid*, 161.
3. *ibid*, 102.
4. *ibid*, 154.
5. Mountfield, 203–6, Appendix IV.
6. Trade and Navigation Returns for the United Kingdom, ports section, Liverpool and Birkenhead, 1913–14.
7. 'Customs Returns compiled by the Liverpool Chamber of Commerce, 1860–80', from material calculated by William Blood; see also W. O. Henderson, *The Lancashire Cotton Famine* (1934), *passim*.
8. Trade and Navigation Returns for the United Kingdom, 1900–1913; Table 9 for the year 1913.
9. *ibid*.

10. See below, chapter 9, page 160.
11. Freight schedules for the Calcutta, South Africa, West Indian Islands, China, Central and South American Shipping Conferences, 1875–1914. For documented reference see *Blue Funnel* and *Shipping Enterprise*; for a general statement, see D. C. North, 'Ocean Freight Rates and Economic Development, 1750–1913', *Journal of Economic History*, vol 18, no 4 (1958), 537–47.
12. *Blue Funnel*, 176.
13. *ibid*, 65.
14. *Shipping Enterprise*, 112.
15. *ibid*; also *Blue Funnel*, chapters V and VI.
16. Marriner and Hyde, *The Senior*, 115–18.
17. *ibid*, 64.
18. *Blue Funnel*, 56–69.
19. *ibid*, 70–5.
20. *ibid*, 90.
21. *ibid*, 76.
22. *ibid*, 126, showing average net earnings per voyage in the main trades.
23. *Shipping Enterprise*, 76.
24. From information supplied by Dr P. N. Davies, from his thesis 'Sir Alfred Jones'.
25. For details of these struggles, see Davies, 'Sir Alfred Jones', *passim*.
26. *ibid*; see also *Merchant Adventure* (Holt & Co).
27. C. Wilson, *The History of Unilever* (1954), vol 1, 34.
28. *Shipping Enterprise*, 5–9.
29. From information kindly supplied by Mr A. G. E. Jones.
30. A. H. John, *A Liverpool Merchant House* (1959), 96.
31. *ibid*, 102.
32. *Shipping Enterprise*, 45–55.
33. *ibid*, 58–9.
34. Charlotte Erickson, 'The Impact of Push and Pull', *Nordic Emigration*, Uppsala University Research Conference 1969, pp. 34–6.
35. *Shipping Enterprise*, 30.
36. *ibid*, 84.
37. *ibid*, 127.

NOTES TO CHAPTER 7

1. A. G. Kenwood, 'Port Investment in England and Wales, 1851–1913', *Yorkshire Bulletin*, 17 no 2 (1965), 156–67.
2. *ibid*.
3. Mountfield, 83.
4. *ibid*.
5. *ibid*.
6. *ibid*, 86.
7. *ibid*, 87.
8. B. Lubbock, *Last of the Windjammers* (1948 ed), vol I, 78; quoted by Mountfield, 36.
9. Mountfield, 36.
10. *ibid*, 22–3.
11. *Blue Funnel*, 61–6.
12. Mountfield, 37.
13. *ibid*, 38.
14. *ibid*.
15. *ibid*, 53.
16. *Blue Funnel*, 162–4.
17. Mountfield, 79.
18. *ibid*, 100.
19. Harrison Papers, Diary of Sir Thomas Harrison Hughes, 1905; see also Hyde, *Shipping Enterprise, passim*.
20. *ibid*.
21. Sir Rex Hodges, 'The Dock System of the Port of Liverpool', *Merseyside: a Scientific Survey*, 165.
22. *ibid*.
23. Mountfield, 124.
24. *ibid*, 31–2.
25. *ibid*.
26. *ibid*.
27. *ibid*, 33.
28. *ibid*, 118.
29. *ibid*, 119; see also *Blue Funnel*, 141.
30. Holt MSS, Minutes of the Ocean Steam Ship Company, 19 February 1913; see also R. W. Williams, *The Liverpool Docks Problem* (1912) and 'The First Year's working of the Liverpool

Dock Scheme', *Transactions of the Liverpool Economic and Statistical Society, Session 1913–14* (1914).

31. Barker & Harris, *A Merseyside Town in the Industrial Revolution*, 328–30.
32. *ibid.*
33. *ibid.*
34. *ibid.*
35. Holt MSS, Richard Holt's Diary, 12 February 1900.
36. *Hansard*, vol 277 (1883), 685ff; vol 279 (1883), 17–18; vol 282 (1883), 258–60, 512–13; vol 289 (1884), 1,372ff; vol 303 (1886), 233ff; vol 315 (1887), 1,345, 1,719; vol 316 (1887), 26ff.
37. *Blue Funnel*, 106.
38. *ibid*, 108.
39. *ibid*.
40. Holt MSS, Alfred Holt's Diary, under section B, 43ff.

NOTES TO CHAPTER 8

1. For the economic effects of this congestion, see D. H. Aldcroft, 'Port Congestion and the Shipping Boom of 1919–20', *Business History*, vol 3, no 2 (1961), 97–106. In the case of Liverpool, congestion was caused largely by unequal arrivals and disproportionate volumes of commodities.
2. Mountfield, 205, Appendix IV.
3. *ibid*.
4. S. G. Sturmey, *British Shipping and World Competition* (1962), 49, 50, 52, 56.
5. Mountfield, 129.
6. *ibid*, 130.
7. *ibid*, 133.
8. *ibid*, 133–4.
9. Sturmey, *British Shipping*, 36.
10. *ibid*.
11. *ibid*, 46–7.
12. *ibid*, 48.
13. *Liverpool Steamship Owners Association, 1858–1958* (1958), 28.
14. Sturmey, 48.

15. *ibid*.
16. Sturmey, 51–2.
17. Harrison MSS, Minutes of Board meetings, 1919 and 1920.
18. For a detailed account of the Far-Eastern trade, see F. E. Hyde, 'British Shipping Companies and East and South-East Asia, 1860–1939', *The Economic Development of South-East Asia*, (ed) C. D. Cowan (1964), 27–47.
19. A. McLellan, *A History of Mansfield and Company, 1920–33* (1953), part II, 4.
20. H. Leak, 'The carrying trade of British Shipping', *Journal of the Royal Statistical Society*, vol 102 (1939), for an analysis of tonnage figures; see also M. G. Kendall, 'United Kingdom Merchant Shipping Statistics', *Journal of the Royal Statistical Society*, vol 111 (1948), for the measurement of net income.
21. M. G. Kendall, 126.
22. *Shipping Enterprise*, 123ff.
23. A. H. John, *A Liverpool Merchant House*, 135.
24. *ibid*, 136ff; see also *Shipping Enterprise*, chapter VII and VIII, *passim*.
25. John, 141ff.
26. *ibid*, 139.
27. *Shipping Enterprise*, 148, 154, 173.
28. *ibid*, 164.
29. *ibid*, 160.
30. *ibid*, Apendix III.
31. Davies, 'British Shipping and the Growth of the West African Economy'.
32. *ibid*; P. N. Davies, PhD thesis.
33. Estimated from the statement of accounts and balance sheets for 1938–9.
34. Files of *Fairplay* for 1932 and 1933, *passim*.
35. Anderson, *White Star*, 165.
36. *ibid*, 181.
37. Wardle, *Steam conquers the Pacific*, 175–6.
38. Chandler, *Liverpool Shipping*, 134.
39. *Shipping Enterprise*, 155, 159.

NOTES TO CHAPTER 9

1. Trade and Navigation Returns of the United Kingdom, 1919–1939; imports expressed c.i.f. (ie including transport costs) and exports free on board (ie excluding transport costs).
2. *ibid*, relevant tables for individual ports.
3. G. C. Allen, F. E. Hyde, D. J. Morgan and W. J. Corlett, *The Import Trade of the Port of Liverpool* (1946), 20–4.
4. *ibid*.
5. A. Redford (ed), *Manchester Merchants and Foreign Trade; vol 2, 1850–1939* (1956), 285; see also *Import Trade*, 30.
6. *Import Trade*, 39.
7. *ibid*, 48.
8. Wilson, *History of Unilever*, vol 2, 326, 342.
9. *Import Trade*, 74–6.
10. *ibid*, 66–7.
11. *ibid*, 84.
12. Trade and Navigation Returns, 1919–39, ports section, tables relevant to Liverpool and Birkenhead.
13. Mountfield, 155.
14. *ibid*, 156.
15. *ibid*, 157.
16. *ibid*, 158.
17. Wilson, *History of Unilever*, vol 1, 277–8; also Mountfield, 159.
18. See Mountfield, 160, for a fuller account of these arrangements.
19. This figure included approximately 2 million tons of naval vessels applicable to previous years.
20. Figures supplied by kind permission of the Mersey Docks and Harbour Board.
21. *ibid*.
22. For more specific details, see D. E. Baines and R. Bean, 'The General Strike on Merseyside, 1926', *Liverpool & Merseyside*, 239–66.
23. *ibid*, 250.
24. *ibid*.
25. *ibid*, 253.
26. W. Smith, 'The Location of Industry', *Merseyside: a Scientific Survey*, 170–1.
27. *ibid*.

28. *ibid*.

29. From information kindly supplied by the Housing Department of Liverpool Corporation; also *Housing Progress, 1864–1951: City of Liverpool Housing* (1951), *passim*.

30. *The Port of Liverpool* (1950–1), compiled and edited by the Public Relations Department of the Mersey Docks and Harbour Board, 93.

31. V. E. Cotton, *The Book of Liverpool Cathedral* (1964), 7–8.

32. This included £24·6 millions for housing, at least £2 millions for dock schemes, £7·5 millions for the Mersey Tunnel, over £1 million for Speke Airport, and about £1·5 millions for the Philharmonic Hall and the new University Library; in addition, some £4 millions was expended on general works and improvements in the area.

NOTES TO CHAPTER 10

1. Mountfield, 169.
2. *ibid*, 171.
3. *ibid*.
4. Mersey Docks and Harbour Board, Annual Reports and Accounts, 1940–5.
5. *ibid*.
6. *ibid*.
7. Mountfield, 173.
8. *ibid*.
9. *ibid*, 174.
10. Mersey Docks and Harbour Board, Annual Reports and Accounts, 1946.
11. Mountfield, 179.
12. *ibid*, 180.
13. *ibid*, 182.
14. *ibid*, 183–4.
15. *ibid*, 189.
16. Trade and Navigation Returns of the United Kingdom, 1949–1950.
17. *ibid*.
18. Trade and Navigation Returns, 1950–60.
19. *ibid*.

20. *ibid*.
21. Joyce Bellamy and Martyn Webb, 'The Foreign Trade of Humberside' (1952), part III, Statistical Appendices, together with supplementary information kindly supplied by Dr Bellamy.
22. *ibid*.
23. *ibid*.
24. Trade and Navigation Returns, 1950–60, relevant tables for Liverpool.
25. *ibid*, comparative tables for Liverpool and London.
26. *ibid*.
27. From information kindly supplied by the Mersey Docks and Harbour Board.
28. *Import Trade*, 96.
29. *ibid*.
30. Smith, *Merseyside: a Scientific Survey*, 179.
31. *ibid*, 179–80.
32. F. E. Hyde and Sheila Marriner, 'The Economic Functions of the Export Merchant', *The Manchester School* (1952), 216.
33. *ibid*.
34. *ibid*, 217–20.
35. *ibid*.
36. *ibid*.
37. *ibid*, 221.
38. *ibid*.
39. Sturmey, *British Shipping*, 365ff.
40. *ibid*. It is true that most of the amalgamations had taken place before the end of the 1930s, but in recent years there have been some further mergers.
41. *ibid*, 293–4.
42. *ibid*.
43. Mersey Docks and Harbour Board, Annual Reports and Accounts, 1954–5.
44. See below, chapter 11, page 205, for an analysis of the various projections.
45. Hyde, 'British Shipping Companies and East and South-East Asia', 41.
46. *ibid*.
47. *Blue Funnel and Glen Lines Bulletin*, centenary edition, 1865–1965, 183.

48. From information kindly supplied by Mr Brian Watson Hughes.
49. P. N. Davies, *A Short History of the ships of John Holt and Company (Liverpool) Ltd, and the Guinea Gulf Line Ltd* (1965), 9–10.
50. *ibid.*
51. *ibid*, 11.
52. *ibid*, 12.
53. *ibid.*

NOTES TO CHAPTER 11

1. Twemlow, LTB, vols 1 and 2. A further volume of the Town Books has been published by G. Chandler, *Liverpool under James I* (1960).
2. These opinions were repeated by Celia Fiennes.
3. This statement gives a very broad picture. A more detailed examination of the census returns gives a high degree of fluctuation for specific areas of the city.
4. See above, chapter 7, p. 140.
5. See above, chapter 10, p. 197.
6. For the period before 1860, the conversion to constant prices is extremely difficult. One can only compare (not even legitimately) with the Rousseaux Index allied with the Schumpeter-Gilboy Index. From 1860 onwards, the Blue Book Index of capital goods prices, an Index from *Key Statistics*, and the Maywald Index of Building Costs have been used.
7. Calculated on imports c.i.f., exports f.o.b. If export and re-export figures are adjusted in accordance with balance of payment accounts, the percentage share of Liverpool's export trade is slightly lower.
8. For a discussion of these points, see R. O. Goss, *Studies in Maritime Economics* (1969), 'The Turn-Round of Cargo-Liners and its effect on Transport Costs', *passim*; also by the same author, 'The Size of Ships', written for the Colloquium on the Future of European Ports, College of Europe, Bruges, April 1970.
9. As quoted in the *Liverpool Daily Post* following statements of the directors of Oceans for the half-year ending 30 June 1969.

10. 'The Next Decade', a copy of a speech delivered by Sir John Nicholson to a Conference on Future Port Development, March 1970. The author is greatly indebted to Sir John for permission to quote.

11. *ibid.*

12. *ibid.*

13. *ibid.*

Appendices

APPENDIX I

(a) Shipping entering and clearing Liverpool 1709–51

	(Thousand tons)	
	Inwards	Outwards
1709	14·6	12·6
1716	17·9	18·9
1723	18·8	18·4
1730	18·1	19·1
1737	17·5	22·4
1744	22·1	20·9
1751	29·2	31·2

Source: Enfield, 67. These figures agree with those in British Museum, Add MS 11256.

(b) Shipping entering and clearing Liverpool 1752–93

	(Thousand tons)	
	Inwards	Outwards
1752	29·1	31·8
1753	34·2	34·7
1754	32·3	33·4
1755	33·2	30·7
1756	29·8	35·4
1757	32·4	37·9
1758	36·3	38·5
1759	33·0	35·1

1760	36·9	37·2
1761	32·9	40·3
1762	45·5	39·3
1763	39·7	44·9
1764	46·4	50·7
1765	53·0	53·8
1766	51·6	51·0
1767	51·7	57·4
1768	54·9	60·4
1769	58·3	62·5
1770	46·1	66·5
1771	59·7	73·4
1772	68·8	81·7
1773	70·4	76·6
1774	79·3	76·9
1775	86·4	76·7
1776	74·1	68·5
1777	70·8	71·3
1778	76·3	63·4
1779	57·1	64·8
1780	58·8	61·6
1781	58·9	65·5
1782	66·3	64·5
1783	96·1	105·1
1784	122·3	113·5
1785	127·4	122·2
1786	140·2	128·8
1787	153·6	159·8
1788	140·8	186·4
1789	171·7	170·4
1790	205·4	201·6
1791	220·3	225·6
1792	225·2	231·3
1793	188·3	169·8

Source: Troughton, p. 260 quoting figures in agreement with those in Add MS 11255, and 11256. After 1781 Troughton's figures were taken from a similar but not identical source.

(c) Shipping entering Liverpool and paying dock dues 1800–55

(Thousand tons)

1800	450·1	1827	1,225·3
1801	459·7	1828	1,311·1
1802	510·7	1829	1,387·9
1803	494·5	1830	1,412·0
1804	448·8	1831	1,592·4
1805	463·5	1832	1,540·1
1806	507·8	1833	1,590·5
1807	662·3	1834	1,692·9
1808	516·8	1835	1,768·4
1809	594·6	1836	1,947·6
1810	734·4	1837	1,959·0
1811	611·2	1838	2,026·2
1812	446·8	1839	2,158·7
1813	547·4	1840	2,445·7
1814	549·0	1841	2,425·5
1815	709·9	1842	2,425·3
1816	774·2	1843	2,445·3
1817	653·4	1844	2,632·7
1818	754·7	1845	3,016·5
1819	867·3	1846	3,096·4
1820	805·1	1847	3,351·5
1821	839·8	1848	3,285·0
1822	892·9	1849	3,639·1
1823	1,010·8	1850	3,536·3
1824	1,180·9	1851	3,737·7
1825	1,223·8	1855	4,096·1
1826	1,228·3		

Source: Baines, quoting returns of the Dock Trust.

(d) Shipping entering the Mersey and paying dock dues 1858–1968

| | (Thousand net registered tons) | | |
	paying tonnage rates	paying harbour rates only	Total
1858	4,005·1	436·9	4,441·9
1860	4,372·0	325·2	4,697·2
1865	4,186·2	526·3	4,712·5
1870	5,210·7	517·8	5,728·5
1875	6,089·5	499·2	6,588·7
1880	6,763·8	760·8	7,524·5
1885	7,546·6	1,024·8	8,571·4
1890	8,421·4	1,232·6	9,654·0
1895	9,061·3	1,715·8	10,777·1
1900	10,021·7	2,359·2	12,380·9
1905	12,830·5	3,165·9	15,996·4
1910	12,899·9	3,754·1	16,654·1
1915	15,001·1	3,979·9	18,980·9
1920	13,434·4	3,086·9	16,521·4
1925	15,078·7	4,556·4	19,635·1
1930	16,184·5	5,130·3	21,314·8
1935	15,486·5	4,991·9	20,478·5
1940	14,305·7	4,756·2	19,061·9
1945	16,299·1	3,800·4	20,099·5
1950	15,372·2	5,756·7	21,128·9
1955	17,203·2	8,892·7	26,095·9
1960	19,838·1	9,463·9	29,302·0
1965	23,078·5	8,234·1	31,312·6
1968	20,153·6	9,046·6	29,200·2

(e) Tonnage of Ships entering and clearing the Port of Liverpool
from Foreign Ports—1816–1845

| | Inwards | | Outwards | |
| | British | Foreign | British | Foreign |
	TONS	TONS	TONS	TONS
1816	201,895	98,778	221,895	119,495
1817	192,511	140,123	226,619	141,211
1818	255,409	187,778	278,697	204,512
1819	248,984	143,513	230,908	163,074
1820	228,235	166,821	266,875	171,800
1821	242,322	149,151	248,239	155,387
1822	261,137	174,607	275,237	190,557
1823	296,710	199,866	291,076	216,989
1824	327,198	174,593	336,855	194,543
1825	315,115	222,187	316,170	238,961
1826	299,037	181,907	292,780	186,629
1827	306,369	231,863	331,751	237,021
1828	340,644	179,514	369,572	190,648
1829	326,311	210,713	351,101	228,275
1830	368,268	272,463	389,276	268,839
1831	413,928	265,037	440,418	278,569
1832	397,933	227,087	432,544	237,845
1833	410,502	250,360	454,772	258,225
1834	438,515	261,747	503,353	275,752
1835	517,172	269,837	521,924	274,842
1836	500,952	256,334	545,877	291,668
1837	484,253	313,534	484,500	320,553
1838	507,791	403,687	555,446	417,909
1839	559,920	362,605	558,130	386,051
1840	573,359	468,873	623,007	480,949
1841	656,629	338,438	678,130	351,264
1842	618,624	369,966	637,005	385,664
1843	691,707	417,621	779,071	437,194
1844	760,597	367,918	874,753	398,380
1845	914,352	492,189	924,097	488,376

Source: Parliamentary Papers—Return to an Order of the Honourable The House of Commons, dated 19 January 1847.

APPENDIX II

Dock Revenue from Port Traffic

(These figures are only indicative of growth, if changes in schedules of rates are taken into account. See references in text)

	£		£
1724	810	1813	50,177
1725	847	1814	59,741
1752	1,776	1815	76,915
1762	2,527	1816	92,646
1772	4,552	1817	75,889
1782	4,249	1818	98,538
1792	13,243	1819	110,127
1802	28,192	1820	94,412
1805	33,364	1821	94,556
1806	44,560	1822	102,403
1807	62,831	1823	115,783
1808	40,638	1824	130,911
1809	47,580	1831	183,455
1810	65,782	1837	173,853
1811	54,752	1841	175,506
1812	44,403	1851	269,020 (excluding Birkenhead)

Under the Mersey Docks and Harbour Board

Dues paid on tonnage, graving docks, dock rent, on goods (dock rates and town rates), applicable on conservancy account (harbour rates and portion of dock tonnage rates)

Total in £

1861	667,567	1933	2,314,142
1871	867,756	1937	2,603,930
1881	1,051,928	1939	2,583,460
1891	1,117,925	1945	4,240,251
1901	1,190,994	1950	5,147,851
1911	1,417,661	1955	7,174,071
1913	1,685,176	1960	8,768,616
1920	2,641,470	1963	11,109,681
1921	2,571,512	1965	11,874,118
1929	2,855,843	1966	12,227,173
1930	2,789,951	1967	12,104,807
1931	2,459,738	1968	11,477,244
1932	2,433,622		

NB The above figures do not include such items as rents from allocated berths and are, therefore, not an accurate representation of total income to the Dock Board. They are, however, indicative of port usage.

APPENDIX III

Some shipping companies associated with the Port of Liverpool

1. *To Europe and the Mediterranean*

Bahr Behrend & Co Ltd, founded by Lorentz Hansen in 1790.

Ellerman and Papayanni Lines, 1901. See Bibby, Leyland and Papayanni Lines.

Glynn Line, founded by John Glynn in 1811; amalgamated with MacAndrew Line in 1922.

Moss Line, founded by James Moss in 1815; amalgamated with Moss and Hampson in 1823; James Moss & Co established a line of steamships to the Mediterranean in association with Lamport & Holt 1848–9. 1873, Moss Steamship Co Ltd; taken over by Royal Mail Steam Packet Co Ltd during first world war; amalgamated with J. & P. Hutchison Ltd in 1934 to form Moss-Hutchison group.

Bibby Line. John Bibby came to Liverpool in 1801; in 1807 was joint founder of Highfield and Bibby; began business in 1817 as John Bibby and Co. Engaged in packet service from Parkgate to Dublin; later extended services to Mediterranean. Bibby Line sold to Frederick Leyland in 1873.

The Cunard Steam Ship Co Ltd (Mediterranean service) started by Charles MacIver in 1851.

Johnston Line, founded by Willam and Edmund Johnston in 1872; absorbed into Johnston-Warren Lines in 1934; now part of Furness group.

The Larrinaga Steamship Co Ltd, originally Spanish, registered Bilbao 1773; moved to Liverpool early 1860s.

British and Continental Steam Ship Co Ltd, founded 1922.

2. *To North America*

Cunard Steam Ship Co Ltd (qv).

The American Black Ball Line of sailing packets.

The White Diamond Line, founded by Enoch Train of Boston, 1839. In 1853, George Warren came from Boston to Liverpool to manage the Liverpool office. He gained control of the line and it became associated with his name. During the American Civil War the ships were transferred to the British flag and Liverpool became the headquarters.

The Collins Line, founded in 1848 in America; competed with Cunard. The last Collins liner left Liverpool in 1858.

The Inman Line, established in 1850; secured part of mail contract in 1875. The line was sold twenty years later to the Inman and International Steamship (Red Star) Co. The US government gave a mail contract to this company (which became American) though the ships were British.

The White Star Line. The flag was purchased by T. H. Ismay in 1867 from H. T. Wilson and J. Pilkington. Ismay founded the Oceanic Steam Navigation Co Ltd in 1869; this was known as the White Star Line. The share capital was taken over by the International Mercantile Marine in 1902, but in 1927, the Royal Mail group acquired the capital. After the Royal Mail crash the White Star was amalgamated with the Cunard Steam Ship Co, under the title of Cunard-White Star. The title White Star was dropped in 1949.

The Guion Line, founded in 1866 by Messrs Williams and Guion. Registered as the Liverpool and Great Western Steamship Co, the line competed with Cunard and White Star in the transatlantic emigrant trade. The last Guion ship sailed from Liverpool in 1894.

The National Line, founded by a group of Liverpool business men in 1863; competed in North Atlantic emigrant trade; abandoned Liverpool–New York service in 1894 and, by 1914, the company ceased to exist.

The Leyland Line, founded out of the earlier Bibby Line in 1873. Extended services from the Mediterranean to the Atlantic. A new company was formed in 1900, but in 1902, the fleet was split, one half going to the Morgan combine. In 1934, the line returned to British ownership through purchase by Messrs T. & J. Harrison.

Cunard Line (Canadian service) 1840–67; re-entered Canadian trade through purchase of Thomson Line in 1911.

Canadian Pacific Steamships Ltd, started with three steamships from Liverpool to Vancouver via Suez and Hong Kong in 1891. In 1902, Canadian Pacific acquired interests in Beaver Line which gave access to berths from Liverpool, Avonmouth and London via Antwerp to Canada. In 1915, Canadian Pacific took over Allan Line.

3. To West Indies, Central and South America

Pacific Steam Navigation Co, founded by William Wheelwright and incorporated by royal charter in 1840. Taken over by Royal Mail in 1910. After Royal Mail crash, it was reorganised in Furness group.

Lamport and Holt, established in 1845 by William James Lamport and George Holt. Traded first in Mediterranean, but in 1866, started direct service between Antwerp and River Plate. Engaged in South American meat trade. Later became part of Royal Mail group and is now part of Vestey shipping interests.

Harrison Line (Charente Steam Ship Co) founded by Thomas and James Harrison. Began direct services to Bombay and New Orleans in 1860s, and with South Africa in 1904. West Indian and Brazilian trade of importance after 1885.

Booth Steamship Co Ltd, founded by Alfred and Charles Booth in 1866. Traded with North Brazil and, in 1901, absorbed the Red Cross Line. In 1903, acquired Liverpool and Maranham Steam Ship Co, thus creating a powerful domination of Brazilian trade. Has now become part of Vestey group but still functions as a separate line.

The Booker Line, founded by Josias Booker, though shipping firm established by George Booker. Traded with Demerara and, to date, with British Guiana.

4. To West Africa

Elder Dempster, incorporating the African Steam Ship Co, founded in 1852 and the British and African Steam Navigation Co founded in 1869. This company came under the active genius of Alfred Jones who created a virtual shipping monopoly in British shipping to West Africa. After his death in 1909, Elder Dempsters were taken over by the Royal Mail Group. The company was reorganised after the Kylsant crash and is now part of the Ocean group.

The Guinea Gulf Line (John Holt & Co (Liverpool) Ltd) formed in 1954 after reorganisation in 1949, and now part of Elder Dempsters in Ocean group.

The Palm Line, founded in 1949 by United Africa Company (Lever Bros) to separate shipowning activities from main group.

5. *To South and East Africa, the Persian Gulf, India and Pakistan*

Brocklebank Line, founded 1770; at first a shipbuilding firm at Whitehaven; shipping merchanting developed and in 1820 the Brocklebanks opened their own office in Liverpool; Thomas Brocklebank taking charge in Liverpool, leaving John Brocklebank to supervise shipbuilding at Whitehaven. Ships traded with India, Singapore, and China (also some ships to South America). In 1905, a service was started between Antwerp, China and Japan and half the shares in the Shire Line purchased; sold half the shares in Brocklebank Line to Edward Bates and Sons in 1911, and in 1912, took over Calcutta service of Anchor Line. In 1919, Cunard Steam Ship Co purchased all shares in Brocklebank Line held by Brocklebank and Bates families.

Harrison Line (qv) purchased Rathbone ships engaged on Calcutta route in 1889 and obtained access to Indian tea trade. Also entered East African trade after 1911.

The Hall Line Ltd, formed by Robert Alexander in association with Liston, Young and Co in 1864, to sail ships to India and Australia. Alexander moved to Liverpool in 1868, main business with India. Sun Shipping Co (official name of Hall Line) created in 1874; later managed by Alexander and Radcliffe. 1883, fleet divided into three ownerships (Sun Shipping Co Ltd, Messrs Alexander and Radcliffe and Messrs Robert Alexander & Co). 1901, Hall Line and Alexander ships sold to Ellerman group.

Anchor Line, founded in Glasgow by Capt. Thomas Henderson with agency house in Liverpool since 1869.

The Clan Line, founded by Charles William Cayzer in 1878. Traded with India and, after 1881, with South Africa. Now part of British and Commonwealth Shipping Co Ltd.

Castle Line (later Union Castle) founded by Donald Currie in 1862. Traded with South Africa. Mail contract divided between Union and Castle Lines after 1876. Fleets of the two companies were joined in 1905 to form Union-Castle. Joined with Clan Line in British and Commonwealth group after second world war (together with King Line, the Houston Line, the Thompson Steamshipping Co, the Scottish Shire Line and Bullard, King & Co).

6. *To the Far East*

Blue Funnel Line (Ocean Steam Ship Co Ltd) incorporating China Mutual Steam Navigation Co, Glen Line, etc, now part of larger Ocean group. For details see text *passim*.

The Glen and Shire Lines (qv).

The Bibby Line (qv). Present Bibby Line dates from 1889, services to Rangoon via Mediterranean.

7. *To Australia and New Zealand*

Beazley Line, founded by James Beazley shortly after 1845. In 1864, he founded British Shipowners Co to extend services to Australia. Company managed by Gracie, Beazley and Co. This latter firm now loading brokers for Shaw Savill-Blue Funnel joint service to Australia.

Blue Funnel (qv) joint service with Shaw Savill and Albion companies.

Port Line, created to run services acquired by Cunard in 1916 when Commonwealth and Dominion Line was purchased.

Black Ball Line, founded by James Baines to trade with Australia. By 1860, this company owned 86 ships. Unsuccessful with steamships, Baines died in 1889 in poverty.

APPENDIX IV

A list of principal Liverpool docks (excluding graving docks, alterations and extensions)

Name	Original water area (approx) (acres)	Opened	Surveyor or Engineer-in-Chief
1. Old dock	4¾	1715 (completed 1720)	Thomas Steers
2. Salthouse	4¾	1753	Planned by Thomas Steers executed by Henry Berry
3. George's	3	1771	Henry Berry
4. Duke's	1¼	1773	(James Brindley)
5. King's	7¾	1788	Henry Berry
6. Queen's	6½	1796	Thomas Morris
7. Canning	4+	1813	John Foster
8. Union (with basin, subsequently Coburg)	2¾	1816/17	John Foster
9. Prince's	11⅓	1821	John Foster and son
10. Clarence	6+	1830	Jesse Hartley
11. Brunswick	12⅔	1832	,, ,,
12. Waterloo	5½+	1834	,, ,,
13. Victoria	11⅔	1836	,, ,,
14. Trafalgar	11⅔	1836	,, ,,
15. Albert	7¾	1845	,, ,,
16. Canning half-tide	2½	1844–45	,, ,,
17. Salisbury	3⅓	1848	,, ,,
18. Collingwood	5+	1848	,, ,,
19. Stanley	7+	1848	,, ,,
20. Nelson	7⅞	1848	,, ,,
21. Bramley Moore	9⅔	1848	,, ,,
22 Wellington	7⅚	1849	,, ,,
23. Wellington half-tide	3+	1849	,, ,,

24. Sandon	10+	1851	,,	,,
25. Huskisson east lock and west lock	1¾	1851	,,	,,
26. Huskisson	13+	1852	,,	,,
27. Canada	18	1859	,,	,,
28. Canada half-tide (later Brocklebank)	10¾	1862	G. F. Lyster	
29. Herculaneum	3½	1864	,,	,,
30. Langton	18¼	1881	,,	,,
31. Alexandra	17⅚	1881	,,	,,
32. Harrington	9	1883	,,	,,
33. Hornby	17	1884	,,	,,
34. Toxteth	11	1888	,,	,,
35. Gladstone and branches	58¼	1927	T. M. Newell	

Docks at Birkenhead

Name	Original Water area (approx)	opened	Surveyor or Engineer-in-Chief
	acres		
1. Morpeth	11⅔	1847	J. M. Rendel
2. Egerton	4+	1847	,, ,,
3. Great Float (later separated into East Float and West Float)	111 (including Alfred and other docks	1851–60	Planned by J. M. Rendel
4. Low Water Basin (subsequently converted into wet-dock and called Wallasey dock)	12¾	1863 1877–78	Planned by J. M. Rendel G. F. Lyster
5. Alfred	8⅔	1866	,, ,,
6. Vittoria	11+	1909	A. G. Lyster
7. Bidston	10⅔	1933	T. L. Norfolk

Select Bibliography

Aldcroft, D. H. 'Port Congestion and the Shipping Boom of 1919–1920', *Business History*, 3 no 2 (1961), 97–106.

Allen, G. C., Hyde, F. E., Morgan, D. J. and Corlett, W. J. *The Import Trade of the Port of Liverpool* (1946).

Anderson, R. *White Star* (1964).

Anonymous. *A General and Descriptive History of Liverpool* (1797).

Anonymous. *Housing Progress, 1864–1951: City of Liverpool Housing* (1951).

Anonymous. *Remarks on the Salt Trade of the counties of Chester and Lancaster* (1804).

Ashton, T. S. *Economic Fluctuations in England, 1700–1800* (1959).

Baines, D. E. and Bean, R. 'The General Strike on Merseyside, 1926'; see Harris, J. R.

Baines, T. *History of the Commerce and Town of Liverpool* (1852).

Barker, T. C. 'Lancashire Coal, Cheshire Salt, and the rise of Liverpool', *Transactions of the Historic Society of Lancs and Cheshire*, vol 102 (1951).

Barker, T. C. 'The failure of Sir Thomas Johnson', *Transactions of the Historic Society of Lancs and Cheshire*, vol 105 (1953), 203–4.

Barker, T. C. *Pilkington Brothers and the Glass Industry* (1960).

Barker, T. C. 'The Sankey Navigation', *Transactions of the Historic Society of Lancs and Cheshire*, vol 100 (1948).

Barker, T. C. and Harris, J. R. *A Merseyside Town in the Industrial Revolution: St Helens, 1750–1900* (1954).

Broadbridge, S. *Studies in Railway Expansion and the Capital Market in England, 1825–93* (1970).

Brooke, R. *Liverpool during the last quarter of the eighteenth century* (1853).

Stewart-Brown, R. *Liverpool Ships in the eighteenth century* (1932).

Buck, N. S. *The Development of the Organisation of the Anglo-American Trade, 1800–50* (1925, reprinted 1969).

Calvert, A. F. *Salt in Cheshire* (1915).

Cammell Laird & Co. *Builders of Great Ships* (1959).

Carlson, R. E. *The Liverpool and Manchester Railway Project, 1821–31* (1969).

Chaloner, W. H. *The Social and Economic Development of Crewe* (1950).

Chandler, G. *Liverpool in the reign of James I, 1603–25* (1960). This work is a continuation of the LTB published by Twemlow, qv.

Chandler, G. *Liverpool Shipping* (1960).

Checkland, S. G. 'Corn for South Lancashire and Beyond, 1780–1800', *Business History*, 2 no 1, 4–20.

Cotton, V. E. *The Book of Liverpool Cathedral* (1964).

Craig, R. and Jarvis, R. *Liverpool Registry of Merchant Ships* (1967).

Davies, P. N. 'British Shipping and the Growth of the West African Economy, 1910–50' (Unpublished PhD thesis, Liverpool, 1967).

Davies, P. N. *A Short History of the Ships of John Holt & Co (Liverpool) Ltd, and the Guinea Gulf Line Ltd* (1965).

Davies, P. N. 'Sir Alfred Jones and the Development of West African Trade' (Unpublished MA thesis, Liverpool, 1963).

Davis, R. *A Commercial Revolution* (Historical Assn Pamphlet, 1967).

Davis, R. *The Rise of the English Shipping Industry* (1962).

Emery, P. J. 'Wallasey Pool—the birth-pangs of a Port' (Unpublished MA thesis, Liverpool, 1959).

Enfield, W. *An Essay towards the History of Liverpool* (1774).

Farnie, D. A. *East and West of Suez* (1969).

Gibson, T. E. (editor). *Diary of Nicholas Blundell of Crosby* (1895).

Hardie, D. W. F. *A History of the Chemical Industry in Widnes* (1950).

Harley, J. B. 'Ogilby and Collins: Cheshire by Road and Sea', *Cheshire Round*, 1 no. 7 (1967), 210–25.

Harris, J. R. (editor). *Liverpool and Merseyside: essays in the Economic and Social History of the Port and its Hinterland* (1969).

Harris, S. A. and Barker, T. C. 'Henry Berry (1719–1812): an inventory of his professional papers', *Transactions of the Historic Society of Lancs and Chesire*, vol 112 (1960).

Henderson, W. O. 'The American Chamber of Commerce in

Liverpool', *Transactions of the Historic Society of Lancs and Cheshire*, vol 85 (1935).

Henderson, W. O. *The Lancashire Cotton Famine* (1934).

Henderson, W. O. 'The Liverpool Office in London', *Economica*, vol 42 (1933).

Hodges, R. 'The Dock System of Liverpool', in Smith, *Merseyside*, qv.

Holt, C. R. (editor). *The Diary of John Holt and the Voyage of the Maria* (1948).

Hyde, F. E. *Blue Funnel: a History of Alfred Holt & Co of Liverpool, 1865–1914* (1956).

Hyde, F. E. 'British Shipping Companies and East and South East Asia, 1860–1939', in C. D. Cowan (ed), *The Economic Development of South-East Asia* (1964).

Hyde, F. E. and Marriner, S. 'The Economic Functions of the Export Merchant', *Manchester School* (1952).

Hyde, F. E. *Mr Gladstone at the Board of Trade* (1934).

Hyde, F. E. and Marriner, S. *The Senior: John Samuel Swire, 1825–98* (1967).

Hyde, F. E. *Shipping Enterprise and Management: Harrisons of Liverpool* (1967).

Hyde, F. E., Parkinson, B. B., and Marriner, S. 'The Port of Liverpool and the Crisis of 1793', *Economica*, vol 18 (1951).

Hyde, F. E., Parkinson, B. B. and Marriner, S. 'The Nature and Profitability of the Liverpool Slave Trade', *Economic History Review*, 2nd series, vol 5 (1953).

Irvine, W. F. *Liverpool in the Reign of Charles II* (1899).

John, A. H. *A Liverpool Merchant House* (1959).

Kellet, J. R. *The Impact of Railways on Victorian Cities* (1969).

Kendall, M. G. 'United Kingdom Merchant Shipping Statistics', *Journal of the Royal Statistical Society*, vol 111 (1948).

Kenwood, A. G. 'Port Investment in England and Wales, 1851–1913', *Yorkshire Bulletin*, 17 no 2 (1965), 156–67.

Leak, H. 'The Carrying Trade of British Shipping', *Journal of the Royal Statistical Society*, vol 102 (1939).

Lobley, D. (editor). *The Cunarders* (1969).

McLellan, A. *A History of Mansfield & Co, 1920–33* (1953).

Marriner, S. *Rathbones of Liverpool, 1845–73* (1961).

Merritt, J. E., 'The Triangular Trade', *Business History*, vol 3 (1960).

Mersey Docks and Harbour Board. *The Port of Liverpool* (1950–1951).

Mountfield, S. 'Liverpool Docks and the Municipal Commissioners' Inquiry of 1833 for Liverpool', *Transactions of the Historic Society of Lancs and Cheshire*, vol 115 (1963), 163–74.

Mountfield, S. *Western Gateway: A History of the Mersey Docks and Harbour Board* (1965).

North, D. C. 'Ocean Freight Rates and Economic Development, 1750–1913', *Journal of Economic History*, vol 18 (1958).

Ormerod, H. A. *The Liverpool Free School, 1515–1803* (1951).

Ormerod, H. A. *The Liverpool Royal Institution* (1953).

Pares, R. *A West Indian Fortune* (1950).

Parkinson, B. B. 'A Slaver's Accounts', *Accountancy Research*, vol II (1951), 144–50.

Parkinson, C. N. *The Rise of the Port of Liverpool* (1952).

Peet, H. *Liverpool in the Reign of Queen Anne* (1908).

Peet, H. *Liverpool Vestry Books*, vol 1 (1912) vol 2 (1915).

Picton, J. A. *Memorials of Liverpool* (1873).

Picton, J. A. *Selections from the Municipal Archives and Records* (1883).

Pollins, H. 'The Finances of the Liverpool and Manchester Railway', *Economic History Review*, 2nd series, vol 5 (1952).

Poole, B. L. 'Liverpool's Trade in the Reign of Queen Anne' (Unpublished MA thesis, Liverpool 1960).

Redford, A. *Manchester Merchant and Foreign Trade, vol 2: 1850–1939* (1956).

Smith, W. (editor). *Merseyside: A Scientific Survey* (1953).

Smithers, H. *Liverpool, its Commerce, Statistics, and Institutions, with a History of the Cotton Trade* (1825).

Stephenson, R. 'The Development of the Liverpool Dock System', *Transactions of the Liverpool Nautical Research Society*, vol 8 (1953–4, 1954–5), 61–75.

Sturmey, S. G. *British Shipping and World Competition* (1962).

Touzeau, J. *Rise and Progress of Liverpool* (2 vols, 1910).

Troughton, T. *The History of Liverpool* (1810).

Twemlow, J. A. *Liverpool Town Books, 1550–1862* (1918).

Veitch, G. S. *The Struggle for the Liverpool and Manchester Railway* (1930).

Walford, C. *A Review of the Causes which have led to the Commercial Greatness of Liverpool* (1883).

Wardle, A. C. *Steam Conquers the Pacific* (1940).

Webster, T. *The Port and Docks of Birkenhead* (1848).

Webster, T. *Minutes of Evidence of the Proceedings on the Liverpool and Birkenhead Dock Bills in the Sessions of 1848–52 and 1855–6* (2 vols 1857).

Willan, T. S. *The Navigation of the River Weaver in the Eighteenth Century* (Chetham Society, 3rd series, 1951).

Williams, R. W. 'The First Year's Working of the Liverpool Dock Scheme', *Transactions of the Liverpool Economic and Statistical Society, Session 1913–14* (1914).

Williams, R. W. *The Liverpool Docks Problem* (1912).

Wilson, C. *The History of Unilever* (2 vols, 1954).

Acknowledgements

The author is greatly indebted to many personal friends on Mersey-side for help in the writing of this book. In particular, he has received the most generous co-operation from officers in the Mersey Docks and Harbour Board in the supply of statistical information and from Mr Stuart Mountfield, author of *Western Gateway* and former General Manager of the Dock Board; his kind help and criticism greatly improved the text. Sir John Nicholson, chairman of the Ocean group, read chapter 11. Professor A. R. Myers of the Department of Mediaeval History in the University of Liverpool, helped the author to decipher a seventeenth-century document from the Moore papers. To the author's colleagues in the Departments of Economics and Economic History in the University of Liverpool, especial thanks are due to Mr George Peters for advice and help in the determination of rates of growth; to Dr J. R. Harris for information about eighteenth-century Liverpool; to Dr Peter N. Davies for permission to use material from his forthcoming book on the history of Elder Dempster and Co, and to Mr Philip Cottrell for directing his attention to source material on investment and other related topics.

In many cases due acknowledgement is made to individual acts of kindness and generosity in the permission to use manuscript and other primary sources. To his former post-graduate students, Mr Neville Syder, Mr P. J. Emery, and Mrs Brenda Poole, the author is greatly indebted for permission to use material from their un-published theses; to Mr T. Whitley Moran for permission to use abstracts of title-deeds to various Liverpool properties; to Dr George Chandler, City Librarian, for extracts from the Moore papers and to Dr Alan Smith for information about the Herculaneum pottery. Mr R. Bastin generously allowed information from his forthcoming thesis on Liverpool's emigrant trade to be used.

Finally, to those whose help in technical matters greatly facilitated the production of this book; to Dr Gordon Jackson and Dr

Harley for editorial work on the text; to Mr Paul Laxton, Mr D. H. Birch and Mr Alan Hodgkiss of the Department of Geography in the University of Liverpool for the use and reproduction of maps; to Mrs Jean Girling who prepared the material and typed the text and to his wife who read it, corrected and revised it and helped in the compilation of the Index, the author extends his gratitude.

Index